Human Capital

T0328323

At a time when governments and policy-makers put so much emphasis on 'the knowledge economy' and the economic value of education, human capital theory has never been more important. However, research in this area is often very technical and therefore not easily accessible to those who wish to use it as a guide to policy formation. This book provides an interface between such research and its potential applications in government, education and business. Reporting on a major research initiative, new findings are presented in a non-technical way on three major themes: measuring the benefits from human capital, applications of the human capital model, and policy interventions. Aimed at academic researchers and professionals concerned with the problems and techniques of human capital theory, it will also be useful for graduate courses on the economics of education as a complement to standard textbooks.

JOOP HARTOG is Professor of Economics at the University of Amsterdam.

HENRIËTTE MAASSEN VAN DEN BRINK is Professor of Economics at the University of Amsterdam.

Human Capital

Advances in Theory and Evidence

edited by

JOOP HARTOG AND
HENRIËTTE MAASSEN VAN DEN BRINK

CAMBRIDGE
UNIVERSITY PRESS

CAMBRIDGE UNIVERSITY PRESS
Cambridge, New York, Melbourne, Madrid, Cape Town, Singapore, São Paulo, Delhi

Cambridge University Press
The Edinburgh Building, Cambridge CB2 8RU, UK

Published in the United States of America by Cambridge University Press, New York

www.cambridge.org
Information on this title: www.cambridge.org/9780521117562

First published 2007
This digitally printed version 2009

A catalogue record for this publication is available from the British Library

ISBN 978-0-521-87316-1 hardback
ISBN 978-0-521-11756-2 paperback

Contents

List of figures   *page* vii

List of tables   viii

Notes on contributors   ix

Prologue
Joop Hartog and Henriëtte Maassen van den Brink   1

Part I   Measuring the benefits from human capital

1   What should you know about the private returns
    to education?
    Joop Hartog and Hessel Oosterbeek   7

2   The social returns to education
    Mikael Lindahl and Erik Canton   21

3   Returns to training
    Edwin Leuven   38

4   Human capital and entrepreneurs
    Justin van der Sluis and C. Mirjam van Praag   52

5   The effects of education on health
    Wim Groot and Henriëtte Maassen van den Brink   65

6   Are successful parents the secret to success?
    Erik Plug   81

Part II   Applying and extending the human capital model

7   Overeducation in the labour market
    Wim Groot and Henriëtte Maassen van den Brink   101

8   Underinvestment in training?
    Randolph Sloof, Joep Sonnemans and Hessel Oosterbeek   113

9   Human capital and risk
    Joop Hartog and Simona Maria Bajdechi   134

Part III   Policy interventions

10 Using (quasi-)experiments to evaluate education
    interventions
    Hessel Oosterbeek   155

11 Unemployment duration: policies to prevent human
    capital depreciation
    Bas van der Klaauw   170

12 Can we stimulate teachers to enhance quality?
    Ib Waterreus   189

13 Optimal tax and education policies and investments
    in human capital
    Bas Jacobs   212

    Epilogue: some reflections on educational policies   233

A note on econometrics   236
Index   238

Figures

1.1   Education as an investment   *page* 8

1.2   Returns to schooling in Europe, men and women
      (year closest to 1995)   9

1.3   Mincer estimates of return to schooling for the
      Netherlands, 1962–99 males   13

10.1   Relation between age and training participation   161

Tables

2.1 Summary of cross-country literature on social
returns to education *page* 30

6.1 Various family background estimates. The effects
of parent's income, schooling and IQ on schooling
on birth children using the Wisconsin Longitudinal
Survey 84

6.2 Various family background estimates. The effects of
parent's income, schooling and IQ on schooling on
adoptees using the Wisconsin Longitudinal Survey 86

7.1 Average values by characteristics of the survey and
characteristics of the sample used in the study 105

8.1 Number of points (gross of investment costs) for
employer and worker 117

8.2 Percentages of efficient decisions 120

9.1 Percentage change in income if risk and skew are
reduced from sample mean values to zero 145

12.1 Characteristics of different pay criteria 195

12.2 Comparison of the estimated costs (in millions of
euros) of an increase in the number of hours worked
of a general wage increase and a full-time premium 205

Notes on contributors

Simona Maria Bajdechi received her master's degree in applied statistics and optimizations in 1998 from the University of Bucharest, Romania. In 2005, she got her PhD in economics from the University of Amsterdam with the thesis entitled 'The Risk of Investment in Human Capital'. During her work as a PhD student she was affiliated to the Tinbergen Institute, Amsterdam. Her current research interests focuses on education and wages and income distribution.

Erik Canton wrote his PhD dissertation on 'Economic Growth and Business Cycles' at Tilburg University. Thereafter he joined the CPB Netherlands Bureau for Economic Policy Analysis, and worked mainly in the area of education, R&D, and science policy. As of 2005 he is on detachment at the European Commission, where his activities concentrate on the Renewed Lisbon Strategy. He has also worked as a consultant for the World Bank.

Wim Groot has been Professor of Health Economics at Maastricht University since 1998 and a coordinator of the 'NWO Prioriteitprogramma' SCHOLAR on 'Schooling, Labour Market and Economic Development' at the University of Amsterdam since 1997. His research interests are in the field of health economics and the economics of education. His research is focused on willingness to pay for health and health care, the evolution of health capital, and on the (social) returns to human capital. As author and co-author, he has published more than 120 articles in national and international scientific journals and books. He has written over 200 reports, newspaper articles and columns. Since 2003 he has been writing a column for a national newspaper *Het Financieele Dagblad*.

Joop Hartog studied economics at the Netherlands School of Economics, where he got his PhD in 1978 with a thesis on income distribution. In 1981 he became Professor of Micro-economics at the University of Amsterdam. He has published widely on labour economics and the economics of education, co-founded the journal *Labour Economics* and held many visiting positions (including at Stanford, Cornell, Wisconsin and the World Bank). In 2001 he was elected to the Royal Dutch Academy of Sciences.

Bas Jacobs studied economics at the University of Amsterdam where he also did his PhD. His research combines public finance, macroeconomics and labour economics. He has written theoretical papers on optimal labour and capital taxation, optimal subsidies on education, human capital risk, economic growth, and the optimal financing of higher education. In addition, he has done empirical research on productivity growth, technological change and wage inequality. Jacobs has worked at the CPB Netherlands Bureau for Economic Policy Analysis and Tilburg University. He has been a research fellow at the University of Chicago and the European University Institute in Florence. He is assistant professor at the Universities of Amsterdam and Tilburg and member of the Tinbergen Institute and CentER.

Edwin Leuven is a senior researcher at the Department of Economics, University of Amsterdam, where he received his PhD in 2001. Before this he worked for two years as a full-time consultant at the OECD. His main research interests are the economics of education and labour economics. His work has been published in several leading international academic journals.

Mikael Lindahl is Assistant Professor in Economics at the Swedish Institute for Social Research (SOFI), Stockholm University. He is also a research fellow at IZA, Bonn. After receiving his PhD in economics from Stockholm University in 2000, he spent three years as a postdoctoral researcher at SCHOLAR, University of Amsterdam. His main research interests are in the areas of empirical labour economics and the economics of education, and his work has been published in several international academic journals including the *Journal of Economic Literature*, the *Journal of Human Resources*, the *Quarterly Journal of Economics* and the *Scandinavian Journal of Economics*.

Henriëtte Maassen van den Brink is Professor of Economics at the Department of Economics and Econometrics of the University of Amsterdam. She is the Scientific Programme Director of SCHOLAR, a research institute on 'Schooling, Labour Market and Economic Development'. She obtained her PhD in economics (*cum laude*) at the University of Amsterdam in 1994. She also obtained an MSc in psychology (*cum laude*) at the same university.

Her research interests are in the areas of microeconomics, labour markets and human capital. She has been a visiting professor at Stanford University, Cornell University and the European University Institute. She has received several research grants from the Netherlands Organization for Scientific Research.

Hessel Oosterbeek is Professor of Economics of Education at the University of Amsterdam. Besides education, his research interests include labour economics, economics of training and experimental economics.

Erik Plug is a senior researcher at the University of Amsterdam, where he also obtained his PhD in 1997. He is further affiliated as a research fellow to the Tinbergen Institute. His current research interests relate to family, education and labour economics.

Randolph Sloof obtained his PhD in economics from the University of Amsterdam in 1997. After a short stay at the General Court of Audit in The Hague he joined SCHOLAR in 1998 as a postdoctoral researcher to work on a project entitled 'The Experimental Evaluation of the Holdup Problem'. In 2002 he joined the Department of Economics of the University of Amsterdam as an assistant professor in economics of organization and personnel, and from 2006 onwards as associate professor.

Joep Sonnemans is Professor of Behavioural Economics at the University of Amsterdam. He is interested in (experimental) research in which insights from economics and other social sciences (e.g. psychology) are combined or contrasted: expectation formation, bargaining, social behaviour, individual search behaviour, behavioural finance and behavioural economics.

Bas van der Klaauw obtained his PhD in 2000 from the Free University of Amsterdam, where he is currently working as an associate professor. He is affiliated to the Tinbergen Institute and SCHOLAR. His research is in the field of empirical microeconometrics and is mainly concerned

with policy evaluation and labour economics. He has recently published articles in the *Economic Journal, International Economic
Review* and *Journal of Labor Economics.*

Justin van der Sluis has a master's degree in work and organizational
psychology from the University of Amsterdam. Later he worked for a
short while as a consultant in 'strategic decision-making'. In 2002 he
returned to the University of Amsterdam for a PhD project where he
also joined the SCHOLAR research group. His PhD thesis discusses the
role of education for the development of successful entrepreneurs.

C. Mirjam van Praag is Professor of Entrepreneurship and
Organization at the University of Amsterdam (UvA). She is also the
founding director of the Amsterdam Centre for Entrepreneurship
(ACE) of the UvA. Previously she was an associate professor of the
Economics of Organization and Personnel (UvA) and a consultant with
the Boston Consulting Group. Mirjam van Praag's research interests
are in the field of the economics of entrepreneurship and organization.

Ib Waterreus is a scientific member of staff at the Netherlands
Education Council. He earned a master's degree in economics (1997)
and a PhD (2003) from the University of Amsterdam. Between 1997
and 2003 he was a research worker at SCHOLAR and the Max Goote
Expert Centre at the University of Amsterdam, with an interval at the
Institute for Social and Economic Research of the University of Essex,
Colchester (UK) in 2001 on a Marie Curie fellowship.

Prologue

JOOP HARTOG AND HENRIËTTE
MAASSEN VAN DEN BRINK

HUMAN capital theory was born some four decades ago, under the strong and inspiring leadership of Theodore Schultz, Gary Becker and Jacob Mincer. It has been flourishing ever since, with many new theoretical and empirical developments. Human capital is now a familiar concept, used daily in public debates, and a favourite phrase of many politicians who want to stress the relevance of developing and disseminating new knowledge for maintaining high levels of welfare.

Research on human capital, both theoretical and empirical, is often very technical and therefore not easily accessible to those who want to use the insights in applied work, in developing government policies, human resource policies in organizations and in contributions to social debates. The same holds for students with different types of education. In many curricula, students should attain an understanding of concepts, issues and approaches without digging into all the technical details.

This book aims to be an interface between the technical research in the workshop and applications in government, education and business organizations. The book is written by staff of SCHOLAR (an acronym for Schooling, Labour Market and Economic Development), a research institute at the University of Amsterdam focusing on the economic relation between education and the labour market. SCHOLAR was founded in 1997 with a grant from the Dutch science foundation NWO. Its mission was to undertake original academic research on important issues in this area, and to disseminate the results to a wider audience than just academic specialists.

In this book, we highlight our research findings in a non-technical way, focusing on key results and implications for understanding the role of education in the labour market, and on policy implications. At a time when everybody talks about 'the knowledge economy' and the prime importance of education (including on-the-job training), these are obviously interesting issues. We present the results in thirteen chapters, in a fixed framework: introduction, existing knowledge, new findings and implications. The brief summary of the literature in each chapter (plus references for further reading) adds the element of a reference book, but the focus is on an accessible account of new research findings. These features, we hope, will also make the book useful as course reading in the economics of education, complementary to a standard textbook.

The book is based on original research on human capital that has been undertaken because the questions and approaches were seen as relevant, interesting and promising. As such it is the fruit of a fairly recent research agenda. It covers all the core issues on which active research is going on at present.

A strong methodological undercurrent connects many contributions in this book. *It ain't what you think it is.* Empirical work is about measuring the strength of relationships and thereby testing theories that predict how variables are interrelated, thus being able to make sensible judgements about the effects of policy interventions. Recent empirical work in economics is drenched in the awareness that reliable estimates of the strength of relationships are not easily obtained. Selective instead of random observations, endogenous rather than exogenous explanatory variables and measurement errors all undermine the classical method of ordinary least squares to estimate coefficients in regression equations. With an economy full of agents that seek their best alternative in the myriad of choices they have to make, it is not easy to find samples where individuals have been randomly assigned to one situation or another. Increasingly, researchers are made responsible for the quality of the data they employ. Thus, they may make the special effort to create a dataset from deliberate random assignment of cases to alternatives, as in medical experiments where patients are randomly divided between the group that gets the new pill and the group that has the placebo. Or they look for datasets where nature has taken care of the assignment, as if a boat had sunk and the new pills had washed ashore on one island but not on the next. As a last resort they may restrict themselves to work with datasets that allow econometric correction, thereby remaining closest to the econometric tradition.

The impact of econometric methodology is prominent in many chapters of this book. It is a key issue in the chapters on measuring returns to education, on the effect of parental background, on educational achievement and on the effects of policy interventions. The methodological innovations have substantial consequences. The methodological concerns have high policy relevance. If one really aims for true effects of policy interventions, rather than just demonstrating an activist attitude, one should be seriously interested in the reliable estimation of these effects. This would imply the desire to accompany policy interventions by investigating the impact right from the beginning and to design testing procedures in tandem with designing the policy intervention itself. And it would imply interest in and awareness of the methodological pitfalls, not necessarily in the full technical details, but certainly in the conceptual issues and their implications. The contributions in this book illustrate quite vividly what is at stake here.

The density of research varies strongly between issues. For some questions there are a large number of studies to base conclusions on; for other questions the field has just been opened up. Right from the invention of the human capital model there has been wide interest in estimating the rate of return to education, and this means that by now there are an enormous number of estimates. So we have a good picture of the crude, average return to an average year of education. New information can be presented and interpreted against the backdrop of all these earlier studies. Hence, in chapters 1 and 3, we can document the development of the private rate of return to education and training in the Netherlands over several decades in this perspective, in chapter 8 we can draw on these estimates to document variability of returns, as a background to assessing the risk of investment in schooling, and in chapter 4 the novel research findings on return to schooling accruing to entrepreneurs can be contrasted with the massive evidence on returns for employees. The same holds for our contributions to the issues of overeducation. In fact, in this case we use the amassed evidence for a meta-analysis to detect structure in the estimated returns to over- and undereducation. Our analyses of the impact of parental background on children's schooling (chapter 6) also stand in a long tradition of the nature–nurture discussion.

In some fields very little is known, and we contribute to ploughing new fields. New experimental evidence in chapter 8 shows that hold-up in firms is much less of a problem than it has been predicted to be. The role of risk in human capital issues (chapter 9) is empirically heavily under-researched. Incentive systems for secondary school teachers (chapter 12) have not frequently been studied. Non-monetary returns to education (chapter 5) are routinely acknowledged but empirical evidence is not abundant. Chapter 5 explores the effects of education on health. What exactly in education affects health and how can we impart health benefits through education? Social returns to education (external effects) is the argument always invoked to justify policy interventions (chapter 2) without solid empirical foundation; in general we claim the social return is not much different from the private return.

The case for government intervention ultimately rests largely on cost-benefit analysis, quasi-experiments and equity arguments. (Quasi-) experiments and equity arguments are extensively and carefully analysed in chapters 10 and 13. The key innovation is the joint analysis of several types of taxes and subsidies, with the prime result that deadweight welfare losses that are always stressed in separate analyses of one kind of tax or subsidy can be reduced substantially by a balanced combination of tax–subsidy instruments. In particular, the conclusion that subsidies to education are an instrument to counter efficiency losses from equity-based income taxes puts a new perspective on an old debate.

Some questions remain open. Old fields need maintenance and upkeep, to fight the ever-returning weeds. We know a lot about crude average returns to education, very little about specific returns to specific types of programmes, schools or students. We have many studies on returns to training, yet little is known about the mechanism that produces the returns and how it varies with circumstances and specifications. The basic model of human capital is well developed, but we know little of investments under uncertainty. And just in case anyone doubts that there are still interesting questions waiting to be explored, each chapter concludes with a list of suggestions for further work.

Research is like an addiction. The more you have used it, the more you want. Human capital, its theory and applications remain a growth industry, as they have been for the last forty years.

PART I

Measuring the benefits from human capital

1 | What should you know about the private returns to education?

JOOP HARTOG AND HESSEL
OOSTERBEEK

1.1 Basic schooling model

In this chapter, we focus on schooling as an investment in human capital. We present the core model in its most basic specification and derive implications for interpreting wage differentials by education as reflecting returns on the schooling investment. We briefly survey international evidence on estimated private rates of return and summarize our own contributions to that literature.

The basic human capital model of schooling envisages two options: (1) go to school for s years and earn an income Y_s every year after leaving school, or (2) go to work right away and earn annual income Y_0 (see figure 1.1). This makes the choice for schooling an investment problem. While in school, the student has forgone earnings of Y_0 for every year in school and direct outlays for tuition, books, etc. of K per year. After leaving school the individual has benefits: in every working year, earnings are Y_s rather than Y_0. The gap in annual earnings is the dividend flowing on his investments.

The internal rate of return is the discount rate that equates the present values of the two lifetime earnings flows. But as the above suggests, we can also take it as the dividend rate $Y_s - Y_0$ relative to the investment cost, composed of forgone earnings Y_0 and direct outlays K for every year in school. To calculate the rate of return, one may follow the instructions implicit in the definition above by tabulating earnings for comparable individuals with and without a particular education at every age and then solve for the internal rate of return. This is indeed how some early researchers did it.

Jacob Mincer (1974) has simplified the estimation of rates of return from cross-sections with an elegant formula. Mincer's formula derives straightforwardly from equating the present value of two earnings streams, each consisting of constant annual earnings, but only differing in the time when they start flowing: Y_0 starts right now, Y_s only starts

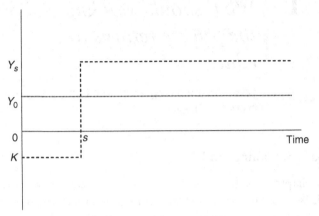

Figure 1.1. Education as an investment

after s years. The model predicts that for every year in school earnings are augmented by the discount rate, multiplicatively. With a discount rate of 5%, an extra year of schooling raises annual earnings by 5%, basically as compensation for postponing earnings.[1] Applying this formula in reverse, we may estimate the rate of return as the coefficient of schooling years in a cross-section regression for individual earnings. Thus, all one needs is an earnings survey of individuals with different educations (and work experience). The regression coefficient of earnings on education is interpreted as the return to education. Following Mincer, the effect of experience on earnings is estimated using a parabola (i.e. using experience and experience squared). The experience effect is supposed to be the same for all education levels.

There is an abundant literature on estimated rates of return to education based on Mincer's approach. Generally, these returns are estimated to be somewhere between 5 and 15%. Psacharopoulos (1985) has collected many of these studies and drawn some general conclusions. He concludes that returns are higher in developing countries than in developed countries, that highest returns accrue to primary education, and that returns to university education may be higher than those for secondary education. While these results certainly make sense, we should note that they have been derived by straightforward averaging of very diverse studies, without any adjustment for differences in data or methodology.

A recent attempt to estimate comparable estimates of Mincer rates of return across Europe from comparable datasets and a uniform

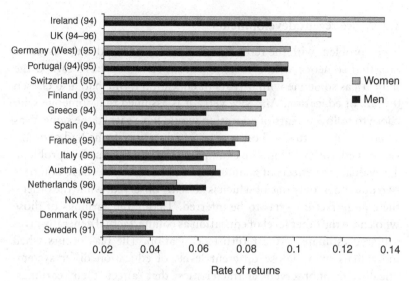

Figure 1.2. Returns to schooling in Europe, men and women (year closest to 1995)
Source: Harmon, Walker and Westergaard-Nielsen (2001)

methodology finds that minimum rates over the sample period (the 1990s) varied between countries from 4.0 to 10.7%, while maximum rates are between 6.2 and 11.5%. Returns estimated in or around 1995 are shown in figure 1.2 (from Harmon, Walker and Westergaard-Nielsen, 2001). Trostel, Walker and Woolley (2002) use data from twenty-eight countries covering the period 1985–95, from a common questionnaire applied in all countries. Averaged over the twenty-eight separate country estimates, the mean return is 5.8% for men, with an unweighted standard deviation of 3.5%. For women, the mean return is 6.8%, with standard deviation 3.9%. Returns in the United States are markedly higher than in Europe. Heckman, Lochner and Todd (2003) estimate returns between 10 and 13% for white men and between 9 and 15% for black men in the 1940–90 period. In recent research attention is focused on an increase in the rate of return that has been observed in the United States but not generally elsewhere (see Trostel, Walker and Woolley, 2002). The increase is linked to lower demand for the poorly educated, due to relocating low-skilled work to developing countries, and increased demand for the more highly educated, due to knowledge-intense new technologies.

1.2 More recent developments

A key problem with the return estimates just described is the assumption that someone with s years of education would have earned the same Y_0 as someone with 0 years of education if s/he had also chosen 0 years of education. And vice versa it is assumed that someone who chose to follow 0 years of education would have earned the same Y_s as someone who actually chose s years of education if s/he had chosen s years of education. This is an example of the basic evaluation problem. To evaluate the effects of an intervention one ideally needs to compare two outcomes, only one of which is actually observed, while the other – the counterfactual – has to be inferred. Taking the earnings of those who chose the other level of education as counterfactual generally gives a biased estimate of the return to education. The bias occurs when individuals who choose different levels of education differ systematically in unobserved characteristics that affect their earnings. Differences in relevant dimensions of ability and motivation are obvious candidates for such characteristics. The problem of unobserved heterogeneity does not disappear if one adds measurable characteristics, such as IQ scores or parental background. Datasets are limited and one cannot pretend to measure all the relevant variables.

To properly identify the counterfactual one either wants to randomly assign individuals to different levels of education, or to clone individuals so that identical individuals can attend different levels of education. During the past fifteen years, different researchers have come up with approaches that mimic these two ideal identification strategies. In the approach that mimics random assignment, researchers have looked for situations or events that treat otherwise identical persons very differently in a way that affects their education decisions but not their later earnings. Such situations or events are referred to as natural experiments and in statistical terms create instrumental variables. This idea was developed and first applied by Angrist and Krueger (1991), mimicking the random assignment obtained from US compulsory school laws. They imply that individuals born in different quarters of the year have different amounts of schooling if they start school on the first day that they are required to do so and stop the first day they are allowed to do so. The quarter of birth thus creates differences in the amount of schooling among individuals that is as good as random. The identifying assumption is then that the quarter of birth has no direct effect on earnings. Others have followed Angrist and Krueger's example using different natural experiments, like proximity to college, gender composition of a girl's siblings and changes in compulsory school laws. Almost without exception these studies find returns to education that are at least as high as the returns obtained with a Mincer regression.

The approach that mimics cloning of people uses information from (identical) twins. The underlying idea is that identical twins share the same genetic and social characteristics so that there will be no systematic difference in their earnings when they obtain the same level of education. Consequently, if they have acquired different levels of education, any observed earnings difference can be attributed to this education difference. Twin studies of the returns to schooling have been conducted for the United States, the United Kingdom, Sweden and Australia. The results by and large confirm the findings from the natural experiment studies that the return is at least as high as the returns obtained with a Mincer regression. An important contribution in this line of research is the paper by Ashenfelter and Krueger (1994) who ask each twin the level of education of his/her twin brother/sister so that they can deal more satisfactory with the problem of measurement error in education.

The finding that the corrected return to education was at least as high – and sometimes even much higher – than the Mincer return came somewhat as a surprise. It was believed that the Mincer return was biased upwards because it also captures the earnings effects of unobserved ability and motivation. Studies that include an ability measure like IQ indeed tend to find a reduction in the rate of return, on average by about one-third. In explaining this counterintuitive result it was realized that the various situations that have been used as natural experiments might have had an impact on specific groups. Changes in compulsory school laws, for instance, affect in particular those individuals who want to stay in school as short a time as possible, and are unlikely to affect individuals who would in any case pursue a higher education. This insight makes clear that there is no such thing as 'the' return to education. The effect of an additional year in school may be very different for different individuals (some may benefit more from the same intervention than others) and may be very different depending on whether the extra year is the fourth year or the tenth year. Moreover, the effect of an extra year will depend on the exact curriculum that is taught during the extra year.

Some studies test the validity of the instrumental variables using an over-identification test. Such a test can only be performed when there are more instruments than potentially endogenous variables. In this test the residual of the earnings equation is regressed on all the instruments. The instrument set is said to be valid if the instruments are unrelated to the residual. (In an exactly identified model, this holds by construction.) What this test basically does is test whether different (combinations of) instruments would have given the same estimate for the return to education. Two remarks are in order. First, as should be clear from the discussion above, rejecting this test does not necessarily invalidate the instruments. If the instruments affect different individuals or affect decisions at different levels of education, it is perfectly conceivable that they give different estimates. Second, passing the over-identification test does not prove that the instruments are valid. The test assumes that the model is at least exactly identified and thus that at least one of the instruments is valid. This assumption cannot be tested. In our view the use of the over-identification test in this field of research is somewhat misleading.

Two recent studies investigate the heterogeneity of returns. Aakvik, Salvanas and Vaage (2003) use an increase in the amount of compulsory schooling from seven to nine years in Norway to identify the wage effect of an extra year of schooling. To identify the returns to an extra year for different levels of education, they interact the reform indicator with information about local availability of schools of different levels. For an extra year of the lowest level of vocational education a return of 0.7% is reported. For the next level of vocational education a return is reported of 8.6% for a two- or three-year programme. For higher levels of education (upper secondary to university) returns are substantially larger.

Meghir and Palme (2003) evaluate a social experiment in Sweden. The experiment had three ingredients: the number of years of compulsory schooling was increased from seven or eight to nine years, streaming was delayed, and means-tested subsidies for education were provided. The experiment started in just a few municipalities and was then extended to others. The key findings are (1) that the reform increased participation in education among students with unskilled fathers, especially for such students with *below* median ability, and (2) that overall earnings increased, which is mainly due to a large impact of the reform on earnings of individuals with *above* median ability and unskilled fathers.

Besides highlighting the heterogeneity in returns along various dimensions, the results of the two studies show that an extra year of education can have a negligible effect on earnings.

1.3 Contributions to the international literature

We have made several contributions to the international literature: a long time series of returns to education, an analysis of international differences in wage inequality by education (market forces or institutions?), a discussion of the causal effects of education, and attention to the skill content of schooling.

Using a succession of datasets, we have estimated Mincer rates of return in the Netherlands from 1962 to 2001. The estimates are reproduced in figure 1.3. The substantial drop in the returns to education between the early 1960s and the mid 1980s, one of the largest observed in the empirical literature, can be attributed to an equally substantial increase in the supply of educated labour. In 1960, 57% of the male labour force had only basic education and 4% had a higher vocational degree. In 1979 22.9% had just basic education and 13.6% had a higher vocational degree. For women, these figures changed from 54 and 1% to 20.5 and 11.9%. Although the increase in education levels

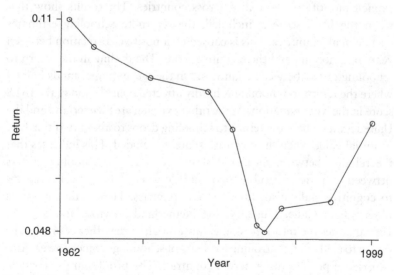

Figure 1.3. Mincer estimates of return to schooling for the Netherlands, 1962–99 males

of the workforce has continued, we observe a stabilization of the returns to education between 1985 and 1995 and a fairly rapid increase after 1995. This pattern is commonly explained by changes on the demand side. Skill-biased technological change and changes in the international trade patterns are often mentioned as forces causing more demand for high-skilled workers and a declining demand for low-skilled workers. Hence market forces seem largely responsible for increased earnings inequality between educational levels within the Netherlands (cf. Hartog, Oosterbeek and Teulings, 1995; Leuven and Oosterbeek, 2000). We elaborate on this interpretation below.

Leuven, Oosterbeek and Van Ophem (2004) present Mincer estimates of returns to education for various countries. These returns differ substantially across countries, from 3.4% in Sweden to 10.3% in Chile. For the United States the return to schooling according to the IALS (International Adult Literacy Survey) dataset equals 9.2%, which is an estimate well within the range commonly found for this country. For eight out of fifteen countries the point estimate of the return to schooling falls in the narrow range of 4.4 to 6.4%, consistent with results reported elsewhere. The paper also presents returns from Mincer equations augmented with the IALS test score measure. The IALS includes a skills measure based on various tests that have been developed with the explicit aim of comparability across countries. The results show that when the IALS score is included, the return to schooling estimates decline in all countries. This is caused by a positive correlation between years of schooling and the cognitive score. The decline in the return to schooling differs between countries. On the one extreme stands Poland where the return to schooling is hardly affected by inclusion of the IALS score in the wage equation. At the other extreme are Switzerland and the United States where the return to schooling drops to about two-thirds of its initial value when the cognitive score is included. This indicates that the relation between measured skills and years of schooling differs between countries, a result we exploit below. The labour market returns to cognitive skills also differ across countries. Here a dichotomy is observed: in Chile, Hungary, the Netherlands, Switzerland and the United States the return to skill is substantial; in the other countries the return to skill after controlling for years of schooling is much lower. Also experience profiles differ across countries. The profiles are steepest in Switzerland, Italy, Canada and the United States, and are (relatively) flat in Chile, Hungary, the Czech Republic and Slovenia.

While increased earnings inequality between education and skill groups within countries is frequently ascribed to demand and supply forces, an often-cited paper by Blau and Kahn (1996) claims that market forces are unable to explain differences in earnings inequality between skill groups across countries. Instead they attribute them to differences in labour market institutions. Leuven et al. (2004) challenge this conclusion. The key point is that Blau and Kahn define skill groups in terms of attained levels of education. While this is a legitimate procedure when analysing developments within a country, this need no longer be the case when examining differences across countries (as we noted above). Blau and Kahn's procedure assumes that a year of education in the United States has exactly the same meaning in terms of skills as a year of education in Germany. A consequence of this procedure is that 50% of the German workforce would belong to the lowest one-third of the US workforce in terms of skill level. Instead of measuring skills in terms of levels of education, Leuven et al. use the IALS score as a direct measure of cognitive skill. Redoing the Blau and Kahn analysis with a skill measure based on education leads Leuven et al. to the same conclusion as Blau and Kahn. But once they measure skill based on internationally comparable test results, the conclusion completely reverses. International differences in wage inequality between skill groups across countries are to a large extent consistent with differences in demand and supply of different skill groups. Or, to put it differently, low-skilled workers in the United States earn relatively low wages compared to low-skilled workers in other (mainly continental European) countries because they are in abundant supply. This has important implications for policy. While the Blau and Kahn result suggests that the relative position of the low-skilled can be improved by protective labour market institutions, the conclusion of Leuven et al. is that the best policy for improving the position of the low-skilled is to reduce their relative supply. This can be achieved by expansion of education participation.

Systematic comparison of returns to education, with the aim of understanding the difference, is not well developed. Ashenfelter, Harmon and Oosterbeek (1999) make a contribution by performing a meta-analysis of ninety-six results extracted from twenty-seven different papers that give estimates of the return to schooling. In a meta-analysis the units of observation are individual studies, and variables typically included in the database are the estimated effect along with its standard error, the number of observations, and year and country of study. The main point of their analysis is testing for the presence of publication bias. Publication bias refers to the possibility that the observed sample of published results was selected solely because they were 'statistically significant'. Publication or reporting bias may exist even without the authors of individual studies being aware of it. The potential problem arises because of the desire to report useful results. Results against the null hypothesis of no effect are usually considered more valuable and more likely to be reported. To analyse publication bias, Ashenfelter et al. split their sample of results into three groups: straight Mincer returns, returns based on instrumental variables, and returns obtained from twin studies. While they find no indication for publication bias in the first group of studies, they show that there is strong evidence for such bias in instrumental variables estimates: on average, the estimates with larger standard errors (IV) also tend to be larger. This accounts for most of the often-cited result that IV estimates are higher than usual Mincer estimates.

Trying to get closer to the true causal effects of schooling, Webbink (2006) and Oosterbeek and Webbink (2004) attempt to identify the earnings effects of specific extra years of education. Webbink (2006) analyses what happened to the earnings of university graduates after a reduction of the length of university programmes from five to four years in 1984 relative to what happened to the earnings of graduates from unchanged higher vocational programmes. Similarly, Oosterbeek and Webbink (2004) analyse the earnings differential due to an extension of lower vocational programmes from three to four years, and compare the before/after earnings difference of graduates from these extended programmes with the before/after earnings difference of graduates from programmes that were unaffected by the change. According to these studies, an extra year of university education boosts earnings by 7 to 9%, whereas an extra year of lower vocational education has no effect on earnings.

Jonker (2001) looks in the black box of human capital measured in years of schooling and compares different educational tracks for chartered accountants: a regular, full-time university programme or a dual track where part-time schooling is combined with junior work as an accountant. The two tracks end up in exams with the same requirements, but the university programme contains a broader set of fields, providing graduates with more general skills. University-trained accountants indeed embark on somewhat broader careers, and have somewhat steeper earnings profiles, as human capital theory predicts (from the greater emphasis on general skills relative to job-specific skills). But generally, the differences in labour market performance are very small. However, the dual track is more often chosen by students from lower socioeconomic backgrounds, indicating that the main difference between the two tracks is accessibility for students with poorer family backgrounds. Due to the lack of a credible source of exogenous variation in factors that affect the choice of type of track, Jonker does not purge her estimates from possible endogeneity bias.

Oosterbeek and Van Ophem (2000) deviate from the almost universally assumed log linear effect of schooling on earnings. With a quadratic specification they find that marginal returns decline for successive years of education. They also find that returns are higher for individuals with higher IQ scores (measured at age 12). A male with IQ 100 has a marginal rate of return of 10.0% at six years of schooling and of 6.8% at twelve years of schooling; with an IQ of 120, these marginal returns are 12.0 and 8.8%. Such results can explain why abler individuals have a longer education; international evidence on the relationship between ability and returns is mixed (Hartog, 2001).

1.4 Conclusion and discussion

This chapter provided a brief and non-technical summary of the developments in the field of measuring the private financial return to education. While there is reason to suspect that the simple Mincerian estimates are biased, more sophisticated studies show that this is probably not the case. One should be well aware what these estimates exactly represent. They measure the average percentage earnings differential per year of schooling between individuals with different levels of education based on cross-sectional observations. As such these estimates provide a useful summary of earnings inequality associated with schooling in a particular year in a given country. The cross-section average return to a year of education has been estimated many times, at different times and different places. Internationally, the estimates are in the interval between 5 and 15%, with values in Europe clustering at the low end of the interval. We have contributed to understanding international differences by showing that conventional supply and demand arguments make a strong contribution and that institutional wage compression in Europe is not the dominant factor to explain differences with the United States. Still, the literature on explaining international differences is remarkably thin. One might suspect that differences in the structure of the school system and in financial aid to students have consequences for the returns to education. However, we have no evidence on these issues. Similarly, we have no reliable evidence on variations in the rate of return across types of education (vocational versus academic, across academic disciplines), levels of education and across individuals (e.g. by ability or family background). There are good reasons to suspect that abler individuals benefit more from higher education and that contributions of ability and schooling to earnings are not independent. We find support for this assumption, and thus contribute to internationally mixed evidence.

The human capital earnings function has a standard specification, based on Mincer's formulation: log linear in years of schooling, returns to experience independent of returns to school years. But this specification only holds under tight restrictions, which certainly need not hold.[2] Indeed, we found evidence of marginal returns declining in school years.

In Hartog, Van Ophem and Bajdechi (2004) we find that the effect of experience is not independent of education: higher education leads to steeper earnings profiles. This can easily add four percentage points to the rate of return on a university education. Much remains to be done to uncover stable patterns in variation of the rate of return across time, place and individuals.

One should be cautious in using the estimated private rates of return for policy conclusions. A popular interpretation is that high returns to education justify increased investments in education, and that low returns have the opposite implication. This interpretation is not warranted. The Mincer returns typically measure private returns to investments in education, whereas policies should be based on the social return (see chapter 2 for more about social returns). While this may seem a trivial observation, recent Dutch policy discussions show the contrary. Even academically trained economists have argued for more public expenditure for education with reference to the increased private return.

Private returns are primarily of interest for private decision-making. In that sense, more detailed information about variation in rates of return, across studies and over time, can be quite useful. In particular, information on the riskiness of the investments may be welcome (see chapter 9). Yet, properly assessed private returns are also useful as policy guidance.

High private returns may justify higher private contributions, either as lower subsidies to tuition, or as higher contributions ex post, e.g. student loans rather than scholarships (see chapter 13). These issues too demand more detailed information. The average cross-section return to an average year of education is insufficient guide to lay out the details of a student support scheme. The same need for detailed information holds for other questions. For example, low returns to schooling may be countered by higher public expenditure on schooling if the low returns are due to poor quality of education. Increasing quality may then very well pay off to individuals and society. Thus, while we have abundant evidence on the average earnings effect of additional schooling, and we can safely conclude that on average schooling is a very rewarding investment, we have no systematic body of evidence on variation of returns by length of schooling, quality of schooling, type of schooling or type of individual. In that sense, after all these decades of estimation, there is still more work to do.

Notes

1. One may also bring in compensation for direct outlays K, but often these are very small relative to earnings forgone: a tuition fee of 1,500 euros does not weigh heavily if the opportunity cost is 20,000 euros. But this may differ between countries, depending on the extent to which tuition is subsidized.
2. See Card (1999) for a more general specification.

References

Aakvik, A., K. Salvanas and K. Vaage (2003). Measuring heterogeneity in the returns to education in Norway using educational reforms. IZA Discussion Paper 815, Bonn.

Angrist, J. and A. Krueger (1991). Does compulsory schooling attendance affect schooling and earnings? *Quarterly Journal of Economics*, 106: 970–1014.

Ashenfelter, O. and A. Krueger (1994). Estimates on the economic returns to schooling from a new sample of twins. *American Economic Review*, 84(5): 1157–73.

Ashenfelter, O., C. Harmon and H. Oosterbeek (1999). A review of estimates of the schooling/earnings relationship, with tests for publication bias. *Labour Economics*, 6: 453–70.

Blau, F. and L. Kahn (1996). International differences in male wage inequality: institutions versus market forces. *Journal of Political Economy*, 104: 791–837.

Card, D. (1999). The causal effect of education on earnings, in O. Ashenfelter and D. Card (eds.), *Handbook of Labor Economics*, vol. IIIA. Amsterdam: North-Holland, pp. 1801–63.

Harmon, C., I. Walker and N. Westergaard-Nielsen (2001). *Education and Earnings in Europe*. Cheltenham: Edward Elgar.

Hartog, J. (2001). On human capital and individual capabilities. *Review of Income and Wealth*, 47 (4): 515–40.

Hartog, J., H. Oosterbeek and C. Teulings (1995). Age, wages and education in the Netherlands, in P. Johnson and K. Zimmermann, *Labour Markets in an Ageing Europe*. Cambridge: Cambridge University Press.

Hartog, J., H. van Ophem and S. Bajdechi (2004). How risky is investment in human capital? CESifo Working Paper 1261, Munich.

Heckman, J., L. Lochner and P. Todd (2003). Fifty years of Mincer earnings regressions. IZA Discussion Paper 775, Bonn.

Jonker, N. (2001). Job Performance and Career Prospects of Auditors. PhD thesis, Tinbergen Institute.

Leuven, E. and H. Oosterbeek (2000). Rendement op scholing stijgt. *Economisch Statistische Berichten* 23-6-2000: 523–4.

Leuven, E., H. Oosterbeek and H. van Ophem (2004). Explaining international differences in male skill wage differentials by differences in demand and supply of skill. *Economic Journal*, 114: 466–86.

Meghir, C. and M. Palme (2003). Ability, parental background and education policy: empirical evidence from a social experiment. Working Paper 5/03, IFS, London.

Mincer, J. (1974). *Schooling, Experience, and Earnings*. National Bureau for Economic Reseach. New York: Columbia University Press.

Oosterbeek, H. and H. van Ophem (2000). Schooling choices: preferences, discount rates and rates of return. *Empirical Economics*, 25 (1): 15–34.

Oosterbeek, H. and D. Webbink (2004). Wage effects of an extra year of lower vocational education: evidence from a simultaneous change of compulsory school leaving age and program length. Working Paper.

Psacharopoulos, G. (1985). Returns to education: a further international update and implications. *Journal of Human Resources*, 20: 583–97.

Trostel, P., I. Walker and P. Woolley (2002). Estimates of the return to schooling for 28 countries. *Labour Economics*, 9: 1–16.

Webbink, D. (2006). Returns to university education: evidence from a Dutch institutional reform. *Economica*, forthcoming.

2 | *The social returns to education*

MIKAEL LINDAHL AND ERIK CANTON

2.1 Introduction

The most frequently estimated relationship in labour economics is the one between wages and education using micro data on working individuals. The general finding is that an additional year of education increases wages by 5–15%. The figure is at the lower end for egalitarian countries such as the Netherlands and Sweden and at the upper end for many developing countries. The general consensus is that such an interval estimate quite well resembles the causal effect of education on wages, i.e. the private return to education (cf. chapter 1).

Is the estimated private return averaged over individuals a good indicator of the social return to education? Two conditions need to be fulfilled. First, the estimated private wage return needs to be equal to the effect of education on productivity. This is not the case if, for instance, institutions compress the wage structure or if education is just a signal of ability to employers. Second, there should be no (non-internalized) externalities to education. Education externalities exist if the education level of others affects the productivity of the individual. We may here differentiate between static externalities, when education has a one-time effect on output (Lucas, 1988), and dynamic externalities, where a higher education level makes the economy grow faster, perhaps because more human capital increases the number of innovations (Romer, 1990), or makes it easier to imitate technologies developed by others (Nelson and Phelps, 1966). There are also effects of education on outcomes other than productivity. For instance, a higher level of education has been shown to decrease mortality (Lleras-Muney, 2005), affect voting behaviour (Milligan, Moretti and Oreopoulos, 2004) and reduce criminal activity (Lochner and Moretti, 2004) (cf. chapter 5).[1]

If the social return to education is larger than the private return, there are positive externalities to education. If the average education in a country (or a firm, city or region) has an effect on average wages, and that effect is bigger than the estimated relationship for individuals, we have some evidence of positive static externalities to education. If the average education in a country has an effect on the growth of output, conditional on the growth of education, we have some evidence of positive dynamic externalities to education. These externalities are also of interest for policy purposes (see Aghion and Howitt, 1998).

This chapter focuses on two strands of literature: cross-country regressions and cross-region/cities regressions. Before we turn to an overview of the empirical literature, we first recapitulate some macro-economic theory on economic growth, essential for understanding the empirical results. We then review the early empirical growth literature. Third, we go through the main findings of the contribution by Krueger and Lindahl (2001) (henceforth referred to as K&L) and, fourth, we review the new literature on social returns to education published in the last couple of years. We end with policy implications.

2.2 Human capital and macroeconomic theory

When studying the social returns to education, we need to distinguish between level and growth effects of educational attainment, and between static and dynamic externalities. To illustrate the various mechanisms, we start with some textbook macroeconomic theory. Before we consider human capital in a macroeconomic framework, it is helpful to first consider the standard neoclassical growth model as developed by Solow (1956). This theory assumes a production function of the type

$$Y = Af(K, L) \tag{2.1}$$

where Y is output, A is total factor productivity (TFP), K is physical capital, and L is labour. Labour productivity is defined by Y/L. Changes in TFP (A) are called Hicks neutral technological changes. Another widely used neoclassical production function takes the form

$$Y = f(K, EL) \tag{2.2}$$

where E is an efficiency index. For a given capital stock K and labour input L, changes in E lead to changes in labour productivity. Increases in E are thus referred to as labour-augmenting technological progress, also called Harrod neutral technological change.

Let x denote the rate of technological progress (either Hicks or Harrod neutral). Population growth increases the labour force at rate n. Long-run economic growth is equal to population growth and technological progress, $n + x$. As n and x are exogenously determined, this class of models is referred to as exogenous growth models. The short-run rate of economic growth can deviate from the balanced growth rate when the economy is adjusting to a new equilibrium (transition dynamics). In the neoclassical view, each country has access to the world technology (A or E). New knowledge immediately spreads around the world without costs. An important prediction of this model is international convergence in output levels: poor countries grow faster than rich ones. Another prediction is that when capital is mobile, advanced economies should invest in poor countries where capital is scarce and the marginal returns to investment are high.

Human capital in a neoclassical framework

According to human capital theory (developed by Schultz (1961) and Becker (1964)), education enhances a person's skill level and thereby his or her human capital. A higher skill level in the workforce increases the production capacity. Although this sounds very straightforward, systematic research on how to incorporate human capital in theories of growth only started about two decades ago.

As especially the neoclassical prediction of international convergence in per capita production levels is not supported by the data, Robert Lucas asked 'Why doesn't capital flow from rich to poor countries?' (Lucas, 1990). His answer is that international differences in returns to physical capital (as implied by the neoclassical growth model) become much smaller when account is taken of differences in human capital across countries: physical capital tends to move towards countries with more human capital. In the 1990s the standard neoclassical growth model was revised by introducing human capital. For instance, Mankiw, Romer and Weil (1992) propose a Cobb-Douglas production function of the form

$$Y = K^{\alpha} H^{\beta} (EL)^{1-\alpha-\beta} \tag{2.3}$$

where H is the human capital stock of the workforce, α is the production elasticity of physical capital, β is the production elasticity of human capital ($\alpha + \beta < 1$ to maintain exogenous balanced growth), and $1 - \alpha - \beta$ is the production elasticity of labour. Mankiw, Romer and Weil use enrolment rates to proxy the human capital stock, but it can also be determined from a macro-Mincer equation of the form

$$H = e^{\pi(s)} \tag{2.4}$$

where s is average years of schooling.

The inclusion of human capital in a neoclassical growth model has several implications. First, the average skill level in the workforce has an impact on the production level. An increase in the average years of schooling in the population increases the human capital stock H, and thereby the production level Y. Second, when markets are competitive (so that factor returns are given by their marginal product), the human capital stock not only affects the wage rate, but also the interest rate. Increases in the human capital stock thereby also lead to increases in the interest rate, and to adjustments in the physical capital stock. Third, changes in the stock of human capital only have a temporary impact on the growth rate; the balanced growth rate is again determined by the exogenous rate of labour-augmenting technical progress and population growth.

Human capital and endogenous growth

So far we have assumed that long-run economic growth is exogenous. An increase in human capital leads to higher production levels, but does not affect the balanced growth rate. Policies and deliberate actions to build human capital only have a transitory impact on economic growth, and the balanced growth rate is determined by parameters that cannot be manipulated. Lucas (1988) proposes to introduce endogenous growth through human capital accumulation. We will be brief in our summary; for an elaborate treatment of the analysis the reader is referred to Lucas (1988) and to Barro and Sala-i-Martin (1995). Suppose that the production function takes the form

$$Y = K^{\alpha}(uH)^{1-\alpha} \tag{2.5}$$

where u is time devoted to production. How is human capital accumulated? Schooling and experience gained on the shop floor are two well-known ways of building human capital. The former is often labelled learning-or-doing (as time devoted to schooling competes with production time), and the latter as learning-by-doing (Lucas, 1988). Suppose that each employee is allotted one unit of time, which can be used for production or learning. Learning-or-doing can be modelled as

$$\gamma_H = B(1 - u) - \delta \tag{2.6}$$

where γ_H is the growth rate of human capital for a representative individual (so aggregated across individuals γ_H also denotes the macroeconomic growth rate of human capital), $1 - u$ is the time devoted to learning, B is the transformation rate of learning into human capital and δ is depreciation of human capital. The core of the model responsible for endogenous growth is that there are constant returns to scale with regard to reproducible factor inputs, physical capital and human capital. Investments in physical and human capital entail a trade-off between current and future consumption. The optimal consumption path is derived from maximization of the consumer's intertemporal utility function. In this model, consumer preferences and the human capital accumulation technology together determine the long-run growth rate. As economic growth is determined from structural parameters, growth is called endogenous. Notice that human capital is a purely private commodity in this analysis. Increases in human capital translate into higher wages, and there are no external effects. So there is no reason (in terms of economic efficiency) for government interference in this framework. The widely invoked argument that the government should support education because education is good for growth is therefore not valid in the Lucas economy without spillovers.

Lucas also considers a model with human capital externalities. Production is affected by the average human capital stock $\overline{H}$, i.e.

$$Y = K^{\alpha}(uH)^{1-\alpha}\overline{H}^{\psi} \tag{2.7}$$

where ψ captures the size of the spillover effect. As average educational attainment has a one-time effect on the output level, this is sometimes referred to as a static externality. Individuals base their human capital investment decision on the private marginal product of human capital, taking the average human capital stock as given. The social marginal product of human capital takes the effect of individual human capital investments on the average human capital stock into account. In the presence of human capital spillovers there is a wedge between the private and the social marginal product of human capital. Without government action, there will be underinvestment in human capital from a social viewpoint.

Human capital and technology adoption

In the endogenous growth model by Lucas (1988), sustained economic growth is due to the accumulation of human capital over time. An alternative view is that a country's human capital stock affects the rate of economic growth. For instance, in Romer's (1990) analysis, innovations are generated by the human capital stock, and Nelson and Phelps (1966) assume that the human capital stock determines the ability to assimilate new technologies. One way to model the idea that human capital builds absorptive capacity is to link the growth rate of total factor productivity to the human capital stock, i.e.

$$\gamma_A = \gamma_A(H) \tag{2.8}$$

with $\gamma_A' > 0$. This type of spillover is also referred to as a dynamic human capital externality. Whether it is the stock of human capital or its accumulation that is important for growth is a testable empirical question, to which we turn next.

2.3 Main findings from the early growth literature

Much of the literature prior to K&L found the level of education to have a positive impact on the growth in output, with the change (or growth) in education having no impact on output growth. This is in accordance with dynamic, but not static, externalities. Barro and Sala-i-Martin (1995) estimate ten-year growth in output 1965–85 as a function of average years of schooling and a number of variables such as life expectance, political instability and initial output.[2] Male (female) secondary and higher education is found to have positive (negative) effects on growth if specified in levels, whereas there appears to be no effect of change in education.[3] Barro and Sala-i-Martin explain the somewhat peculiar result that female educational attainment is bad for economic growth by arguing that less female attainment signifies more backwardness, and a higher growth potential through the convergence mechanism. Another explanation is that the regression results suffer from multi-collinearity when both male and female attainment are included (cf. K&L).

As discussed in section 2.2, Mankiw, Romer and Weil (1992) extend the standard neoclassical growth model with human capital. Investments in human capital are measured by using a schooling variable, namely the percentage of the labour force enrolled in secondary education (primary and tertiary education are not considered). The econometric results show that the inclusion of human capital improves the fit of the model. A representative outcome of their analysis is the following production function

$$Y = K^{1/3}H^{1/3}L^{1/3}. \tag{2.9}$$

This implies a production elasticity of human capital of $\frac{1}{3}$: 1% more human capital translates into $\frac{1}{3}$% higher production. It is important to note that in equilibrium, the human capital stock affects a country's production level, but not the rate of economic growth. Changes in the stock of human capital will lead to transition dynamics, and this predicts a positive relationship between human capital accumulation and economic growth during the transition period. While Mankiw, Romer and Weil do find evidence for such a positive relationship for the total country sample, their results are not robust to changes in the country sample. No significant relationship between human capital investments and GDP growth (per working-age person) is found for the OECD countries.

Benhabib and Spiegel (1994) estimate growth in output 1965–85 as a function of growth in labour force participation, in capital and in years of schooling, as well as initial log output level, in seventy-eight countries. They find a negative but insignificant effect of growth in education. When they also include the initial level of years of schooling (measured in logs), they find this variable to have a significant positive effect on growth. Pritchett (2001) finds similar results for growth in education (using an improved education measure) to Benhabib and Spiegel, controlling for investment growth rates.[4]

2.4 Measurement errors and specification issues

Krueger and Lindahl (2001) attempt to solve the conflict between micro and macro estimates. Micro studies show a robust positive private return to education; macro studies display a lack of association between growth in GDP per capita and education changes in cross-country data. K&L show that by simply aggregating the micro-Mincer relationship to the country level (under some assumptions and after correcting for the labour share in the economy), one would expect a similar estimate of the association between growth in GDP per capita and changes in average years of schooling as between log wages and years of schooling. The micro estimate should tell the same story as a macro-Mincer relationship: see also Heckman and Klenow (1998), Topel (1999), and Bils and Klenow (2000). Hence, it is puzzling that the cross-country regressions have found a positive association between growth and the initial level of education, but no association with changes in education.

There are several reasons why estimation of education effects using micro-Mincer and macro-Mincer growth specifications differ, but K&L conclude that the combination of controlling for the change in the capital stock and a high degree of measurement error in the change in schooling variable across countries, explains this finding.[5] If the coefficient on capital growth is restricted to have a more plausible value (one minus the labour share), change in schooling has an effect on growth closer to what one would have predicted (around 8%, and significant). This is also the case if measurement error in schooling is corrected for (producing an estimate around 7% but with a very large standard error). K&L (2001: 1126) conclude that 'unless measurement error problems in schooling are overcome, we doubt the cross-country growth equations that control for capital growth will be very informative insofar as the benefit of education is concerned'.

In fact, K&L have put a lot of effort into the question of the extent of measurement error in cross-country schooling data. K&L find that the Barro-Lee data (used in Barro and Sala-i-Martin, 1995) and the Kyriacou data (used in Benhabib and Spiegel, 1994) are very reliable if the data is in *levels*, but that especially the Kyriacou data has very low reliability if the data is in *changes*.

K&L also estimated less restrictive versions of the macro growth model. First, they investigated the assumption that all countries have the same relationship between growth and education at the start of the period, by allowing for country-specific effects. K&L found that the average effect of initial education on growth is negative and statistically insignificant for years of schooling and negative and statistically significant for male secondary and higher education. Second, K&L investigated the importance of the linearity assumption of initial education. They find that initial education had a significant positive impact on growth for the countries with the lowest education and a negative impact for the countries with the highest education.[6]

K&L conclude that change in education is positively associated with economic growth when measurement error in education is accounted for, and that this association is often greater than what would be expected from the micro-Mincer literature. This is either because of reverse causality or omitted variables at the country level, or because of externalities not captured by the micro-Mincer estimations. They argued that unless researchers find credible sources of identification and deal explicitly with measurement error, we are unlikely to learn much about human capital accumulation and growth from cross-country data.

2.5 The new literature on social returns using cross-country data

Before turning to a growing strand of literature that utilizes within-country variation across areas, we sum up the development in the cross-country literature of education and growth in the last couple of years. None of these studies deals satisfactory with the endogeneity issue but they make several other important contributions.

De la Fuente and Doménech (2006) improve the data on education for OECD countries and find a strong positive correlation between the quality of education data and the size and significance of education coefficients in GDP and growth regressions. For instance, they investigate and remove sharp breaks in previous data series. Comparing the improved data and its performance with the data in Barro and Lee (1993, 1996), Kyriacou (1991) and with other utilized data series on education, they find that their own data and a dataset by Cohen and Soto (2001) perform best. The elasticity of GDP per worker and years of schooling appears to be around 1, implying a social return to education of about 10%, slightly above the average private returns in OECD countries.

Cohen and Soto (2001) also spend much effort on improving the cross-country data on education. They do this for ninety-five countries and estimate school attainment for five-year age groups in ten-year

Table 2.1 *Summary of cross-country literature on social returns to education*

Study	Human capital data	Dependent variable	Human capital stock	Change in human capital
Barro and Sala-i-Martin (1995)	Barro and Lee (1993)	Growth in GDP per capita	+ for males – for females	0
Benhabib and Spiegel (1994)	Kyriacou (1991)	Growth in GDP per capita Growth in TFP	+	0
Cohen and Soto (2001)	Own data constructed from several sources	GDP per capita Growth in GDP per capita	+ 0	+
De la Fuente and Doménech (2006)	Own data constructed from several sources	GDP per worker Growth in GDP per worker	+ (OECD)	+ (OECD)
Heckman and Klenow (1998)	Barro and Lee (1993)	GDP per capita	+	
Krueger and Lindahl (2001)	Barro and Lee (1993) and Kyriacou (1991)	Growth in GDP per capita	+ 0 (average of country-specific education estimates)	+
Mankiw, Romer and Weil (1992)	UNESCO	Growth in GDP per worker		+
Portela, Alessie and Teulings (2004)	Revised version of Barro and Lee (2001)	Growth in GDP per worker	+	+
Pritchett (2001)	Barro and Lee (1993) and Nehru, Swanson and Dubey (1995)	Growth in GDP per worker		0
Topel (1999)	Barro and Lee (1993)	Growth in GDP per worker		+

Note: When a coefficient estimate is reported to have 0 return, it means that the estimate was statistically insignificant.

intervals, utilizing OECD, national or UNESCO censuses, extrapolating missing observations. Sometimes they rely on enrolment data when census data is missing. Their data is probably the best existing dataset on education for a large number of countries to date. Regressing GDP per capita on years of schooling, controlling for the investment rate, they find a social return to education of 8–10%. Regressing GDP growth on the change in years of schooling, social returns turn out to be about 8–9%. Such social returns are very similar to the typical private return in most countries.

Teulings and van Rens (2003) extend the analysis in K&L in two ways. They include general equilibrium effects because of imperfect substitution between well-educated and poorly educated workers (by including quadratic terms of education levels) and they allow for skill-biased technological change (by including interaction terms between time dummies and initial education). They show that it is important to separate the returns to education into a short-run and long-run return, showing that the latter consistently exceeds the former. They also find evidence of skill-biased technological progress.

Portela, Alessie and Teulings (2004) put a lot of effort into the measurement of education in the Barro-Lee data. They find that measurement error is systematic instead of classical. Specifically, Barro and Lee use census information, and when this information is not available the authors generate a forward flow or a backward flow by using a perpetual inventory method based on enrolment data. Portela, Alessie and Teulings show that the perpetual inventory method smoothes observations, thereby compressing the data. They correct the Barro-Lee data, and use the improved series in growth regressions. Their econometric results suggest that both the level and change in education are important for growth.

2.6 The new literature on social returns using individual and within-country data

K&L argued at the end of their paper that because of the problem of unreliable cross-country data on education and the difficulty of solving the reverse causality/omitted variable issues, the most promising path for future research in this field would be to focus on using variation across regions within a country instead of cross-country data. In their own words: 'it might be more promising to examine growth across regions of countries with reliable data' (K&L, 2001: 1131). Whereas much improvement in the issue of measurement errors in cross-country educational data has been seen in the last couple of years, the literature on cross-country regressions has not dealt with the reverse causality and omitted variable issues. We will therefore survey the newest development in the field of social returns, where the focus has been on finding credible exogenous variation across areas within a country.[7]

Acemoglu and Angrist (2001) estimate log wages on years of schooling and state average years of schooling, controlling for year, state of birth and residence effects, using US individual data. Simple OLS estimates find private returns of about 7% and externalities of about the same magnitude.[8] Acemoglu and Angrist argue that a serious problem with these simple OLS estimates is that economic growth in a state might increase wages as well as the demand for education. They therefore use state-specific indicators of compulsory schooling laws as instruments for state average education.[9] To deal with endogenous migration across states, they use these laws in state of residence at age 30 instead of in state of birth. To deal with the endogeneity of individual years of schooling they also use quarter of birth as an additional instrument. They find that when endogeneity is taken into account the private return to schooling is about 7% and the external return is small and statistically insignificant. Hence, the social return is found to roughly equal the private return to education.

Moretti (2004) estimates the relationship between individual wages and the fraction of individuals with college degrees in US cities. He attempts to deal with endogeneity by including city dummies and simultaneously instrumenting average education with the lagged age structure in the city. The baseline estimate shows that a one percentage point increase in the college share in a city is associated with about 1.1–1.2% higher average wages. Using lagged age structure as an instrument generates higher estimates on average and about 2% higher wages for poorly educated groups. Moretti translates the coefficient estimated for college share into an estimate for average years of schooling. An education externality of about 1% increase in average wages of a one percentage point increase in the college share is equivalent to one college year of schooling generating 25% higher wages, and the effect would be even bigger for the poorly educated. Assuming the private return to one college year to be about 8%, this would mean education externalities of the size of 17%, a very large estimate indeed.

The very large externalities found by Moretti (2004) deviate from the findings in Acemoglu and Angrist (2001). One reason is that even though the private return appears to be linear, the social return is higher at higher levels of education. The different identification strategies probably also explain at least part of the difference.

In existing work in this area it is mostly assumed that workers with different human capital are perfect substitutes in production. Under this assumption one can interpret the effect of average human capital or the college share on individual wages as externalities. This is no longer the case if workers with different skill levels are imperfect substitutes. Imperfect substitutability implies that an increase in the aggregate supply of skilled workers tends to increase the wages of unskilled workers and decrease the wages of employees with high levels of education. Ciccone and Peri (2006) develop a method to distinguish human capital externalities from imperfect substitutability in production. This is done by replacing the dependent variable (the wage growth in the region) with a measure of wage growth which is adjusted for the composition of workers with different education in the beginning of the period. They find that average schooling externalities in US cities are close to zero and insignificant. They also show that the very large externalities found in Moretti (2004) might be driven by a lack of control for imperfect substitutability.

2.7 Conclusions and discussion

We conclude that there is not much evidence of any sizeable static externalities to education. The importance of dynamic externalities is more uncertain. Much work remains to be done on these issues, but the reading of the literature so far points towards the conclusion that the social return to education is about the same or maybe slightly higher than the private return. External effects provide no firm basis for extra government subsidies to education.

This means that large subsidies to education and compulsory schooling laws should be based on other grounds. They may be justified, for instance, on the effects that education has on civic participation, reduced crime and longer life expectancy (cf. chapter 5), as well as because of an effect on the opportunities and outcomes of the next generation (cf. chapter 6). Indeed, De la Fuente and Ciccone (2003: 4) conclude that 'when a reasonable allowance is made for non-market returns to education and for its benefits for social cohesion, human capital becomes a rather attractive investment alternative from a social point of view'.

One area where more work needs to be done is on the question whether there are positive externalities for some levels and types of education. We know something about the former but very little about the latter issue.

Notes

1. There is also evidence of a positive link between educational investments across generations (cf. chapter 6).
2. The apparent advantage of these so-called Barro regressions is that the method can be useful to detect mechanisms that have been ignored by theorists. However, the inclusion of indicators is to some extent ad hoc. Also, the empirical results may depend on the included list of variables. Indeed, Levine and Renelt (1992) have shown that only a few variables appear with robustly significant coefficients.
3. In an earlier paper, Barro (1991), running similar regressions but measuring education in enrolment rates, found both primary and secondary enrolment rates to have a positive impact.
4. The studies reviewed here are only a few of the many studies estimating cross-country growth regressions focusing on education effects. For more extensive reviews, see Pritchett (2006), De la Fuente and Ciccone (2003) and Sianesi and Van Reenen (2003).
5. Even though one would like to control for the growth in the capital stock in GDP growth regressions, it makes estimation of the effect of change in education very difficult if education is poorly measured. If growth in capital and change in education are highly correlated, the estimate for the change in education is too low if this variable is also poorly measured. Simultaneously including growth in capital and change in education in growth regressions is also complicated by capital growth to some degree probably being determined by increased availability of educated workers and by expected GDP growth.
6. See Vandenbussche, Aghion and Meghir (2005) for a theoretical explanation of this finding.
7. See Moretti (2004) for a more extensive review.
8. This is similar to results found in an early paper by Rauch (1993), who estimates individual log wages as a function of individual and average years of schooling across US cities (controlling for other individual and city variables). He estimates the private return to be about 5% and the additional return from city average education to be 3–5%.
9. See chapter 3 for an explanation of the use of instruments.

References

Acemoglu, D. and J. Angrist (2001). *How Large Are Social Returns to Education? Evidence from Compulsory Schooling Laws.* NBER Macroeconomics Annual 2000. Cambridge, MA: MIT Press.

Aghion, P. and P. Howitt (1998). *Endogenous Growth Theory.* Cambridge, MA: MIT Press.

Barro, R. J. (1991). Economic growth in a cross-section of countries. *Quarterly Journal of Economics*, 106 (2): 407–43.

Barro, R. J. and J. W. Lee (1993). International comparisons of educational attainment. *Journal of Monetary Economics*, 32 (3): 363–94.

(1996). International measures of schooling years and schooling quality. *American Economic Review Papers and Proceedings*, 86 (2): 218–23.

(2001). International data on educational attainment: updates and implications. *Oxford Economic Papers*, 53 (3): 541–63.

Barro, R. J. and X. Sala-i-Martin (1995). *Economic Growth.* Cambridge, MA: MIT Press.

Becker, G. S. (1964). *Human Capital: A Theoretical and Empirical Analysis with Special Reference to Education.* New York: NBER.

Benhabib, J. and M. M. Spiegel (1994). The role of human capital in economic development: evidence from aggregate cross-country data. *Journal of Monetary Economics*, 34 (2): 143–73.

Bils, M. and P. J. Klenow (2000). Does schooling cause growth? *American Economic Review*, 90 (5): 1160–83.

Ciccone, A. and G. Peri (2006). Identifying human capital externalities: theory with applications. *Review of Economic Studies*, 73 (2): 381–412.

Cohen, D. and M. Soto (2001). Growth and human capital: good data, good results. CEPR Discussion Paper 3025, London.

De la Fuente, A. and A. Ciccone (2003). *Human Capital in a Global and Knowledge-Based Economy.* Brussels: European Commission.

De la Fuente, A. and R. Doménech (2006). Human capital in growth regressions: how much difference does data quality make? *Journal of the European Economic Association*, 4 (1): 1–36.

Heckman, J. J. and P. J. Klenow (1998). Human capital policy, in M. Boskin (ed.), *Policies to Promote Human Capital Formation.* Hoover Institution, Stanford University.

Krueger, A. B. and M. Lindahl (2001). Education for growth: why and for whom? *Journal of Economic Literature*, 39 (4): 1101–36.

Kyriacou, G. (1991). Level and growth effects of human capital: a cross-country study of the convergence hypothesis. C. V. Starr Center for Applied Economics Working Paper 91–26, New York University.

Levine, R. and D. Renelt (1992). A sensitivity analysis of cross-country growth regressions. *American Economic Review*, 82 (4): 942–63.

Lleras-Muney, A. (2005). The relationship between education and adult mortality in the United States. *Review of Economic Studies*, 72 (1): 189–221.

Lochner, L. and E. Moretti (2004). The effect of education on crime: evidence from prison inmates, arrests and self-reports. *American Economic Review*, 94 (1): 155–89.

Lucas, R. E. (1988). On the mechanics of economic development. *Journal of Monetary Economics*, 22 (1): 3–42.

(1990). Why doesn't capital flow from rich to poor countries? *American Economic Review Papers and Proceedings*, 80 (2): 92–6.

Mankiw, N. G., D. Romer and D. N. Weil (1992). A contribution to the empirics of economic growth. *Quarterly Journal of Economics*, 107 (2): 407–37.

Milligan, K., E. Moretti and P. Oreopoulos (2004). Does education improve citizenship? Evidence from the United States and the United Kingdom. *Journal of Public Economics*, 88 (9–10): 1667–95.

Moretti, E. (2004). Estimating the social return to higher education: evidence from longitudinal and repeated cross-sectional data. *Journal of Econometrics*, 121 (1–2): 175–212.

Nehru, V., E. Swanson and A. Dubey (1995). A new data base on human capital stock in developing and industrial countries: sources, methodology and results. *Journal of Development Economics*, 46 (2): 379–401.

Nelson, R. and E. Phelps (1966). Investment in humans, technological diffusion, and economic growth. *American Economic Review*, 56 (1–2): 69–75.

Portela, M., R. Alessie and C. Teulings (2004). Measurement error in education and growth regressions. Tinbergen Discussion Paper 04–040/3, Amsterdam.

Pritchett, L. (2001). Where has all the education gone? *World Bank Economic Review*, 15 (3): 367–91.

(2006). Estimating the aggregate returns to education, in E. Hanushek and F. Welch (eds.), *Handbook of the Economics of Education*. Amsterdam: North-Holland.

Rauch, J. (1993). Productivity gains from geographic concentration of human capital: evidence from cities. *Journal of Urban Economics*, 34 (3): 380–400.

Romer, P. (1990). Endogenous technological change. *Journal of Political Economy*, 98 (5): S71–S102.

Schultz, T. W. (1961). Investment in human capital. *American Economic Review*, 51 (1): 1–17.

Sianesi, B. and J. Van Reenen (2003). The returns to education: macroeco-
nomics. *Journal of Economic Surveys*, 17 (5): 157–200.
Solow, R. M. (1956). A contribution to the theory of economic growth.
Quarterly Journal of Economics, 70 (1): 65–94.
Teulings, C. and T. van Rens (2003). Education, growth and income inequal-
ity. CEPR Discussion Paper 3863, London.
Topel, R. (1999). Labor markets and economic growth, in O. Ashenfelter
and D. Card (eds.), *Handbook of Labor Economics*. Handbooks in
Economics, vol. V. Amsterdam: North-Holland.
Vandenbussche, J., P. Aghion and C. Meghir (2005). Growth, distance to
frontier and composition of human capital. CEPR Discussion Paper
4860, London.

3 | *Returns to training*

EDWIN LEUVEN

3.1 Introduction

There is a steadily growing literature that investigates the determinants of individual wage growth over the lifecycle. Understanding wage growth is important for a number of reasons: first, wages are the major determinant of individual welfare; second, because observed wage growth can have several theoretical explanations and distinguishing between these increases our understanding of the functioning of labour markets; and finally, an often mentioned reason is that different components of wage growth are informative about the extent to which wages are tied to jobs, which in turn is a measure of the cost of worker displacement.

The two basic wage growth patterns that have been studied in this context are (i) how wages increase with experience, and (ii) how wages increase with tenure, keeping experience constant. The observed patterns can, however, have many sources. A first explanation is human-capital-based and conjectures that wage growth mirrors productivity growth. A second mechanism that generates wage growth is job search and matching (Jovanovic, 1979a, b; Mortensen, 1978). The intuition is simple: good matches are more likely to survive which generate a positive relation between experience/tenure and wages. All wage growth comes from mobility between jobs rather than from increases in productivity because of human capital investment. Finally contractual considerations can cause wage profiles to slope upwards because postponing rewards can provide an incentive to workers to exert effort early on.

Distinguishing between these alternative explanations of lifecycle wage patterns has proved to be a daunting task. There seems, however, to be consensus that there are true returns to tenure, although these seem to be much lower for low-skilled workers. At the same time Brown (1989) finds that firm-specific wage growth occurs mainly during periods of on-the-job training. This latter finding emphasizes the importance of studying the incidence and effects of more direct measures of training instead of tenure which, in the end, is just a proxy for (firm-specific) human capital.

This chapter therefore reviews the literature on the wage effects of formal private sector training. Many studies find very large returns, several orders of magnitudes larger than returns to regular education. Some have therefore argued that this points to underinvestment in training and is evidence for liquidity constraints or hold-up (see chapter 8 for a more in-depth discussion of hold-up and its implications for investment). The review will highlight the endogeneity problems that hamper the identification of causal effects of training. It will discuss at some length recent studies that put more effort into solving for self-selection of training and consequently find much smaller returns. The chapter will then conclude that the case for underinvestment is weaker than previously thought and will discuss some alternative mechanisms that might explain this result.

The outline of this chapter is as follows. The following section briefly discusses recent insights from the theoretical literature that studies training. Section 3.3 turns to the operationalization of training on an empirical level. Section 3.4 outlines the estimation issues surrounding the recovery of causal effects of training on wages. Section 3.5 briefly summarizes the standard literature based on fixed effects models and then section 3.6 more extensively looks at two recent studies that take an alternative identification approach using Dutch data. Finally section 3.7 concludes and discusses the implications for the case for underinvestment.

3.2 Theory

Standard competitive theory, as put forward by Becker (1962), distinguishes between general training and specific training. General training is of equal value in many firms, whereas specific training is only useful in one firm. One common concern with respect to training was the so-called poaching externality. It was argued that if firms trained their workers, competing firms would poach these valuable employees. This would be possible since training firms would need to pay workers less than their marginal product in order to earn back investment costs. Training firms would recognize the threat of losing their investment, and the common view was that this would lead to underinvestment in training: the possibility of turnover leads to underinvestment.

Becker argued that because in a competitive world workers reap all the returns to general training, they will consequently finance it, either directly or through lower wages. Since the worker and not the firms finance general training, the negative poaching externality disappears and underinvestment in general training only occurs when workers are liquidity constrained. A second important insight of Becker's theory was that firms would finance specific on-the-job training but might let workers share in the returns to reduce inefficient turnover.

Recent literature demonstrates that market imperfections may render training that is technologically general de facto specific, because wages will be less than marginal product (Stevens, 1994; Acemoglu and Pischke, 1999). This wedge between productivity and wages gives firms the possibility of earning back training costs. As a consequence, investment incentives for the employer are (partially) restored, and the scope for underinvestment in training because of liquidity constraints on the side of the employee is reduced.

The poaching externality, however, reappears if there is the possibility of labour turnover. Since there is a wedge between the wage and the productivity of the worker, not only the training firm but also future firms may benefit from training. The worker and the firm, however, do not internalize these positive externalities for third parties, and therefore underinvest (Stevens, 1994).

3.3 Measurement of training

Training and, more generally, the stock of human capital is difficult to measure. Initially, studies of training used labour market experience as a proxy for general training and job tenure as a proxy for specific training. In the 1980s datasets containing self-reported measures of training became available.[1] These datasets were typically based on household surveys (e.g. the Current Populations Survey (CPS) and the National Longitudinal Survey of Youth (NLSY)) in which respondents were asked whether they participated in some form of training in a specific reference period. In the CPS this is the period since the start of the respondent's current job, while in the NLSY this is the period since the last interview. Apart from these household surveys, employer-based (see Barron et al., 1987) and matched employer–employee surveys

(Lynch and Black, 1998, for example) are also slowly becoming available. Finally there are a few studies that use administrative data from a single firm (e.g. Bartel, 1995).

First there is the issue of whether to collect stock or flow measures. Most surveys collect flow measures: namely, the amount of training over a particular period. In the CPS, on the other hand, the reference period covers the period since the start of the job. This implies that if all reported training is specific this question would measure the stock of training.

The responses to these training questions are sensitive to the period covered by the training questions (e.g. Loewenstein and Spletzer, 1997): the longer the reference period the more training will be reported. A factor that is likely to introduce measurement error is the retrospectiveness of these self-reported training measures. Recollection problems are expected to increase with both the span of time between the training spell and the interview, and the detail of the training questions. Training questions that measure flows are therefore probably more accurate than training questions that attempt to measure stocks.

Surveys typically ask about training incidence, but increasingly try to measure the length of training spells in an attempt to more accurately measure training effort. The true costs of training are, however, difficult to measure. First, respondents are unlikely to be fully aware of the opportunity cost of training. To the extent that the employer pays for training, the respondents are also unlikely to have information on the direct (monetary) cost of training.

Training is almost inherently heterogeneous and some aggregation is therefore inevitable. The aggregation implicit in the training questions varies between surveys. The types of training measured by these surveys therefore vary and are typically derived from the institutional setting, and often combine mode of delivery and provider. The NLSY, for example, asks about training followed at business schools, apprenticeship programmes, vocational or technical institutes, but also about correspondence courses, formal company training run by the employer, military training, seminars or training programmes run at work by someone other than employer, seminars or training programmes outside of work, and training given by vocational rehabilitation centres. It is not immediately clear to what extent this is an economically sensible classification.[2]

The above illustrates the conceptual and practical complexity of collecting information on training. Little is known about the extent to which these conceptual measurement problems lead to actual measurement error. The only study to date hinting at this is Barron et al. (1997b). These authors use data from a matched employer–employee survey dataset to see to what extent employer and employee responses are consistent. This approach has the drawback that both the worker and the establishment are likely to make mistakes when reporting training. The 'truth' is therefore not observed and the extent of measurement error cannot be determined. Barron et al. (1997b) find that correlations between worker and establishment measures are less than 0.5 and that establishments report 25% more hours of training on average than do workers. On average, incidence rates are similar between worker and establishment reports, although 30% disagree on whether on-site formal training occurred.

These results suggest that training is measured with substantial error. If measurement error is 'classical' (additive and independent of the true value) then this will result in downward biased estimates. But since training has a mixed discrete continuous character the effect is less clear-cut. Frazis and Loewenstein (2003) show that in specifications that include both a participation indicator and training duration, the coefficient on participation will be upward biased and the coefficient on duration downward biased as in the classical case.

3.4 Estimation issues

This section discusses the estimation issues involved in return studies. First the fundamental evaluation problem is briefly explained, after which the methods that are employed in the literature are discussed.

3.4.1 Evaluation framework

There is by now a large literature that estimates returns to private sector training. The fundamental problem in estimating such returns is treated extensively in the evaluation literature. The basic framework is as follows. Assume training is mere participation and denoted by d_i a binary indicator variable. The outcome is the wage. Now denote the wage with training by $w_i(1)$ and without training by $w_i(0)$.

We can define several parameters of interest. A common one is the average effect of training on the trained (ATT): this is simply the average benefit of training, $w_i(1) - w_i(0)$, for those that participated in training, i.e. $d_i = 1$. In a similar way the average effect of training (in the population) and the average effect of training for the untrained can be defined.

The main challenge in estimating returns to training (treatment effects) is that it needs to answer a 'what if' question. To illustrate, suppose we want to estimate the ATT. We observe what the trained earn after training. But in order to calculate the wage return we will need to answer the following question for each training participant: 'What would the trainee have earned without training?'

We do not observe this and one easy answer is to take the average wage of the non-participants as an approximation, but this is only correct if training is exogenous (unrelated to everything else that correlates with the outcome). In practice training is unlikely to be exogenous. and estimating a causal effect then becomes a challenge. Recovering this 'counterfactual', the what-if question, is the fundamental evaluation problem.

3.4.2 The standard regression approach

The prototypical equation that the literature estimates takes the following form:

$$ln\ w_i = x'_{it}\beta + \gamma d_{it} + \varepsilon_{it} \tag{3.1}$$

where w_{it} is the wage of individual i at time t, x_{it} is a vector of control variables, d_{it} a measure of the stock of training and ε_{it} the residual/error term.

Early studies estimated (3.1) by ordinary least squares (OLS). Without covariates x_{it} and d_{it} mere participation, the OLS estimate of the effect of training is simply the difference in average earnings between those that participated in training and those that did not.

The OLS approach assumes that training is exogenous, conditional on the individual characteristics x_i that are included in equation (3.1). OLS therefore ignores the possibility that there are unobserved individual characteristics, such as ability, that affect wages and correlate with training.

This is obviously a very strong assumption and the current state of affairs in the literature is to estimate fixed effect versions of (3.1) where it is assumed that $\varepsilon_{it} = c_i + u_{it}$, where c_i is a time-invariant individual-specific effect that can correlate with training.

This approach effectively estimates (3.1) in deviation of individual means and is comparable to estimating (3.1) in first differences. This so-called fixed-effects estimator takes into account any confounding influence of unobserved individual characteristics that correlate both with wages and training as long as these are fixed over time (they are picked up by c_i). The resulting estimate of γ is now the difference in wage growth between those that trained and those that did not. The crucial identifying assumption here is thus that participants would have experienced the same wage growth as non-participants in the absence of training.

A few studies (Pischke, 2001; Frazis and Loewenstein, 2003) have estimated fixed-effect growth equations by adding individual specific growth rates of earnings $\delta_i t$ to the fixed effects version of equation (3.1).

3.4.3 Exploiting exogenous variation in training

As an alternative to fixed-effect-based approaches, a number of papers have estimated γ using selection models or instrumental variables (IV). The resulting equation (3.1) is now augmented with a participation equation:

$$d_i^* = w_{it}'\eta + v_{it}.$$

Selection models specify a joint parametric distribution for ε, v and can be estimated using maximum likelihood models or control functions. It has been pointed out that selection models can be very sensitive to misspecification of the joint distribution of ε, v and are identified exclusively on functional form and distributional assumptions unless w_{it} includes variables that are not included in x_{it}.

Unfortunately any variable will not do. What is needed is a variable z_{it} that (i) affects training participation but (ii) is independent of all other factors that affect wages for which equation (3.1) does not control. This is commonly referred to as an exclusion restriction and z_{it} as an instrumental variable. With an instrument the common approach is to estimate γ using two-stage least squares (2SLS).

A final thing to note is that when treatment effects are heterogenous, the estimated effect is a so-called local average treatment effect (Imbens and Angrist, 1994). In this case the estimated effect is the average effect for the implicitly defined subpopulation that is induced to participate by the exogenous variation generated by the instrument z_{it}.

3.5 Brief summary of the literature

The initial literature that estimated wage returns to training was based on indirect training measures. These studies regress wages on labour market experience and job tenure (seniority). The coefficient on labour market experience is then interpreted as the return to general training, whereas the coefficient of job tenure is interpreted as the return to specific human capital. Abraham and Farber (1987), Altonji and Shakotko (1987) and Topel (1986) are early attempts to estimate the return to seniority over and above the return to experience. They find only small effects of seniority on wage growth. Topel (1991) re-examined the data and concluded that the findings in these studies are biased because of measurement error and selectivity issues. He finds that ten years of current job seniority raises the wage of a typical male worker in the United States by 25%.

Human capital theory predicts upward sloping productivity profiles. Wage profiles are assumed to proxy these productivity profiles. There are several other theories (e.g. deferred compensation, self-selection and matching theories) besides human capital theory that predict upward sloping wage profiles, and as such it is hard to argue that this is a definitive test. One would like to know to what extent wage growth correlates with productivity growth. Medoff and Abraham (1981, 1980) use performance ratings among professional and managerial employees in three US corporations. Medoff and Abraham do not find any statistically significant correlation between these ratings and wage growth. They conclude that the on-the-job training model explains only a small part of the observed return to labour market experience. This result rests on the assumption that these ordinal performance ratings are unbiased measures of productivity.

Subsequent literature was based on direct measures of training collected in household surveys.[3] If we look at the estimates of the wage returns to private sector training in the literature we see that they are typically very high. As an illustration, take the estimates from two recent studies that use the NLSY data. Parent (1999) estimates both simple OLS regressions and IV regressions. The OLS estimate of the return to one full-time week of training is 18%. This estimate drops slightly in his partial fixed-effect estimation to 12%. Frazis and Loewenstein (2003) estimate various specifications and their preferred estimate, which takes into account heterogeneity in wage growth (fixed-effect wage growth regressions), is a rate of return in the region of 40 to 50% for one full-time week of training.

Estimated returns are also high with data from other sources and countries. Bartel (1995), using company data for example, finds that one day of training increases wages by 2%, which is equivalent to a rate of return of 60%. Blundell et al. (1996) report returns to training incidence for men in the UK in the region of 8% using OLS estimations, 9% for fixed-effects estimations, and 7% for IV estimations; and the returns for women are even higher.

3.6 Our contribution to the international literature

The results illustrate the fact that for a variety of datasets and countries the estimated returns to private sector training are substantial. Moreover, the returns to private sector training are very high compared to, for example, the returns to schooling. The return to a *year* of full-time education is around 10%, where in contrast the literature finds returns at least as high for a *week* of private sector training. This raises the question of whether these estimates are indeed causal effects.

These results can be explained by heterogeneity in returns, selectivity and measurement error. Selectivity, for example, may bias the estimated return to training. If the researcher has information that arguably correlates with training participation but not with wages, then instrumental variable methods potentially offer a way to obtain consistent estimates of the return to training.

To illustrate the issue, consider Leuven and Oosterbeek (2005) (cf. chapter 1), who exploit a provision in the Dutch tax system that allows employers to deduct an extra 40% of the training cost of employees who are 40 years or older from their taxable profits. The structure of the age-dependent tax deduction is therefore discontinuous at age 40. All workers younger than 40 are excluded from this additional deduction, while all workers aged 40 or older are included. This structure constitutes a perfect example of a so-called regression discontinuity (RD) data design (cf. Thistlewaithe and Campbell, 1960). This implies a credible exclusion restriction. Leuven and Oosterbeek (2005) then show that the tax provision significantly shifts participation in a discontinuous way around age 40. This is the second requirement of a valid instrument. The authors then proceed by using the discontinuity as an instrument for training participation. The IV point estimates give no support for substantial returns to employer-provided training. Unfortunately the estimates are too imprecise to warrant firm conclusions.

An alternative approach is followed in Leuven and Oosterbeek (2002). The idea forwarded in that paper is to narrow down the comparison group to those who did not participate due to some random event. This is achieved by using the information obtained through two especially designed survey questions. The first is whether there was any training related to work or career that the respondent wanted to follow but did not. The second asks whether this non-participation was due to some random event such as family circumstances, excess demand for training places, transient illness, or sudden absence of a colleague. Respondents who give an affirmative answer to both questions are arguably a more appropriate comparison group. Under two assumptions this approach gives an estimate of the effect of treatment on the treated.

OLS gives an estimate that is similar in magnitude to those found for the studies cited above, and is 12.5% for participating in one training course (with median duration of 40 hours) during the past 12 months. Restricting the comparison group to workers who wanted to participate in training but did not do so reduces the estimated return to 8.7%. When the comparison group is further restricted to those workers who wanted to participate in training but did not do so due to some random event, the point estimate of the return to training is 0.6%.

Although sample sizes do not allow precise estimation of the latter effect, the credibility of the proposed strategy is supported by the fact that on each subsequent narrowing down of the comparison group, the participants and comparison individuals are increasingly similar on observed characteristics. In line with this increased similarity of trainees and non-trainees the point estimate of the return to training consistently drops. We therefore conclude that the high returns to private sector training previously found in the literature are most likely explained by the spurious correlation of training with confounding factors that affect wages, and that existing methods are not sufficient to take this into account.

3.7 Conclusion and discussion

This chapter has provided a review of the literature that estimates wage returns to training. The emphasis has been methodological. The measurement and estimation issues have been extensively discussed. As argued above, the fundamental problem concerning the recovery of the causal effect of training on earnings lies in the correction for selectivity into training.

Section 3.5 shows that traditional studies that depend on differencing (fixed-effect) methods where non-participants are used as a comparison group results in high return estimates. On the basis of these high returns some have argued that there is substantial underinvestment and therefore scope for public intervention. Such underinvestment could arise because of, for example, hold-up or liquidity constraints.

Studies that exploit arguably exogenous variation in training participation find much smaller wage effects of training. This calls into question the case for underinvestment. Recently literature in experimental economics has shown that individuals are often motivated by reciprocity and fairness considerations which are typically ignored in standard human capital models. In a recent study Leuven et al. (2005) show how reciprocity can alleviate underinvestment. They also provide empirical evidence which supports this case. Recent literature emphasizing market imperfections also shows that this may give employers more incentives than previously thought to invest in the general training of their employees.

To conclude, there seems to be a case for further study of training mechanisms and subsequent outcomes. These studies will need to address recent developments in the theoretical literature emphasizing market imperfections and behavioural considerations such as reciprocity. The literature studying outcomes should incorporate recent developments in the econometrical literature and address selectivity issues in a systematic way.

Notes

1. An early attempt at measuring training more directly is found in the Michigan Panel Study of Income Dynamics (PSID). Respondents were asked: 'On a job like yours, how much time would it take the average new

person to become fully trained and qualified?' This seems to measure a characteristic of the job instead of the amount of training the respondent participated in.

2. Apart from formal training there is a growing interest in measuring informal training (e.g. Barron et al., 1997b; Frazis et al., 1996; Loewenstein and Spletzer, 1999).

3. The following studies are a sample of the literature: Barron et al. (1997a), Barron et al. (1999), Altonji and Spletzer (1991), Autor (2001), Bartel (1995), Bishop (1994), Bishop (1991), Blundell et al. (1996), Booth (1993), Booth (1991), Duncan and Hoffman (1979), Frazis and Loewenstein (2003), Greenhalgh and Stewart (1987), Lengermann (1999), Lillard and Tan (1992), Loewenstein and Spletzer (1997), Loewenstein and Spletzer (1999), Lynch (1992), Blanchflower and Lynch (1994), Pischke (2001), Veum (1995).

References

Abraham, K. G. and H. S. Farber (1987). Job duration, seniority, and earnings. *American Economic Review*, 77 (3): 278–97.

Acemoglu, D. and J.-S. Pischke (1999). The structure of wages and investment in general training. *Journal of Political Economy*, 107 (3): 539–72.

Altonji, J. G. and R. Shakotko (1987). Do wages rise with job seniority? *Review of Economic Studies*, 54: 437–59.

Altonji, J. G. and M. Spletzer (1991). Worker characteristics, job characteristics, and the receipt of on-the-job training. *Industrial and Labor Relations Review*, 45: 58–79.

Autor, D. (2001). Why do temporary help firms provide free general skills training? *Quarterly Journal of Economics*, 116 (4): 1409–48.

Barron, J. M., D. A. Black and M. A. Loewenstein (1987). Employer size: the implications for search, training, capital investment, starting wages, and wage growth. *Journal of Labor Economics*, 5 (1): 76–89.

Barron, J., M. Berger and D. A. Black (1997a). *On the Job Training*. Kalamazoo, MI: W. E. Upjohn Institute for Employment Research.

(1997b). How well do we measure training? *Journal of Labor Economics*, 15 (3): 507–28.

(1999). Do workers pay for on-the-job training? *Journal of Human Resources*, 34 (2): 235–52.

Bartel, A. (1995). Training, wage growth, and job performance: evidence from a company database. *Journal of Labor Economics*, 13: 401–25.

Becker, G. S. (1962). Investment in human capital: a theoretical analysis. *Journal of Political Economy*, 70: 9–49.

Bishop, J. (1994). The impact of previous training on productivity and wages, in L. Lynch (ed.), *Training and the Private Sector: International Comparisons*, NBER Comparative Labor Markets Series. Chicago: University of Chicago Press.

Bishop, J. H. (1991). On-the-job training of new hires, in D. Stern and J. M. Ritzen (eds.), *Market Failure in Training? New Economic Analysis and Evidence on Training of Adult Employees*. New York: Springer Verlag.

Blanchflower, D. and L. Lynch (1994). Training at work: a comparison of U.S. and British youths, in L. Lynch (ed.), *Training and the Private Sector: International Comparisons*, NBER Comparative Labor Markets Series. Chicago: University of Chicago Press.

Blundell, R., L. Dearden and C. Meghir (1996). *The Determinants and Effects of Work Related Training in Britain*. London: Institute of Fiscal Studies.

Booth, A. (1991). Job-related formal training: who receives it and what is it worth? *Oxford Bulletin of Economics and Statistics*, 53: 281–94.

  (1993). Private sector training and graduate earnings. *Review of Economics and Statistics*, 75 (1): 164–70.

Brown, J. N. (1989). Why do wages increase with job tenure? On-the-job training and life-cycle wage growth observed within firms. *American Economic Review*, 79 (5): 971–91.

Duncan, G. and S. Hoffman (1979). On-the-job training and earnings differences by race and sex. *Review of Economics and Statistics*, 61: 594–603.

Frazis, H., M. Gittleman, M. Horrigan and M. Joyce (1996). Formal and informal training: evidence from a matched employee–employer survey. Paper prepared for the conference 'New Empirical Research on Employer Training: Who Pays?' held at Cornell University, 15–17 November 1996.

Frazis, H. and M. Loewenstein (2003). Reexamining the returns to training: functional form, magnitude, and interpretation. Working Paper 367, Bureau of Labor Statistics, Washington DC.

Greenhalgh, C. and M. Stewart (1987). The effects and determinants of training. *Oxford Bulletin of Economics and Statistics*, 49: 171–89.

Imbens, G. W. and J. D. Angrist (1994). Identification and estimation of local average treatment effects. *Econometrica*, 62 (2): 467–75.

Jovanovic, B. (1979a). Firm-specific capital and turnover. *Journal of Political Economy*, 87: 1246–60.

  (1979b). Job matching and the theory of turnover. *Journal of Political Economy*, 87: 972–90.

Lengermann, P. (1999). How long do the benefits of training last? Evidence of long term effects across current and previous employers. *Research in Labor Economics*, 18: 439–61.

Leuven, E. and H. Oosterbeek (2002). A new method to estimate the returns to work-related training. Unpublished Working Paper, Department of Economics, University of Amsterdam.

(2005). Evaluating the effects of a tax deducation on training. *Journal of Human Resources*, 40 (2): 453–76.

Leuven, E., H. Oosterbeek, R. Sloof and C. van Klaveren (2005). Worker reciprocity and employer investment in training. *Economica*, 72 (285): 137–49.

Lillard, L. and H. Tan (1992). Private sector training: who gets it and what are its effects? *Research in Labor Economics*, 13: 1–62.

Loewenstein, M. A. and J. R. Spletzer (1997). Delayed formal on-the-job training. *Industrial and Labor Relations Review*, 51 (1): 82–99.

(1999). Formal and informal training: evidence from the NLSY. *Research in Labour Economics*, 18: 403–38.

Lynch, L. (1992). Private sector training and the earnings of young workers. *American Economic Review*, 82 (1): 299–312.

Lynch, L. M. and S. Black (1998). Beyond the incidence of employer-provided training. *Industrial and Labor Relations Review*, 52 (1): 64–81.

Medoff, J. and K. Abraham (1980). Experience, performance, and earnings. *Quarterly Journal of Economics*, 85: 703–36.

(1981). Are those paid more really more productive? The case of experience. *Journal of Human Resources*, 16 (2): 186–216.

Mortensen, D. T. (1978). Specific capital and labor turnover. *Bell Journal of Economics*, 9: 572–85.

Parent, D. (1999). Wages and mobility: the impact of employer-provided training. *Journal of Labor Economics*, 17 (2): 298–317.

Pischke, J.-S. (2001). Continuous training in Germany. *Journal of Population Economics*, 14: 523–48.

Stevens, M. (1994). A theoretical model of on-the-job training with imperfect competition. *Oxford Economic Papers*, 46: 537–62.

Thistlewaithe, D. and D. Campbell (1960). Regression-discontinuity analysis: an alternative to ex post facto experiment. *Journal of Educational Psychology*, 51: 309–17.

Topel, R. (1986). Job mobility, search, and earnings growth: a reinterpretation of human capital earnings functions. *Research in Labor Economics*, 8: 199–233.

(1991). Specific capital, mobility, and wages: wages rise with job seniority. *Journal of Political Economy*, 99 (1): 145–76.

Veum, J. R. (1995). Sources of training and their impact on wages. *Industrial and Labor Relations Review*, 48 (4): 812–26.

4 | Human capital and entrepreneurs

JUSTIN VAN DER SLUIS AND C. MIRJAM VAN PRAAG

4.1 Introduction

In this chapter, we study the effects of human capital investments for the 10% of the labour force that is often neglected in such studies, i.e. for entrepreneurs. Entrepreneurs are defined as individuals who are self-employed, who have started their own business or who run and own an incorporated business. Policy-makers and academic researchers are increasingly aware of the importance of entrepreneurship in our society. Entrepreneurs are often seen as the engine of the economy, responsible for sustained levels of competition, the creation of jobs, and new innovative processes and products, thereby displacing ageing incumbents in a process of 'creative destruction'. These benefits, which accrue to society at large, justify public expenditure to develop and stimulate entrepreneurship. But it is also recognized that if entrepreneurs face constraints such as limited human capital, then these economic benefits might not be realized. This realization has prompted several governments to devise public programmes to encourage entrepreneurship. Underlying most of these programmes is a belief that human capital in general affects entrepreneurs' performance in practice. The measurement of the return to human capital for entrepreneurs is thus relevant for devising programmes to realize optimal economic benefits from entrepreneurship.

This chapter gives an overview of past and current empirical research measuring the effect of formal education, one of the most prominent manifestations of human capital, on an entrepreneur's performance. We measure education in terms of years of schooling and the entrepreneur's performance in terms of the individual income level. Thus, we can measure the returns to education in the same Mincerian fashion as has been done in numerous studies pertaining to employees: the percentage gain in income one would realize when an additional year of education is completed (see chapter 1). The empirical definition of an entrepreneur is any labour force participant who is mainly active in the labour market on a self-employed basis or who is the director of his or her own incorporated business.

Past research has not yet measured the effect of formal schooling on entrepreneur performance consistently. This lack of consistency is due to shortcomings in the empirical strategies applied so far. The empirical strategies might be improved by applying techniques that are common within the technically more sophisticated literature on the returns to education for employees (see chapter 1). To our knowledge, few studies have been performed that measure the effect of specific schooling types, levels or tracks.

In section 4.2 we proceed with a brief discussion of recent applications of more advanced empirical strategies to estimate the effect of formal education in general on entrepreneurial incomes consistently. We compare the estimates of the returns to education for entrepreneurs with those of employees. As was stated in chapter 1, an abundant literature exists on estimates of the returns to education for employees in both developed and developing countries. These studies serve as a benchmark.

The findings from these studies relating to the effect of education on entrepreneurs' earnings are interesting for two reasons. First, they can be related to comparable estimates for employees, to see whether the returns to education are higher or lower for entrepreneurs than for employees. This will form a basis for private decision-making with regards to schooling and employment mode choice as well as for policy implications under quite broad assumptions about the relationship between private and social returns to education (see chapter 2). Second, if we find evidence that schooling in general has a positive effect on entrepreneurship outcomes, it is all the more relevant to strengthen the research effort aimed at differentiating this effect for various education tracks. After having discussed the results from those recent studies, we present conclusions and policy implications.

4.2 Summarizing the earlier evidence: meta-analysis

The relationship between schooling and entrepreneurship (entry and) performance has been measured in many empirical micro studies. A large portion of these studies measures the relationship between education and entrepreneurship outcomes as a by-product while focusing on different issues. Van der Sluis, Van Praag and Vijverberg (2003, 2005) provide an overview of these studies and they perform a meta-analysis to assess whether there are any consistent findings in the entrepreneurship and economics literature with respect to the impact of education on entrepreneurship in industrial countries and developing countries respectively. Several outcomes result from these meta-analyses. It should be kept in mind, though, that while these results do add value to the existing limited knowledge of the returns to education for entrepreneurs, they have been derived by simply averaging very diverse studies, with little adjustment for differences in data or methodology.

The impact of schooling on entrepreneurial *performance*, as has been measured in terms of various performance measures such as profit, personal income, growth or personnel, is significantly positive for 67% of the observations in industrial countries and for 50% of the observations in developed countries. Thus individuals with more schooling indeed tend to perform better as entrepreneurs.

The meta-analysis gives insight into the level of the returns to education for entrepreneurs. This insight is based on a small sub-sample of studies, using similar measures for education and earnings. For the sample of studies of industrial countries, the sub-sample happens to consist of US studies only. The return to a marginal year of schooling in terms of the income it generates turns out to be 6.1% on average. For developing countries we find a closely similar average: 5.5%. Hence, the comparison of the returns to education between industrial and developing countries seems to lead to different results for entrepreneurs than for employees. As was noted in chapter 1, employees' returns to education are higher in developing countries than in industrial countries. Moreover, comparing the percentages obtained to those mentioned in chapter 1, it seems that the returns to education are lower for entrepreneurs than for employees in both industrial and developing countries.

The meta-analysis for industrial countries allows a more direct comparison of the rate of return to education for entrepreneurs and for employees. The comparison is based on the results from twenty studies that compare the two groups of labour market participants using one dataset and thereby one set of definitions, time period, country and the like. These studies show that the returns to education are of the same order of magnitude for employees and entrepreneurs. More specifically, all studies pertaining to Europe indicate that the returns to education are slightly, but not significantly, lower for entrepreneurs than for employees. For the United States we find the opposite: these studies indicate that the returns to education are slightly higher for entrepreneurs than for employees.

Some other results from the meta-analyses are notable and some are worth a comparison with the evidence for employees (see chapter 1 again). As for employees, the returns to education are higher in the United States than in Europe and they are higher for women than for men (both in industrial and in developing countries). However, they are lower for blacks than for whites.

Moreover, the impact of education on the business *start-up* probability of individuals in industrial countries is mostly, i.e. in 75% of cases, insignificant. This indicates that schooling levels and the choice for self-employment are unrelated. With regards to entrepreneurship choice in developing countries, more educated workers typically end up in wage employment, shunning non-farm entrepreneurship. Relative to farming, however, more educated workers seek out non-farm entrepreneurship opportunities.

The last conclusion from the literature overview concerns two limitations of the research undertaken so far. First, until recently, little effort has been put forth to differentiate the effect on entrepreneurship performance of various types of education. However, recently, various interesting turns have been taken by a couple of researchers on this path, i.e. Lazear (2004), Silva (2004) and Wagner (2002).

They investigate whether entrepreneurs are 'jacks-of-all-trades' relative to employees who would then be relative specialists. They test whether entrepreneurs are indeed more likely than employees to have had various professional roles in their lives (Lazear, 2004; Wagner, 2002; Silva, 2004) and/or to have followed broader and less specialized educational tracks (Lazear, 2004; Silva, 2004). Lazear concludes that Stanford Business School students who have had more various professional roles in their lives and who had chosen more diversified curricula while in business school have indeed had a higher propensity to become entrepreneurs. Wagner (2002) finds support for this conclusion: individuals (included in a representative sample of the German labour force) who have had more various professional roles and/or a more diversified professional training subsequent to their formal education tracks are more likely to become entrepreneurs. However, Silva (2004) uses a panel dataset of graduate students as well as a sample of the general Italian working population to conclude that the causality of the results established by Lazear and Wagner is the other way round. He finds that entrepreneurs are indeed generalists but that changes in the spread of their knowledge across different fields, caused by education or work experience, do not increase the likelihood of becoming an entrepreneur. The 'jack-of-all-trades' characteristic is a form of innate ability that manifests itself in both valid educational and labour market curricula.

As used to be the case with early attempts to estimate the returns to education for employees, most studies have not taken account of the basic evaluation problem, discussed in chapter 1, of properly measuring the counterfactual. Hence, the results obtained and discussed so far are potentially biased. Estimation and identification strategies used to identify the effect of education on performance have merely measured the (conditional) correlation between education and performance by means of OLS rather than the causal effect, the estimate of interest.

Several methods to cope with these problems have been applied recently to estimate the returns to education for employees, see chapter 1. The general conclusion is that OLS estimates of the returns to education for employees are biased downwards (Ashenfelter et al., 1999). It remains to be analysed if and to what extent estimates of the return to education for entrepreneurs have been biased too.

The potential bias also raises suspicion about the comparisons of the returns to education for entrepreneurs and employees. The impact of such a bias on the estimated return to education can be different for entrepreneurs and employees (cf. Griliches, 1977). As a result, the conclusions from such comparisons should be re-evaluated.

In what follows, we shall briefly discuss the first applications of a little more advanced identification strategy to the estimation of the returns to education for entrepreneurs. As noted in chapter 1, the idea of IV (instrumental variables) approaches is to imitate a field experiment where individuals are randomly allocated among 'treatments' to estimate their effects.[1] This would mitigate the 'basic evaluation problem'.

4.3 Our contributions

Besides the above described meta-analyses, we made two contributions to the literature. In the first contribution, Van der Sluis, Van Praag and Van Witteloostuijn (2004) compare the magnitude of the returns to education for American entrepreneurs and employees. The returns for both groups are estimated by means of a 'random effects model' using IV, while including a set of detailed ability proxies.

We use a sample drawn from a large US panel of young adults, the National Longitudinal Survey of Youth (NLSY). The sample is a rich panel consisting of more than 6,000 individuals and nineteen annual waves. We extracted, per year observed, the hourly wage, the total years of education completed and various exogenous variables.

A particularly relevant background variable included in the NLSY is the 'Armed Services Vocational Aptitude Battery' (ASVAB), which is an IQ-like test score. It is included in the income equations for both entrepreneurs and employees. The idea is that such test scores make observable what remains unobserved otherwise, i.e. the effect of certain forms of ability on income.

A second relevant feature of the sample is that it includes both entrepreneurs and employees, and records individuals' switches between these states over time. All entrepreneurship spells, including short ones, are recorded. Therefore, the sub-sample of entrepreneurs does not suffer from survival bias, i.e. the estimate of the returns to education will not pertain to surviving entrepreneurs only. Moreover, the incomes and all other relevant variables are measured in a comparable way for both groups such that the returns to education for employees and entrepreneurs can be estimated in a comparable fashion.

The results show that the OLS estimate of the returns to education, which is estimated in this study as a benchmark, and which can be compared in terms of methodology to previous studies such as the ones included in the meta-analyses, is around 7% for both entrepreneurs and employees. In accordance with previous studies using US data the returns are slightly higher for entrepreneurs (7.1%) than for employees (6.7%), though they are clearly of the same order of magnitude (Fredland and Little, 1981; Tucker, 1985, 1987; Evans and Leighton, 1990; Robinson and Sexton, 1994).

The estimation results from using an IV approach and including the discussed ability proxies are novel and quite different: the returns to education are estimated to be higher for both entrepreneurs and employees. The increase from 6.7% to 10.7% for employees is comparable to increases resulting from applying IV instead of OLS in previous applications, such as Blackburn and Neumark (1993). A novel observation is the even greater jump in the estimated level of the returns to education for entrepreneurs. The IV estimate amounts to 14.2% and is twice as high as the OLS estimate of 7.1%. The result is remarkable. The returns to education are estimated to be significantly higher for entrepreneurs than for employees in the United States. Previous research based on OLS estimates resulted in much smaller and insignificant differences. We perform numerous checks to assess the credibility and robustness of the result. We find that the result is not due to selectivity (i.e. caused by different types of people choosing entrepreneurship instead of wage employment), neither to a higher required *risk premium* obtained by more highly educated entrepreneurs. So why is education more valuable for entrepreneurs?

Our explanation for these results is simple. Entrepreneurs have more freedom to optimize their use of education. Entrepreneurs are not constrained by rules from superiors and can decide for themselves how to put their education to its most productive use. This difference in opportunity to optimize the productivity of education for entrepreneurs and employees might therefore be an explanation for the higher returns to education for entrepreneurs.

Our second contribution is the one by Parker and Van Praag (2004) and pertains to Dutch entrepreneurs. The meta-analysis indicated that the OLS-estimated returns to education for entrepreneurs are higher in the United States than in Europe. Moreover, the returns to education are slightly higher for entrepreneurs than for employees in the United States, while in Europe the return to education seems to be higher for employees. We will now test whether this conclusion is maintained when using a more advanced methodology (i.e. IV) for one particular country, the Netherlands. Parker and Van Praag use an improved modelling strategy by also considering the effect of human capital on borrowing constraints. We thereby measure the distinct contribution of each of the factors' human and financial capital on the incomes of entrepreneurs, taking into account the possibility that human capital might also have an indirect effect on performance by making financial capital easier to access. Both education and financial capital constraints are treated as endogenous decision variables.

The dataset used in this application is a random cross-section sample of Dutch entrepreneurs drawn in 1995. Entrepreneurial income is measured as gross personal income, consistent with entrepreneurs' and employees' incomes in Van der Sluis, Van Praag and Van Witteloostuijn (2004). Education is measured in the usual manner: number of years of education attended.

The key result is that the direct return to schooling is almost 14%, that extra years of schooling decrease capital constraints significantly, and that capital constraints hinder entrepreneurs in their performance. The magnitude of the direct effect of education on performance is a little lower than the IV estimate pertaining to the United States. It is higher than the comparable OLS estimate. Note that the Dutch dataset is limited to entrepreneurs so we cannot compare rates of return for employees and entrepreneurs directly. However, our estimated rates of return to schooling are at the very high end of previous IV estimates obtained for employees. This is contrary to some casual 'conventional wisdom' that entrepreneurs do not need schooling to be successful.

4.4 Discussion and conclusion

Entrepreneurship has so far been a neglected topic in the economics of education. We argue, on the basis of a meta-analysis, that the returns to education for entrepreneurs need to be measured with the same methodological rigour as in the studies on employees. In particular, the neglect of the endogenous nature of schooling is a problem. We briefly discussed two recent studies that both try to deal with this problem. We think studies like these are of intrinsic interest for the academic field of entrepreneurship. Both studies have applied IV to deal with the endogeneity problem. The results from both studies imply that the OLS estimates so far have been biased downwards. Do these results then shed an entirely new light on the conclusions from the meta-analysis conducted on studies of industrial countries?

The first conclusion from the meta-analysis, i.e. that education has a significantly positive impact on entrepreneurs' performance, is supported and thus maintained. The second conclusion was that the estimated rate of return to education for entrepreneurs was 6.1% on average. This conclusion is not supported by the studies that account for endogeneity and unobserved heterogeneity. The return to education for entrepreneurs turns out to be much higher, and comparable, in the two applications discussed. Our estimate of the returns to education is a little higher than 14% for the United States; in our Dutch study the estimate of the direct return to education turns out to be a little below 14%.[2]

The third conclusion of the meta-analysis was that the returns to education are of the same order of magnitude for entrepreneurs and for employees (though insignificantly higher for entrepreneurs in the United States). This conclusion is not supported by our results: the returns for entrepreneurs in the United States are shown to be much higher than the returns for employees (respectively 14.2% and 10.7%).[3] The result of this study is checked to be robust. This novel finding must be somewhat puzzling in the light of the traditional studies that test screening hypotheses: apparently entrepreneurs cannot be maintained as an assumedly unscreened control group. This might explain why we find that capital constraints for entrepreneurs are relieved when the level of education is higher.

The fourth conclusion from the meta-analysis was that most previous studies, utilizing OLS, had generated potentially biased results. This potential bias, it was argued, is due to the neglect of problems related to endogeneity and unobserved heterogeneity. Previous studies that account for such problems when estimating the returns to education for employees had indeed pointed out that the bias was significant in the case of employees. The studies presented in this chapter are the first in the field of entrepreneurship that apply IV techniques and thereby account for potential endogeneity. As it turns out in both applications, the bias is significant in the entrepreneurs' case too. To put it more strongly, the bias is even larger in the case of entrepreneurs. We do not yet understand why this is the case.

Of course, the use of instrumental variables is not without critique. In particular, the choice of instruments is vital (see chapter 3 for the requirements: an instrument should have a strong effect on education and no direct influence on income). We used family background characteristics as instruments and this has been criticized by Card (1999), who states that it is possible that family background variables have an additional and separate effect on income. We therefore argue that, in order to validate our results, more analyses in this spirit should be performed with different sets of instruments. Besides the use of different instruments, the use of other identification strategies such as twin studies and field experiments are of the utmost relevance.

One other, but related, issue of concern is the low 'explanatory power' of the determinants in the entrepreneurs' income equation. We can explain only 28% of the variance in entrepreneurial income by the observed factors compared to almost 50% in the employee part of our US study. In our Dutch study we also explain 28% of the variance in entrepreneurial income. The difference found in the US study can, at least in part, be attributed to the greater cross-sectional variance in entrepreneurs' incomes than in employees' incomes. By nature, entrepreneurial incomes are more variable and less predictable than employees' incomes.

It is still possible that we are missing some important determinants of entrepreneurial performance. The full exploitation of human, social and financial capital as determinants of entrepreneur performance should therefore be developed further. Human capital, for instance, has almost exclusively been defined as the level of education. Future research should also focus on the specific direction and compilation of the education followed (vocational studies, technical studies, subjects studied, or specific entrepreneurship-orientated courses, etc.). Lazear (2004), Wagner (2002) and Silva (2004) have started exploring this interesting path.

Before we discuss policy implications it is important to elaborate on the assumptions we will impose. Not all of these conditions follow from our research, and in that sense, the policy implications are speculative. First, we assume that the difference between the social and private benefits of education is at least as large for successful entrepreneurial activity as it is for employees who do well.[4] A successful entrepreneur is, for example, more likely to influence the competition in a market than an employee. Moreover, entrepreneurs can bring new and innovative ideas more easily into the market than employees.

Second, we assume that individuals invest in schooling at a stage in their lives at which they do not yet know, in general, whether they will become entrepreneurs or employees, or a (sequential) combination of both. As a consequence, investment in schooling is not motivated by the specific expected return when belonging to the group of entrepreneurs, but by some (weighted) average return of both employment modes.

Our third assumption is that individuals, as well as policy-makers, bankers and other parties involved, have no more insight into the returns to education than we as researchers have. This implies that individuals and policy-makers share the knowledge (and common opinion) that the returns to education are similar for entrepreneurs and for employees.

The following policy recommendations result: individual decision-makers should be aware that the returns to education for entrepreneurs are higher than those of employees. The evidence for this difference in returns is more solid for the United States than for the Netherlands.

Given this awareness, a larger proportion of individuals with higher education would choose to become entrepreneurs instead of employees than currently. Moreover, people who have a preference for entrepreneurship would be more inclined to pursue (higher) education. This would be privately beneficial for these individuals.

Many governments strongly believe in the desirability of developing more entrepreneurship. Programmes to develop and foster more entrepreneurship have been developed in many countries. In Europe, the Lisbon Strategy that aims to stimulate innovation largely through entrepreneurship has been influential on this matter.[5]

Given the desirability of promoting entrepreneurship, and the new knowledge that the returns to education are higher for entrepreneurs, governments could take two steps. They could stimulate higher schooling amongst (prospective) entrepreneurs, for instance by including entrepreneurship courses in the curricula of schools. This would make it more attractive for prospective entrepreneurs to follow more education (in schools that are now perceived as mainly educating people to become good employees). Alternatively, governments could invest in encouraging more highly educated individuals to opt for entrepreneurship. This could be accomplished by providing more information about entrepreneurship (perhaps in the form of specific courses) at universities and other institutions for higher education. The first step will make sure that entrepreneurs perform better, and that they will thereby generate more benefits, which will probably not only accrue to the entrepreneur himself but to society as a whole. The second step addresses the fact that, at least in Europe, entrepreneurship does not seem to be a favoured option, or even to be part of the choice set, amongst young people with higher education. They usually favour working in a large multinational company and do not even think about self-employment (see the results from the EU Euro-barometer, 2005).

The result of improved policy measures will be an increased number of potentially successful starters and an increased level of useful support to those starters. This will reduce the social costs of bankruptcy and increase the social benefits of innovative enterprises.

Notes

1. The IV method and the random effects model are also applied and explained in chapter 3.

2. The large difference between these estimates and the estimates based on OLS cannot be attributed to publication bias (see chapter 1): the comparable OLS estimates in our own applications are around 7%, hence very much lower.
3. The second study does not generate such a result for Europe because it analyses a sample of entrepreneurs only.
4. Note that in chapter 2 social returns to education for employees are found to be almost equal to private returns.
5. See, for instance, Commission of the European Communities (2005), stating that 'There are just too many obstacles to becoming an entrepreneur or starting a business, and, therefore, Europe is missing opportunities' (p. 16).

References

Ashenfelter, O., C. Harmon and H. Oosterbeek (1999). A review of the schooling/earnings relationship with tests for publication bias. *Labour Economics*, 6: 453–70.

Blackburn, M. and D. Neumark (1993). Are OLS estimates of the return to schooling biased downwards? Another look. *Review of Economics and Statistics*, 77: 217–30.

Card, D. (1999). Causal effect of education on earnings, in O. Ashenfelter and D. Card (eds.), *Handbook of Labor Economics*, vol. IIIA. Amsterdam: North-Holland, pp. 1801–63.

Commission of the European Communities (2005). Communication to the spring European council, Working together for growth and jobs: a new start for the Lisbon Strategy (communication from President Barroso in agreement with Vice-President Verheugen). Brussels: COM.

EU Euro-barometer on Entrepreneurship (2005). Are entrepreneurs born, made or just encouraged? Press memo, available at: http://ec.europa.eu/enterprise/enterprise_policy/survey/eurobarometer_pressmemo.pdf.

Evans, D. and L. Leighton (1990). Small business formation by unemployed and employed workers. *Small Business Economics*, 2: 319–30.

Fredland, J. and R. Little (1981). Self-employed workers: returns to education and training. *Economics of Education Review*, 1 (3): 315–37.

Griliches, Z. (1977). Estimating the returns to schooling: some econometric problems. *Econometrica*, 45 (1): 1–22.

Lazear, E. (2004). Balanced skills and entrepreneurship. *American Economic Review, Papers and Proceedings*, May.

Parker, S. and C.M. van Praag (2004). Schooling, capital constraints and entrepreneurial performance: the endogenous triangle. Tinbergen Institute Discussion Paper 04–106/3, Amsterdam.

Robinson, P. and E. Sexton (1994). The effect of education and experience on self-employment success. *Journal of Business Venturing*, 9: 141–56.

Silva, O. (2004). Entrepreneurship: can the jack-of-all-trades attitude be acquired? CEP Discussion Paper 665, London School of Economics.

Tucker, I. (1985). Use of the decomposition technique to test the educational screening hypothesis. *Economics of Education Review*, 4 (4): 321–6.

(1987). The impact of consumer credentialism on employee and entrepreneur returns to higher education. *Economics of Education Review*, 6 (1): 35–40.

Van der Sluis, J., C. M. van Praag and W. Vijverberg (2003). Entrepreneurship selection and performance: a meta-analysis of the impact of education in industrial countries. Tinbergen Institute Discussion Paper 04–046/3, Amsterdam.

(2005). Entrepreneurship selection and performance: a meta-analysis of the impact of education in less developed countries. *World Bank Economic Review*, 19 (2): 225–61.

Van der Sluis, J., C. M. van Praag and A. van Witteloostuijn (2004). The returns to education: a comparative study between entrepreneurs and employees. Tinbergen Institute Discussion Paper 04–104/3, Amsterdam.

Wagner, J. (2002). Testing Lazear's jack-of-all-trades view of entrepreneurship with German data. IZA Discussion Paper 592, Bonn.

5 | The effects of education on health

WIM GROOT AND HENRIËTTE MAASSEN
VAN DEN BRINK

5.1 Introduction

Education and health are the two most important investments in human capital individuals make. Their economic value lies in the effects they have on productivity: both education and health make individuals more productive. Education and health have a considerable impact on individual well being as well. The wealth of nations is to a large extent determined by the educational attainment and the health status of their population. Compared to the abundance of empirical studies that document the individual rate of return to education (see previous chapters), we know little about the returns to investments in health.

There is evidence to support the claim that there is a positive relation between education and health. Some of this evidence is surveyed in Grossman and Kaestner (1997). This survey concludes that 'A number of studies in the United States suggest that years of formal schooling completed is the most important correlate of good health' (Grossman and Kaestner, 1997: 73). Not only in the United States, but also elsewhere – and in particular in developing countries – the positive association between education and health is well documented.

According to the 2003 Human Development Report, 'Education, health, nutrition and water and sanitation complement each other, with investments in any one contributing to better outcomes in the others' (UN, 2003: 85). The positive association between education and health can be partly attributed to differences in income between countries.

Education affects health, but investments in health and education have some common attributes as well. Theodore Schultz (1993) argues in his seminal paper 'Investments in human capital' that both education and health involve both consumption and investment, that returns in health and education are uncertain, and that there are third-party effects involved. In both cases the involvement of the public sector in the provision of education and health care is large.

There are three potential explanations for the positive relation between education and health: (1) better health enables more investment in education; (2) common factors – such as genetic endowment, social background or time preferences – affect health and education in a similar way; and (3) education leads to better health.

If education affects health this raises at least two questions: what exactly is it in education that affects health and how can we impart health benefits through education? This chapter intends to answer these two questions. Section 5.2 provides an overview of the literature on education and health. In the literature we find mixed evidence on the endogeneity of education in the health equation. One might ask whether the education effect on health is really a causal effect. In section 5.3 we describe our own contributions to the health and education literature by summarizing the results of a survey and meta-analysis of the literature. Section 5.4 provides some tests for causality between education and health. Section 5.5 presents estimates of the education effect on health as the monetary equivalent of the health effect of a year of education. Section 5.6 concludes.

5.2 A review of the literature on health and education

In the literature a large number of studies suggest that education and health are positively related (for an overview: Groot, 2004; Groot and Maassen van den Brink, 2006). Feinstein (2002) distinguishes six channels by which education affects health:
- Effects due to the development of specific skills. Courses on health promotion or health safety may have a direct impact on health.
- Generic cognitive development. Cognitive skills, such as reasoning and the ability to gather and process data, may be helpful in acquiring, interpreting and applying information on health.
- Personal development. The development of psychological resilience, self-efficacy and well being through education may enhance the capacity to initiate and maintain health. Also other personal characteristics that are fostered by educational achievements, such as self-esteem, a positive outlook on the world and motivation, may contribute to health.

- Peer group effects. Mixing with others who have acquired the above-mentioned specific skills, cognitive and personal development may provide a supportive context in which the individual's attitudes and social norms encourage health.
- Positional effects. Education increases status. A higher status may lead individuals to identify more with attitudes, norms and behaviour that improve health.
- Economic effects. Education increases human capital and human capital increases the (lifelong) earnings potential. A higher earnings potential increases the opportunity costs of unhealthy behaviour and increases the returns to investments in health. Consequently investments in education complement investments in health.

Grossman and Kaestner (1997) present an overview of empirical studies on the relation between education and health. This survey shows that better educated people are less likely to smoke, exercise more, wear seatbelts more often, and are more likely to participate in screening programmes for breast cancer and cervical cancer. We can conclude from this survey that better educated people generally have a healthier lifestyle. The only exception is alcohol use: in most countries the better educated consume more alcohol than the less well educated. However, many studies show that moderate alcohol consumption has positive effects on health (mortality), labour productivity and employment opportunities. As a consequence of their unhealthier lifestyle, less well educated people generally report more health problems and make more frequent use of health care arrangements.

Is the education effect on health a causal effect? One may ask whether the education effect on own health is really a causal effect or a selection effect. Many studies on education and health by epidemiologists and social scientists analyse associations between education and health and either ignore or simply assume a causal relation between the two. Very few studies address whether this association really reflects a causal relation. The relation between education and health is merely a correlation and not a causal relation if:

(a) there is a joint relation between education and health, whereby education not only affects health but there is also a reverse causality where health determines investments in education. A reverse effect would create a positive simultaneity bias in measuring the effect of education on health.

(b) there are other factors – i.e. variables that are either not observable
    or not observed – that affect both education and health.

The causality question is important, not only for determining the exact
relation between education and health, but also from a policy point of
view. Only if the relation between education and health is a true causal
relation can a shift in (public) expenditure from health care to education be effective in improving both the level of education and the health
status of the population.

Acemoglu, Johnson and Robinson (2003) argue for a reverse causality between education and health. A shorter life expectancy because
of poor health conditions shortens the time horizon of individuals.
A shorter time horizon lowers the returns and therefore the investments
in human capital such as education. Furthermore, children who are in
poor health are less able or have less energy to attend school, while
workers with poor health may be less inclined to invest in on-the-job
training.

One reason why a reverse causality might only be a minor source of
bias when estimating the relation between education and health is that
educational attainment is essentially established in early adulthood and
remains stable afterwards. Most health impairments are not incurred
until an adult age. Although, especially in less developed countries,
child mortality and morbidity is a cause for concern, infant and child
health for most children in developed countries does not impact on
their educational attainment.

The latter view is supported by the argument in Hammond (2002).
He argues that the link between education and health increases with
age, i.e. that the association is stronger among older populations than
among younger people. This is explained by the fact that some health
behaviours – such as not wearing a seatbelt or condom use – constitute
a constant risk to health, whereas others – such as smoking and excessive alcohol use – constitute a cumulative risk. This means that the
education differential in the latter type of unhealthy behaviour is only
translated into observable physical health differences later in life
(Hammond, 2002: 557). Empirical support for this claim is found is
Groot and Maassen van den Brink (2006). This study finds that the
effects of education on self-assessed health become stronger as people
get older.

The effects listed in Feinstein et al. (2003) – and that were summarized
above – provide causal mechanisms in the relation between education

and health. Grossman and Kaestner (1997) argue that the causality in the effect of education on health arises because more highly educated people are more efficient in maintaining and fostering their health. Or, as they express it, more highly educated people produce health more efficiently.

Grossman and Kaestner (1997) distinguish between two forms of efficiency in the production of health: productive efficiency and allocative efficiency. Productive efficiency refers to the situation whereby more highly educated people are able to obtain higher health benefits from the same amount of inputs. Allocative efficiency refers to the fact that more highly educated people are better informed about the health effects of certain inputs. One example is that more highly educated people are better informed about the health effects of food.

According to the UN (2003) a cross-country comparison over time shows that increases in educational attainment precede improvements in health status (UN, 2003: 87). This temporal sequencing suggests a causal relation between education and health. As argued above, the causal relation between education and health arises because a higher education leads to a healthier lifestyle and because more highly educated people are better able to gather, process and interpret information about healthy behaviour.

Becker and Mulligan (1994) add a third causal mechanism to this. They argue that education leads to a lower time preference for consumption in the present and a higher time preference for consumption in the future:

Schooling also determines investments in time preferences partly through the study of history and other subjects, for schooling focuses students' attention on the future. Schooling can communicate images of the situations and difficulties of adult life, which are the future of childhood and adolescence. In addition, through repeated practice at problem solving, schooling helps children to learn the art of scenario simulation. Thus, educated people should be more productive at reducing the remoteness of future pleasures (Becker and Mulligan, 1994: 10).

Education may alter time preferences, but a lower time preference may cause individuals to invest more in education and health as well. So time preferences may be an intermediate in the relation between education and health – as argued by Becker and Mulligan – but may also be a common (unobserved) causal factor for investments in both education and health. Fuchs (1996) argues that education is correlated with time preference, and that it is time preference that affects health rather than education. This hypothesis is tested by Sander (1998). The study includes cognitive ability and future education as covariates in an equation where the likelihood of smoking tobacco and marijuana is explained by college attendance. Future education and cognitive ability are viewed as correlates of time preference. This study finds both support for the argument that education affects health and for the hypothesis that time preference matters.

As was mentioned above, very few studies actually test whether the effect of education on health is a causal relation. Most of the studies that do test for causality use some sort of 2SLS with appropriate instrumental variables for education to test whether the effect of education on health is truly a causal one (see chapter 3 for an explanation of instrumental variables and two-stage least squares). Aside from the fact that good-quality instruments for education are difficult to obtain and that many of the IV studies suffer from the limitations caused by weak instruments, IV estimations enable the researcher to reject the hypothesis that the effect is a causal one, but the reverse – that it is indeed a causal relation – is almost always difficult to prove. By consequence, IV estimations are biased towards rejecting the notion that education causes better health (see chapters 1 and 3).

Education has both direct and indirect effects on one's own health, but education may affect the health of one's children as well. A number of studies have looked at the effects of parental education on the health status of their children. A distinction has to be made between the effects of parental education on infant health and the effects on the health when children have reached an adult age. More highly educated parents are better informed about what is good for the health of their children. They also attach a higher value to their children's health.

Leigh (1998) finds that – if the education level of the respondent is not controlled for – health is determined by the education level of the mother but not by the education level of the father. If the education level is controlled for, this study no longer finds a statistically significant relation between parental education and health. Similar findings are reported by Groot and Maassen van den Brink (2006). These findings suggest that the education level of the parents has an indirect effect on health – through the education level of the respondent – but not a direct effect.

5.3 Our contributions to the international literature

Both the survey and the meta-analysis in Groot and Maassen van den Brink (2004) show that there are strong links between education and health. Our reading of the literature is that the effect of education on health represents a genuine causal effect, that the reverse effect running from health to education is relatively small (at least for adults), and that there are common factors – most notably time preferences – that affect investments in both health and education. The relationship found in the literature might actually be an underestimate of the real magnitude of the effect. This is because lower levels of education appear to be associated with under-reporting of illness by patients (see Mackenbach et al., 1996).

One important aspect that should not be overlooked is the role of intermediate variables in the relation between education and health. One example is that through intermediate variables parental education affects health. As noted above, most studies do not find a direct linkage between parental education and health at an adult age if the respondent's educational attainment is controlled for. These studies do, however, find that one's own education has a positive effect on health and that parental education is an important factor explaining one's own education.

In this section we also report the results of some tests for causality in the relation between education and health in the Netherlands. We further test whether results are affected by scale of reference bias or reporting heterogeneity and we test whether results are affected by unobserved heterogeneity. We use the results to calculate the Quality Adjusted Life Years (QALYs) weight effect of a year of education in order to obtain an estimate of the education effect on health that is comparable to the wage effect of a year of education. QALYs are measured by multiplying life expectancy in years by the QALY weight of each year of life expectancy. The QALY weight measures quality of health on a 0 to 1 scale, where 0 is the worst possible health (near death) and 1 represents the best possible (perfect) health. To the best of our knowledge there are no prior estimates in the literature of the monetary equivalent of the health effect of a year of education.

In Groot and Maassen van den Brink (2006) we find for women and men in an ordered probit regression that more highly educated people are in better health than less well educated people: the number of years of education has a positive effect on the quality of health. If we control for the prevalence of diseases and handicaps, the size of the education coefficient is 0.018 for men and 0.011 for women. Controlling for the prevalence of diseases and handicaps thus reduces the health effect of education by roughly a third for men and 50% for women. If we do not include any control variables in the equation – i.e. estimate an equation with only the years of education variable – the point estimate is 0.040 (with a standard error of 0.004) for both men and women. Controlling for diseases and handicaps and other individual characteristics thus reduces the point estimate of the years of education variable by more than half for men and by nearly three-quarters for women.

The effect of education on health is larger for men than for women. The QALY weight of a year of education is 0.006 for men and 0.003 for women. For both groups the standard errors of the estimates of the QALY weights are 0.003, i.e. for men the point estimate of the QALY weight is twice the standard error, while for women the point estimate and its standard error are almost identical. The point estimates of the QALY weights imply that if we measure the quality of health on a 0–1 scale, a year of education improves the health state of men by 0.6% and for women by 0.3%.

The results further show that the education level of the mother has an effect on the health of her daughter, but not on the health of her son. The number of years of education of the father does not have a statistically significant effect on the health of his children. The country of origin of the parents does have an effect on the health of the children. Men whose father was born abroad and women whose mother was born abroad are in worse health than people whose parents were born in the Netherlands. It is remarkable that the effects seem to run from father to son and from mother to daughter. Country of birth of the father does not have a statistically significant effect on the health of the daughter, while country of birth of the mother does not have an impact on the health of the son.

To evaluate the reliability of our findings – in particular of the effect of education on health – a number of tests were performed. First, we tested whether the effects of education, diseases and handicaps and other individual characteristics differ between women and men. This is a test on equality of coefficients between women and men. The likelihood ratio tests show that the coefficients differ between women and men. It is thus relevant to treat both groups separately.

Next we tested whether the relation between education and health is linear or (inverse) U-shaped. For both women and men there appears to be a linear relation between years of education and quality of health.

The effects of education on health may vary with age. It is conceivable that the effect of one's own education may decline with age, i.e. decreases the more years have passed since finishing one's education. For similar reasons, the impact of parental background – the years of education of the parents – may also decline with age. It appears that the effects of education of oneself and of one's parents on quality of health do not change with age. In a second test we looked at whether the effects of years of education of the respondent differ between age cohorts. The test statistics indicate that the null hypothesis that there are no differences between age cohorts is rejected for men but cannot be rejected for women. This indicates that the effect of years of education on quality of health varies between age cohorts for men, but not among women.

Our results show that there is a clear and robust relation between education and health. The question remains, however, whether this is also a *causal* relation.

The education effect on self-reported health may not be a causal effect, but merely reflect that more highly educated people answer questions about their health in different ways from less well educated people. A similar health condition may be evaluated differently by people of higher or lower education. This phenomenon is known in the literature as scale of reference bias (Groot, 2000), state-dependent-reporting bias (Kerkhofs and Lindeboom, 1995) or reporting heterogeneity (Shmueli, 2002, 2003; Lindeboom and Van Doorslaer, 2004). We use a generalized version of the ordered probit model as proposed by Bolduc and Poole (1990). The results show that accounting for scale of reference bias does not change the point estimate of the years of education coefficient for men. For women, however, the coefficient becomes larger and more similar to the coefficient for men, after correcting for scale of reference bias. These findings mean that the education effect is not due to scale of reference bias. This suggests that a higher education reduces the borderline between reporting very poor and poor health and between poor and fair health.

The test statistics have shown that among men the effect of education on health changes when one gets older. If the effect between education and health is a causal relation, we expect that both among younger people and among older people education has an effect on health. If, on the other hand, there is a reverse causality – whereby healthier people invest more in education – we only expect a relation between education and health among young people but not among older people.

Our results indicate that among men the effect of years of education on the quality of health is *larger* for older men than for younger cohorts. The effect of education on health increases – and does not decrease – with age for men. Among women we do see that the education effect decreases with age, but – as we have shown above – a test on equality of the age cohort effects of education on health among women cannot be rejected. These findings provide support for the assumption that the effect of education on health is a causal effect.

As we have argued above, it is possible that there are common hereditary or social factors that affect both education and health. If we do not account for these common factors, we may wrongly conclude that there is a causal relation between education and health. In the estimations of the effect of education on health we have controlled for the educational attainment of both parents and for the country of birth of the parents.

Our results show that only years of education of the mother has a statistically significant effect on the quality of health of her daughter. The education level of the parents does not have an effect on men's health. The education level of the father also does not have a statistically significant effect on women's health. This last finding – father's education does not have an effect on his children's health – is important because we may expect that if education is a proxy for unmeasured hereditary or genetic effects, the effect of father's education on health is the same as the effect of mother's education (see Grossman and Kaestner, 1997: 94 for similar findings). If the effect of education is a proxy for social background, we may expect the impact of mother's education on health to be larger than the effect of father's education, as mothers spend more time and care on (the health of) children.

We also expect that if parental education is a proxy for social background that the effect of education of the mother on the health of her children is the same for boys and for girls. However, the results show that mother's education does have an effect on women's health but not on men's health. Summarizing, we do not find evidence of a direct effect of the education level of both parents on health. This suggests that the effect of education on health cannot be ascribed to non-measured hereditary ('nature') or social ('nurture') effects on health and supports the assumption that the relation between education and health is a causal one.

5.4 Instrumental variable approach

If there is a joint causal relation between education and health, education is an endogenous variable in the health equation. We test for the endogeneity of education by applying an instrumental variable (IV) approach. The instruments we use are whether the father had a managerial job and the number of workers supervised by the father when the respondent was 14 years old, and whether the mother of the respondent (ever) had a paid job. We expect that people whose father had a managerial job or whose mother was in paid employment have attained a higher education level. We also expect that these instruments do not have a statistically significant effect on the current health status of the individual. Both conditions are required for instruments to be valid (see chapter 3).

One possible objection to the validity of these instruments is that they refer to the socioeconomic status of the parental household, and may reflect socioeconomic differences in access to health care (at least at a young age). However, in the Netherlands access to health care is universal, as virtually every citizen is covered by health insurance. Therefore socioeconomic differences in access to health care are negligible.

The instrument 'father had a managerial job when the respondent was 14 years old' has a strong effect on educational attainment. Compared to men whose father did not have a managerial job, men with a father who was a manager have obtained about 1.5 years more education. Among women, this is 1–1.5 years depending on whether the father supervised more or less than ten workers. For the other instrument – 'mother had a paid job' – we only find a statistically significant effect for men and women whose mother never had a paid job. Children of mothers who never had a paid job received 0.3–0.6 years less education than children of mothers who only had a paid job before their marriage.

The IV estimates differ between women and men. For men we find that using instrumental variables doubles the effect of a year of education on quality of health. Among women the use of IV yields a statistically insignificant parameter estimate for years of education.

Before we can accept the results of the IV analyses we first have to check whether it is necessary and useful to use IV (the relevance of the instruments), whether we have used the right instruments (the validity of the instruments) and whether the quality of the instruments is good enough. To answer these questions we perform the tests proposed in Bound, Jaeger and Baker (1995) and some other tests. The conclusion that we draw from our test is that we have used valid and good-quality instruments, but that it is not relevant to use instrumental variables. This implies that we can base our interpretation on the specifications where we use actual years of education.

A final test on the robustness of the results concerns the impact of unobserved heterogeneity. The effect of education on health may be due to unobserved variables – such as time preference – that affect both education and health. We correct for unobserved heterogeneity by adding a random effect to the quality of health equation. This random effect captures unobserved factors that determine health and may otherwise be captured by the education variable in the equation. To estimate the random effect health equation, we follow the finite mixture approach described in Heckman and Singer (1984) for random effects duration models. In this approach the distribution of the random effect is proxied by a discrete function: a step function. Essentially, this procedure aims at distinguishing different groups in the sample by estimating different intercepts for each of these groups. The size of these groups is determined by the probability mass, which is estimated along with the intercept points. For a more detailed description of the application of this method to an ordered probit model, see Gilleskie and Harrison (1998).

For both women and men, the estimate of the effect of years of education on quality of health becomes larger after correction for unobserved heterogeneity. For men the coefficient increases by about a quarter, for women it increases by about a third. Qualitatively, correction for unobserved heterogeneity does not alter our conclusions on the impact of education on health: years of education have a statistically significant effect on quality of health. The hypothesis that this effect is a causal effect cannot be rejected.

5.5 A monetary measure of the health effect of education

Without some monetary measure of the effect of education on health, it is difficult to establish whether this is a large effect or not. Conversion to a monetary metric gives more insight into the magnitude of the effect. It also allows us to compare the health effects of education with the wage effects. By this we can estimate the rate of return to education – i.e. the returns in the labour market and in health – more precisely.

As was explained above, to calculate the monetary value of the education effect of the quality of health, we used the literature on the value of a Quality Adjusted Life Year (QALY). QALYs combine quality and quantity (mortality and morbidity) in one unified measure of quality of life corrected life years. A much used measure for the value of a QALY is Laupacis et al. (1992). This study calculates that the value of a QALY is about $100,000.[1]

An alternative estimate of the value of health gains can be obtained from the literature on the value of life. Moore and Viscusi (1988) estimate that the value of a statistical life is $5 million.[2] From this it can be calculated that the properly discounted value of a statistical life year is about $230,000. We assume that the value of a QALY is between $100,000 and $230,000.

The estimates in Groot and Maassen van den Brink (2006) imply that the QALY weight of a year of education is 0.006 for men and 0.003 for women, i.e. a year of education increases the QALY weight by 0.3–0.6%. If we use a QALY value of 100,000 euros, the value of the health gain due to one year of education is $600 for men and $300 for women. If we use a value of a statistical life year of $230,000, the value of the health gain of a year of education becomes $1,380 for men and $690 for women per year.

More insight into the size of the health effect of education can be obtained by relating the value of the health gain to the average income per capita. This also enables us to compare the effect to the wage effect of education. In 1999 the average GDP per capita in the Netherlands was approximately $23,000. For men we estimate that the health gain of a year of education is $600–1,380. For women this is $300–690. For men the value of the health gain is 2.5–5.8% of the average GDP per capita. For women this is 1.3–2.8%.

5.6 Conclusion and discussion

Like education, health has large economic benefits. Better health and a better education increase labour productivity. The investments to increase one's health are not limited to health care alone. Investments in education are equally important for maintaining people's health. In previous chapters it is concluded that the average individual return to a year of education – i.e. the direct wage effect of education – is 6–8%. Our indicative calculations suggest that we have to add another 1.3–5.8% if we also include the value of the education effect on the value of health. In other words, the value of the education effect of health is an additional 15–60% of the wage return to education. We conclude that the education effects on health are substantial.

A crucial question is whether education has a causal effect on health or not, not only for determining the exact relation between education and health, but also from a policy point of view. Only if the relation between education and health is a true causal relation can a shift in (public) expenditure from health care to education be effective in improving both the level of education and the health status of the population.

Both the survey and the meta-analysis show that there are strong links between education and health. Some tentative calculations suggest that the cost-benefit ratio of investments in education on health is highly positive. The evidence in our empirical work strongly suggests a causal relation, although actual causality is difficult to prove. For public policy this implies that a more integrated approach to education and health policies should be taken.

Notes

1. In a meta-analysis of thirty-three studies that have calculated the value of a statistical life, Mrozek and Taylor (2002) infer that the value of statistical life is between $1.5 million and $2.5 million. At a 5% discount rate this would make the value of a statistical life year somewhere between $76,500 and $127,500. An estimate of $100,000 for a QALY is exactly in the middle of these two estimates.
2. Viscusi (1992, 1993) summarizes twenty-four studies and concludes that the appropriate range for the value of a statistical life is between $4 million and $9 million, as this is the range in which most estimates lie. In a regression of 'best estimates' of values of a statistical life year on a number of characteristics of the studies and countries included, Miller (2000) finds that the value of a statistical life year is $4 million.

References

Acemoglu, D., S. Johnson and J. Robinson (2003). Disease and development in historical perspective. *Journal of the European Economic Association* 1: 397–405.

Becker, G. and C. Mulligan (1994). On the endogenous determination of time preference. Discussion Paper 94–2, Economics Research Center/National Opinion Research Center, University of Chicago.

Bolduc, D. and E. Poole (1990). Ordinal probit models with random bounds. *Economics Letters*, 33: 239–44.

Bound, J., D. Jaeger and R. Baker (1995). Problems with instrumental variables when the correlation between instruments and the endogenous explanatory variable is weak. *Journal of the American Statistical Association*, 90: 443–50.

Feinstein, L. (2002). Quantitative estimates of the social benefits of learning, 2: health (depression and obesity). Wider Benefits of Learning Research Report 6, Centre for Research on the Wider Benefits of Learning, Institute of Education, London.

Feinstein, L., C. Hammond, L. Woods, J. Preston and J. Bynner (2003). The contribution of adult learning to health and social capital. Wider Benefits of Learning Research Report 8, Centre for Research on the Wider Benefits of Learning, Institute of Education, London.

Fuchs, V. (1996). Economics, values, and health care reform. *American Economic Review*, 86: 1–2.

Gilleskie, D. and A. Harrison (1998). The effect of endogenous health inputs on the relationship between health and education. *Economics of Education Review*, 17: 279–95.

Groot, W. (2000). Adaptation and scale of reference bias in self-assessments of quality of life. *Journal of Health Economics*, 19: 403–20.

  (2004). Investing in Public Health, Inaugural Lecture, National University of Kyiv Mohyla Academy, Kiev.

Groot, W. and H. Maassen van den Brink (2004). The health effects of education, survey and meta analysis. SCHOLAR Working Paper, University of Amsterdam.

  (2006). The health effects of education. *Economics of Education Review*, forthcoming.

Grossman, M. and R. Kaestner (1997). Effects of education on health, in J. Behrman and N. Stacey (eds.), *The Social Benefits of Education*. Ann Arbor: University of Michigan Press, pp. 69–123.

Hammond, C. (2002). What is it about education that makes us healthy? Exploring the education-health connection. *International Journal of Lifelong Learning*, 21: 551–71.

Heckman, J. and B. Singer (1984). A method for minimizing the impact of distributional assumptions in econometric models for duration data. *Econometrica*, 52: 271–320.

Kerkhofs, M. and M. Lindeboom (1995). Subjective health measures and state-dependent reporting errors. *Health Economics*, 4: 221–35.

Laupacis, A., D. Feeny, A. Detsky and P. Tugwell (1992). How attractive does a new technology have to be to warrant adoption and utilization? Tentative guidelines for using clinical and economic evaluations. *Canadian Medical Association Journal*, 146: 473–81.

Leigh, J. (1998). Parents' schooling and the correlation between education and frailty. *Economics of Education Review*, 17: 349–58.

Lindeboom, M. and E. van Doorslaer (2004). Cut-point shift and index shift in self-reported health. *Journal of Health Economics*, 23: 1083–99.

Mackenbach, J., C. Looman and J. van der Meer (1996). Differences in the misreporting of chronic conditions, by level of education: the effect of inequalities in prevalence rates. *American Journal of Public Health*, 86: 706–11.

Miller, T. (2000). Variations between countries in values of statistical life. *Journal of Transport Economics and Policy*, 34: 169–88.

Moore, M. and W. K. Viscusi (1988). The quantity adjusted value of life. *Economic Inquiry*, 26: 369–88.

Mrozek, J. and L. Taylor (2002). What determines the value of lives? A meta-analysis. *Journal of Policy Analysis and Management*, 21: 253–70.

Sander, W. (1998). The effects of schooling and cognitive ability on smoking and marijuana use among adults. *Economics of Education Review*, 17: 317–24.

Schultz, T. W. (1993). Investments in human capital, in *The Economics of Being Poor*. Oxford: Blackwell, pp. 97–114.

Shmueli, A. (2002). Reporting heterogeneity in the measurement of health and health-related quality of life. *Pharmacoeconomics*, 20: 405–12.

   (2003). Socio-economic and demographic variation in health and its measures: the issue of reporting heterogeneity. *Social Science and Medicine*, 57: 125–34.

United Nations (2003). *Human Development Report 2003: Millennium Development Goals: A Compact among Nations to End Human Poverty*. New York: United Nations.

Viscusi, W. (1992). *Fatal Tradeoffs: Public and Private Responsibilities for Risks*. Oxford: Oxford University Press.

   (1993). The value of risks to life and health. *Journal of Economic Literature*, 31: 1912–46.

6 | Are successful parents the secret to success?

ERIK PLUG

6.1 Introduction

Almost all studies, varying over countries and times, show that when parents are rich and better educated their children tend to receive more schooling and income as well. In the United States, for example, intergenerational correlations of schooling and earnings are close to 0.4 (Solon 1992). And even in Sweden, where education is heavily subsidized, the intergenerational correlations are substantial and move between 0.2 and 0.3 (Björklund and Jäntti, 1997). Recently Haveman and Wolfe (1995) reviewed the mobility literature and came to the conclusion that the human capital of parents, typically measured by the number of years of schooling attained, is the most fundamental factor in explaining the child's success in school. Apparently the evidence on family background is quite persuasive: if you want to be successful, just have successful parents.

But if parents are indeed the secret to success, does this mean that if we – or policy-makers for that matter – make people more successful, their future children will do better as well? This question will serve as the outline of this chapter. Answers will not come easily as our understanding of why successful parents have successful children is at most tentative (Solon, 1999). There could be many family factors at work. Are, for example, parental abilities responsible for economic success passed on genetically to the next generation? Or are better-educated and richer parents better in providing an intellectually stimulating environment for their children? Or do poorer parents face credit constraints when financing their children's education?

It is rather complicated to study these family factors in isolation. After all, they are all related. Since more able parents are on average better educated than less able parents, they get children who do well in school by virtue of superior genes. More able parents are not only better educated, they usually generate more income as well. If family

81

income matters for educational achievement, then ability effects also run through income. Empirically, the fundamental problem is that we cannot interpret family background estimates without ignoring the strong correlation between observed background characteristics like schooling and income and mostly unobserved ability. To date, however, most intergenerational mobility studies do ignore the role of inherited abilities, just report family background estimates that suffer from what we know as ability bias, and therefore make no distinction between causation and association.

Within the framework of the SCHOLAR research, several studies have been conducted to estimate the causal effects of parental education and income on various school outcomes of children. In this chapter we will summarize these findings along the lines of two different empirical strategies that both aim to tackle the ability bias.

The first strategy treats the concept of ability as it is commonly understood and used by psychologists. Ability is observed and simply defined as IQ test scores, or something that is closely related to them. IQ test scores are then included as ability controls in family background models to infer the true causal relationship of interest. The second strategy treats ability as an unobserved concept and obtains identification from adopted children. This identification strategy is fairly simple. If adopted children share only their parents' environment and not their parents' genes, then any relation between the schooling of adoptees and that of their adoptive parents is driven by the influence parents have on their children's environment, and not by parents passing on their genes.

In this chapter we now turn to several empirical examples of such estimates, based on samples taken from the Wisconsin Longitudinal Survey in the United States. Almost all reported estimates come from recent work by Plug and Vijverberg (2003, 2005) and Plug (2004).

6.2 Estimating family background effects on children's schooling using samples of birth and adopted children

Focusing on the question of how family background variables income and schooling affect the educational attainment of children, we have already discussed two alternative approaches, each tackling the ability bias in its own (limited) way. The first approach is traditional and uses additional ability measures. The other approach negates the genetically based correlation between parental background and children's ability with an adoption experiment. We will frame our tests in terms of combinations of these two approaches.

The first set of estimates is presented in table 6.1 and is based on conventional samples of parents and their birth children.[1] Table 6.1 examines various determinants of years of schooling using censored regression models; the first column highlights the effect of family income on the child's years of schooling; the second column presents the same estimate of family income but in the presence of parental IQ measured when one of the parents was still a child; in the third and fourth columns the family income variable is replaced with parental schooling variables and estimates are presented with and without an ability control; in the fifth, sixth and seventh columns we exclusively focus on the role of parental ability measured as childhood IQ scores; and in the last column we finally see what happens when all parental background variables are included simultaneously. All equations contain controls, like age and gender of the child, but these estimates are not reported.

Looking at table 6.1 we find that our results are rather conventional. And, on the whole, our results are quite insensitive to specification choice. Whether regressions are run with or without ability controls, and whether schooling, income and IQ are included separately or simultaneously, we always find that children who come from better-educated, high-IQ and high-income families receive more schooling.

It is interesting to see that the partial schooling effects of both parents are practically identical, and that among all the observed family background effects the partial schooling effects appear to be the least sensitive to specification choice. It would also be interesting to see how the partial IQ effects of both parents behave, but we must leave that for future research. The current dataset only includes childhood IQ measurements of one of the parents. We therefore have to assume that both parents are in the same IQ class. This assumption is not as great a problem as it might seem. If we estimate the ability regressions on mothers and fathers separately using only mothers and fathers for which we have IQ scores available, the maternal and paternal IQ estimates are virtually the same.

We highlight two additional points. First, when we express the magnitudes of these background effects in elasticities, the results also provide some insights into the relative importance of parent's

Table 6.1 Various family background estimates. The effects of parent's income, schooling and IQ on schooling on birth children using the Wisconsin Longitudinal Survey

	(1)[a]	(2)[a]	(3)[a]	(4)	(5)	(6)[b]	(7)	(8)[c]
Parent's income	0.806	0.639						0.333
	0.040***	*0.039****						*0.037****
Parent's IQ		0.329	0.408				0.167	0.136
		0.016***	*0.016****				*0.017****	*0.017****
Mother's IQ				0.395				
				0.022***				
Father's IQ					0.422			
					0.024***			
Mother's schooling						0.296	0.272	0.244
						0.017***	*0.017****	*0.017****
Father's schooling						0.296	0.271	0.244
						0.011***	*0.011****	*0.012****
Number of observations	17,992	17,992	17,992	9,607	8,385	15,871	15,871	14,552

Notes:

[a] Plug and Vijverberg (2003).

[b] Plug (2004).

[c] Plug and Vijverberg (2005).

All standard errors are in italics;

*** significant at 1% level.

schooling, income and ability measured as IQ in predicting the child's success in school. Depending on specification choice, schooling elasticities range from 0.22 to 0.31, family income elasticities vary between 0.02 and 0.06, and IQ elasticities move from 0.11 to 0.28. Not surprisingly, our results are in line with those reported in Haveman and Wolfe: parent's schooling is the most important factor in explaining their child's success in school. And, second, these results shed some light on the relative importance of ability bias. Table 6.1 indicates little bias from the omission of the childhood IQ variable. With or without ability controls, parental schooling and income retain their positive influence on the schooling of children. As expected, the estimates attached to the left-out variable imply an upward bias. Family income appears to be the most sensitive to the inclusion of the IQ measure. With ability controls, the estimated income effect falls about 20%, whereas the schooling effect of either parent decreases by 8%.

The second set of estimates is presented in table 6.2. Table 6.2 is structured similarly to table 6.1. The difference is that results now come from estimating previous family specifications on a sample of parents and their adopted children. Looking at the results in table 6.2 we see that the estimates attached to father's years of schooling and family income are not strikingly different from those obtained using the sample of birth children. These results indicate that for these particular background variables the role of inherited abilities is not large. But the estimates attached to mother's years of schooling and IQ are very different from those obtained using the sample of birth children. The estimated effects of mother's schooling fall significantly, and now lack statistical significance across all specifications. The large swings exhibited by the IQ coefficients across specifications make it rather difficult to identify a consistent pattern. However, if we estimate the ability regressions on mothers and fathers separately, using only mothers and fathers for which we have IQ scores available, we discover that maternal and paternal IQ estimates behave very similarly to the partial effects observed for parental education. Where the effect of the mother's IQ almost disappears, the IQ effect of her husband remains positive and statistically significant. We will return to this point below.

But before we do that, we address two issues: the relative importance of various background variables and the impact of ability bias. With parent's schooling, income and IQ purged of their inherited abilities, the calculated elasticities of father's schooling now move around 0.25,

Table 6.2 *Various family background estimates. The effects of parent's income, schooling and IQ on schooling on adoptees using the Wisconsin Longitudinal Survey*

	(1)[a]	(2)[a]	(3)[a]	(4)	(5)	(6)[b]	(7)	(8)[c]
Parent's income	0.604	0.530						0.427**
	0.200***	*0.206****						*0.199****
Parent's IQ		0.115	0.176**				−0.139*	−0.140**
		0.076	*0.069****				*0.075****	*0.074****
Mother's IQ				0.095				
				0.122				
Father's IQ					0.221			
					0.024***			
Mother's schooling						0.104	0.114	0.072
						0.075	*0.073*	*0.075*
Father's schooling						0.233	0.261	0.236
						0.043***	*0.044****	*0.045****
Number of observations	685	685	685	282	403	610	610	574

Notes:
[a] Plug and Vijverberg (2003).
[b] Plug (2004).
[c] Plug and Vijverberg (2005).
All standard errors are in italics;
* significant at 10% level
** significant at 5% level
*** significant at 1% level.

the elasticities of the mother's schooling are about 0.10, the IQ elasticities behave somewhat erratic and range from − 0.10 to 0.13, and the income elasticities hardly change and remain very small at between 0.02 and 0.05. For adoptees we still find that parental schooling is the most prominent factor in explaining the child's success in school. But this effect is entirely driven by the father's schooling. Mother's schooling has little if any impact on the schooling of her adopted child. Comparison of the estimates in tables 6.1 and 6.2 suggests that the impact of the parent's schooling, income and IQ is smaller for adoptees than for children who are raised by their own biological parents. This is not unexpected. If family genes are somehow responsible for the child's schooling, the estimates should go down when the inherited abilities of adoptive parents are eliminated. The difference between estimates for own birth and adopted children, which can be interpreted as the impact of ability bias, is not easily generalizable across specifications. According to the barest models (columns (1), (3), (5), (6) and (7)) the reduction is most sizeable for the mother's schooling and IQ: the estimates attached to the mother's schooling and IQ decrease by almost 65 to 75%. The average IQ parameter is reduced by 57%, whereas the father's schooling and income estimates fall by 21 and 27%.

Having reported the results, let us take one step back and reflect on what these estimates might mean.

6.3 But what do these results actually mean?

In this section we try to interpret previous estimates to understand which of the following family factors drives the child's success in school. Is it the inheritance of ability? Or is it that richer parents have a better access to financial resources? Or is it that better-educated parents create the more favourable academic environment?

How important are inherited abilities?

In their famous but widely debated book, *The Bell Curve*, Herrnstein and Murray (1994) claim that intelligence measured as IQ is a highly heritable trait and plays a critical role in predicting economic and social success. They suggest that a society will ultimately become fully stratified, not along the lines of background and income, but by levels of inborn intelligence.

The results in tables 6.1 and 6.2, however, cast some doubt on Herrnstein and Murray's predictions. We begin to disentangle the effect of ability into a nature component and a nurture component on the basis of differences in educational attainment between children that are adopted and children that are raised by their own birth parents. In table 6.1 column (3) the parameter estimates attached to the variable 'Parent's IQ' indicate the degree to which intelligent parents produce intelligent children who are more likely to obtain more schooling: this parameter combines cultural and biological effects. The same parameter in table 6.2 represents the IQ effect from which the direct genetical ability transfers that cannot occur among adoptive parents and their children is removed. Thus, according to these estimates (0.408 for birth children and 0.176 for adoptees), about 57% of all ability transfers relevant for educational attainment measured in years run through genes. In Plug and Vijverberg (2003) this estimate is then further subjected to various sensitivity tests, and a lower bound of 50% is determined. If we decompose the ability effects for mothers and fathers separately, we find that for mothers about 76% of her ability relevant for her child's school success is inherited by her children. For fathers this amounts to 48%. These numbers very much resemble the nature values taken by Herrnstein and Murray. In their book they argue that the genetic component of IQ is unlikely to be smaller than 40% or higher than 80% and adopt an estimate of 60%. Apparently, IQ is a heritable trait, although it is not all that is genetically transmitted.

Herrnstein and Murray then treat intelligence as measured by IQ test scores as the single most relevant determinant of school success. Here our results indicate that the position Herrnstein and Murray take is not built on solid ground. We find that it is the educational attainment of fathers, typically measured by the number of years of schooling attained, and not his IQ, that is the most dominant factor in explaining his child's school success. And because the positive influence of father's schooling on his child's schooling is primarily driven by the family environment he creates and not so much by his genes, it is unlikely that a society will ultimately end up as being fully stratified by levels of inborn intelligence.[2]

6.4 Does family income matter?

Economists put their emphasis on nurture in determining educational outcomes. The mechanism they usually offer to explain this family relation is that children from poor families are restricted in their pursuit of more and higher-quality education merely because their parents face credit constraints when financing their children's education.

In table 6.2, where we regress the years of schooling of adopted children on the characteristics of adopting families, we find that a better access to financial resources improves the educational achievement of adoptees. Our estimates are genetically unbiased, but this does not necessarily prove that family income has a causal effect on schooling. The problem is that parents influence their kids through things other than genetics. If, for example, parents endowed with child-rearing talents also make more money, the estimated income effects remain too high, and research on adoptees does not help.

In Plug and Vijverberg (2005) we have further scrutinized the adoption data approach to estimating the effects of parental income on schooling outcomes for offspring. To tackle this particular child-rearing bias we then use additional ability measures, take advantage of the information available on grandparents,[3] exploit the periodic measurement of family income, and examine income effects in low-, middle- and high-income families. In isolation, each test demonstrates that family income is a significant factor. Taken together, the results strongly suggest that there is a causal relation between family income and school success for adoptees. It should be noted, however, that the income elasticities we find are very small and range from 0.02 and 0.05.[4]

6.5 And how important are educated mothers?

Widely held wisdom is that mother's schooling is important for her child's schooling, and many, though certainly not all, studies demonstrate that mother's schooling is more important than the schooling of her husband (Heckman and Hotz, 1986; Haveman and Wolfe, 1995; Hill and King, 1995). Our schooling estimates in table 6.1 confirm this in part. We do not observe a structural difference between the partial schooling effects of both parents, but we do find that the schooling of both mother and father are significantly positive and dominate all observed IQ and income effects. The estimated marginal schooling effects are much higher than the marginal effects found for IQ and income. Our results in table 6.2, however, clearly undermine the common result that parental effects on schooling derive mostly from mother's educational attainment. With adoptees, we find that the association between the father and child schooling falls slightly but remains positive and statistically significant in all specifications. This is in sharp contrast with maternal schooling effects. The estimate of the effect of mother's schooling on that of her child is much smaller (65% less than indicated by the association between mothers and their birth children) and always lacks statistical significance. In Plug (2004) we find that these results appear to be robust to different samples and schooling measures.

These results contradict the conventional wisdom that maternal schooling has a bigger effect on the child's schooling than that of her husband. Is it perhaps possible that we are misinterpreting our findings? To see whether maternal schooling effects are truly close to zero, our findings must be bolstered with further support. And the answer lies in whether different samples and different empirical strategies tell a similar or a different story.

To date there are six intergenerational mobility studies that focus on years of schooling, use three different approaches, and do make a distinction between causation and association: one identical twins study, two other adoption studies and three instrumental variable (IV) studies. With monozygotic twin mothers from Minnesota, identical in their inborn abilities but different in their amounts of schooling, Behrman and Rosenzweig (2002) identify the maternal schooling effect by taking the difference between the twin mothers' children. They find that the mother's schooling has little if any impact on the schooling of her child. Once they look at monozygotic twin fathers and difference out all the genetic abilities that influence their children's schooling, the influence of father's schooling remains positive and statistically significant. Recent work by Antonovics and Goldberger (2005) shows that these maternal schooling effects are not that sensitive to the coding of the data and always remain insignificant and close to 0. But they call into question the assumption that twins differ in terms of education but not in terms of any other characteristic.

Sacerdote (2000) also considers the effects of unobserved inherited abilities on the child's schooling, but, instead of twinning, obtains identification from adopted children. With relatively small samples Sacerdote finds positive and statistically significant schooling effects when mother's and father's schooling are included as separate regressors. Consistent with the previous twin study, the effect of the mother's schooling turns out to be most sensitive to the inclusion of her partner's schooling.

Björklund, Lindahl and Plug (2004) use about 8,000 Swedish adoptees to estimate the impacts of both mother's and father's schooling on the adopted child's schooling, and find that the partial effect of father's schooling is much higher than that of the mother. But since both mother's and father's schooling retains positive and significant effects on their children's schooling, they conclude that in Sweden both parents' schooling contributes to the schooling of the next generation.

Three recent IV studies exploit reforms in the compulsory schooling legislation to identify the effect of parents' schooling on their children's. Oreopoulos, Page and Stevens (2003) use US reforms, which occurred in different states at different times, and find that when the mother's and father's schooling are included as separate regressors, the influence of the mother's and father's schooling are equally important. When mother's and father's schooling are included simultaneously to allow for assortative mating effects, the estimates are no longer significantly different from zero or from each other. Because of the imprecision of their estimates, however, it is impossible to say anything about the mother's and father's relative importance in the transmission process. Black, Devereux and Salvanes (2005) also use changes in compulsory schooling laws introduced in different Norwegian municipalities at different times during the 1960s and early 1970s. They find no effect for father's schooling and a small but positive effect for mother's schooling (which is primarily driven by a relationship between teenage mothers and their sons). In a similar fashion Chevalier (2004) uses a change in the compulsory schooling law in Britain in 1957. He finds a large positive effect of mother's education on her child's education but no significant effect of paternal education. However, his study suffers from the fact that the legislation was implemented nationwide; as a result, there is no cross-sectional variation in the British compulsory schooling law.

Our results turn out to be most comparable to those obtained in previously mentioned twin and adoption studies. In all, these results give some support to the idea that the influence of mother's schooling on that of her child becomes irrelevant when heritable abilities and assortative mating are taken into account.

We are aware that the available IV studies appear to be telling a different story. Where these differences come from, however, we do not know. Perhaps differences are due to the locality of the treatment. Adoptive parents, and also parents of twins, are, on average, better educated, whereas the parents that are affected by the instruments are always less well educated. Or perhaps it is the case that observed differences are country-specific. Searching for possible answers will indeed be fascinating but will have to be left for future research.

6.6 Conclusion and discussion

In this chapter we offer two research designs to examine three alternative mechanisms that could explain why successful parents have successful children.

Both designs aim to tackle the problem that able parents may obtain more schooling and income, which is consistent with the literature on ability bias. The first research design is a simple and a somewhat naive way of dealing with ability bias in mobility estimates. If one is willing to accept that ability is defined by IQ test scores, or something that is closely related to them, one can then use multi-generational samples with such test scores available, estimate the correct equation, and infer the magnitude of the ability bias that would occur if this particular variable were left out. The question is, of course, whether IQ can be treated as the single relevant ability measure. Probably not. Griliches (1977) borrows from Woody Allen to point out that ability is the *thing with feathers*. It is something that is very hard to define. It is better and more realistic to see ability as something that is not observed.

The second design is relatively new in economics and uses adopted children. As we have already mentioned, the advantage of using adoptees seems obvious. We reduce the ability bias and thereby learn something about why successful parents more often have successful children. The disadvantages of using adoptees, to which we have devoted little or no attention thus far, are obvious as well. There are six potential dangers: (a) small samples; (b) adoptees and adoptive parents are different from other children and their parents; (c) adoptees are not always randomly assigned to their adoptive parents; (d) adoptive parents treat their adopted children differently from their own birth children; (e) relevant information on the biological background and adoption history of adopted children is often not observed; and (f) in many cases, the impact adoptive parents have on their adopted children falls when children are getting older. New adoption research should recognize and treat most of these pitfalls.[5] With new, much larger and qualitatively much richer data on adoptees that are now becoming available (Björklund, Lindahl and Plug, 2004), adoption research will provide better answers to the previously addressed mobility questions.

But for now we shall focus our attention on the adoption approach, ask ourselves the question why it is that successful parents have successful children, and show how possible answers serve the interest of policy-makers.

It is quite obvious that policy-makers would like to unravel the secret to success as well. If genes drive the academic success of children in school, then inequality in opportunity would merely be a reflection of the existing gene pool, leaving scant room for effective pro-education policies. If, on the other hand, the environment were primarily responsible for the child's success in school, then improving the educational achievement would actually reduce the inequality in educational opportunity for future generations. The implications for public policy are thus huge. We will highlight four of them.

- Our results indicate that inherited intelligence measured as childhood IQ test scores matters, but not so much that it would eventually lead to a society that is fully stratified by levels of inborn intelligence. We find that more than half of the intergenerational transfer of ability is genetically determined. The smaller portion suggests that the hands of policy-makers are not completely tied and that there is room for effective educational policies that promote equality of educational opportunity.

- If public resources are spent on educational programmes that are believed to alleviate the financial constraints of students from poor families, it is important to know whether family income is the actual mechanism at work. Similarly, income tax policies may, or may not, have a long-term impact on the distribution of schooling of the next generation. We find that family income does matter, but the small elasticities indicate we should not expect much from income and tax policies as effective instruments to counter both existing and future inequalities.

- We would also like to temper the policy-makers' hopes and expectations that the growth in the number of women going to university (they currently outnumber men) will have a lasting effect on the educational opportunity of the next generations. Our results indicate that the positive influence of mother's schooling on that of her child disappears when heritable abilities and assortative mating are taken into account.

- In fact, our results suggest one policy instrument that could work is through the education of men. If today's generation of men had more equality of educational opportunity, our estimates indicate that the next generation of children would start out more equal as well. Obviously, improving the educational achievement of a whole generation is another goal altogether – one that is easier said than done.

Appendix

At our disposal we have a US dataset, the Wisconsin Longitudinal Survey, that contains detailed multi-generational information about families. Data collection started in 1957 on a group of high school male and female students in Wisconsin all born around 1939. Information was gathered about their IQ, family background, and so on. In 1964, 1975 and 1992, the same students were contacted again and information was collected about their school careers, labour market status, family conditions and the school careers of their children. For these children it is recorded whether they are their parents' own offspring or whether they have been adopted.[6]

Notes

1. We use data from a longitudinal survey of American high school graduates to obtain our estimates. We refer the reader to the appendix for a more detailed description of the Wisconsin Longitudinal Survey.
2. The arguments, evidence and research methods presented in *The Bell Curve* have been widely criticized by economists (Ashenfelter and Rouse, 1999; Currie and Thomas, 1999; Cawley, Heckman and Vytlacil, 1999; Goldberger and Manski, 1995; Korenman and Winship, 2000). These discussions are not new and very much resemble the IQ debate that took place among psychologists in the early 1970s (Jensen, 1973; Herrnstein, 1973; Jencks, 1972).
3. In Plug and Vijverberg (2005) we follow Becker and Tomes (1986) to derive an empirical model where grandparents' income enters with a hypothesized sign that is negative, as an additional control for unobserved child-rearing talents.

4. Although research designs differ in estimation techniques, in the variables used, in variable specifications and in sample designs, the income estimates taken from existing literature are comparable to our estimates. Haveman and Wolfe (1995), for example, review the potential determinants of children's schooling and find that income elasticities range from 0.02 to 0.20.

5. The WLS data on adoptees and their parents suffer from similar limitations. Sensitivity tests reported in Plug and Vijverberg (2003, 2005) and Plug (2004) indicate that adoption results appear fairly robust against points (b), (c) and (d).

6. For an extended data description we refer the reader to Plug and Vijverberg (2003, 2005) and Plug (2004). For more detailed information on the WLS data we refer the reader to Sewell and Hauser (1992). Data and documentation from the Wisconsin Longitudinal Study are available at http://dpls.dacc.wisc.edu/WLS/wlsarch.htm.

References

Antonovics, Kate and Arthur Goldberger (2005). Does increasing women's schooling raise the schooling of the next generation? Comment. *American Economic Review*, 95: 1738–44.

Ashenfelter, Orley and Cecilia Rouse (1999). Schooling, intelligence, and income in America: cracks in the Bell Curve. NBER Working Paper 6902. Cambridge, MA

Becker, Gary and Nigel Tomes (1986). Human capital and the rise and fall of families. *Journal of Labor Economics*, 4: 1–39.

Behrman, Jere and Mark Rosenzweig (2002). Does increasing women's schooling raise the schooling of the next generation? *American Economic Review*, 92: 323–34.

Björklund, Anders and Markus Jäntti (1997). Intergenerational income mobility in Sweden compared to the United States. *American Economic Review*, 87: 1009–18.

Björklund, Anders, Mikael Lindahl and Erik Plug (2004). Intergenerational effects in Sweden: what can we learn from adoption data? IZA Working Paper 1194, Bonn.

Black, Sandra, Paul Devereux and Kjell Salvanes (2005). Why the apple doesn't fall far: understanding intergenerational transmission of human capital. *American Economic Review*, 95: 437–49.

Cawley, John, James Heckman and Edward Vytlacil (1999). Meritocracy in America: an examination of wages within and across occupations. *Industrial Relations*, 38: 250–96.

Chevalier, Arnaud (2004). Parental education and child's education: a natural experiment. IZA Working Paper 1153, Bonn.

Currie, Janet and Duncan Thomas (1999). The intergenerational transmission of intelligence: down the slippery slopes of the Bell Curve. *Industrial Relations*, 38: 297–330.

Goldberger, Arthur and Charles Manski (1995). Review article: *The Bell Curve* by Herrnstein and Murray. *Journal of Economic Literature*, 33: 762–76.

Griliches, Zvi (1997). Estimating the returns to schooling: some econometric problems. *Econometrica*, 45: 1–22.

Haveman, Robert and Barbara Wolfe (1995). The determinants of children attainments: a review of methods and findings. *Journal of Economic Literature*, 33: 1829–78.

Heckman, James and Joseph Hotz (1986). The sources of inequality for males in Panama's labor market. *Journal of Human Resources*, 42: 507–42.

Herrnstein, Richard (1973). *IQ in the Meritocracy*. Boston: Little Brown.

Herrnstein, Richard and Charles Murray (1994). *The Bell Curve: Intelligence and Class Structure in American Life*. New York: The Free Press.

Hill, Anne and Elizabeth King (1995). Women's education and women's well-being. *Feminist Economics*, 1: 21–46.

Jencks, Christopher (1972). *Inequality: A Reassessment of the Effects of Family and Schooling in America*. New York: Basic Books.

Jensen, Arthur R. (1973). *Genetics and Education*. New York: Methuen.

Korenman, Sanders and Christopher Winship (2000). A reanalysis of *The Bell Curve*: intelligence, family background, and schooling, in Kenneth Arrow, Samuel Bowles and Stephen Durlauf (eds.), *Meritocracy and Economic Inequality*. New Delhi: Oxford University Press.

Oreopoulos, Philip, Marianne Page and Anne Hu Stevens (2003). Does human capital transfer from parent to child? The intergenerational effects of compulsory schooling. NBER Working Paper 10164, Cambridge, MA.

Plug, Erik (2004). Estimating the effect of mother's schooling on children's schooling using a sample of adoptees. *American Economic Review*, 94: 358–68.

Plug, Erik and Wim Vijverberg (2003). Schooling, family background, and adoption: is it nature or is it nurture? *Journal of Political Economy*, 111: 611–41.

    (2005). Does family income matter for schooling outcomes? Using adoption as a natural experiment. *Economic Journal*, 115: 879–906.

Sacerdote, Bruce (2000). The nature and nurture of economic outcomes. NBER Working Paper 7949, Cambridge, MA.

Sewell, William H. and Robert M. Hauser (1992). A review of the Wisconsin Longitudinal Study of social and psychological factors in aspiration and achievement, 1963–1993. Center for Demography and Ecology, Working Paper 92–01, University of Wisconsin-Madison.

Solon, Gary (1992). Intergenerational income mobility in the United States. *American Economic Review*, 82: 393–408.

(1999). Intergenerational mobility in the labor market, in Orley Ashenfelter and David Card (eds.), *Handbook of Labor Economics*, vol. III. Amsterdam: North-Holland.

PART II

Applying and extending the human capital model

7 | Overeducation in the labour market

WIM GROOT AND HENRIËTTE MAASSEN
VAN DEN BRINK

7.1 Introduction

One of the most important social developments of the past decades in western countries has been the increase in the educational level of the population. The increase in the education level of the workforce has been accompanied by higher than average growth rates for jobs for better-educated workers. Also, for a number of jobs there has been an upgrade in the skills needed to perform adequately. Despite this increase, we may ask whether the increase in the demand for better-educated labour has kept pace with the increase in the supply of skilled workers. If the growth in the supply of better-educated people outpaces the growth in demand, overeducation of the workforce is the likely result. Overeducation is defined as a job–worker match where the worker actually has more education than is required for the job (and conversely for undereducation). It is commonly measured in years. In 1981 Duncan and Hoffman started the overeducation literature by distinguishing education required for the job and actual education. In the 1980s Hartog (see Hartog and Oosterbeek, 1988) introduced the concept of overeducation in the Netherlands, and later continued to contribute (Hartog, 1993, 1997, 2000). At the end of the 1990s he concluded that the ORU specifications (based on over-, required, and undereducation) are useful extensions of the standard Mincer specification (see also chapter 1) but only if these specifications are embedded in structural labour models.

Surveying the literature of the past twenty-five years several explanations can be given for overeducation. One is that overeducation is a deliberate investment and serves as a compensation for lack of other human capital endowments, such as ability, on-the-job training or experience. Sicherman (1991) and Groot (1996) find that overeducated workers have less experience, tenure and on-the-job training than correctly allocated workers. Groot and Maassen van den Brink

(1996) find that workers who have experienced a career interruption – such as women with children – are more likely to be in jobs for which they are overeducated. Büchel and Mertens (2004) find that overeducated workers have lower wage growth than adequately educated workers. This also indicates that they lack human capital. Furthermore, this study finds that overeducated workers have less access to formal and informal training. This suggests that receiving more training does not close the skills gap.

Another explanation is that overeducation is part of a career mobility or insertion process in the labour market. Workers may enter the labour market in jobs for which they are overeducated and later on move to jobs that better match their educational attainment. Groot (1996) and Groot and Maassen van den Brink (1996) find that – after controlling for experience – younger workers are more likely to be overeducated than older workers. Further, in Sicherman (1991) it is found that overeducated workers change jobs more frequently. This also suggests that overeducation is part of a phase of adaptation in the early stages of the working life. Groeneveld and Hartog (2004) find that in the firm's internal labour market overeducation improves the chances of job promotion, while undereducation hampers them. Both effects, however, diminish with the age at which the worker is observed to be over- or undereducated. Rubb (2003a) draws somewhat different conclusions. This study finds that approximately three out of four overeducated workers in year t will be overeducated in year $t + 1$. This suggests that some workers are overeducated for longer periods of time.

Broadly speaking, the literature on overeducation can be distinguished in:
1. studies that focus on the incidence of overeducation and changes in this incidence over time.
2. studies on the consequences of overeducation. These include the returns to overeducation relative to returns to years of education required, studies on the impact of overeducation on unemployment, job mobility and job satisfaction, etc.
3. studies on the causes of overeducation. These studies address topics that were addressed above, i.e. whether overeducation compensates for lack of other forms of human capital or whether overeducation is part of an initiating phase on the labour market.

In this chapter we focus on the incidence of qualification mismatches in the labour market and on the pay-off for formal educational qualifications that are not fully required for the job, as the incidence and returns to overeducation are the best-researched areas within the overeducation literature. In section 7.2, we review what twenty years of research on the incidence and returns to overeducation has taught us. For this purpose we summarize the findings of a survey of the literature and a meta-analysis of the available studies on overeducation. The overview presented in section 7.2 largely draws on the surveys of the literature by Hartog (2000) and Groot and Maassen van den Brink (2000).

In section 7.3 we address a more detailed and specific question within the overeducation literature, namely what determines the dynamics of job–skill mismatches in the labour market? To answer this question we use data from a Dutch labour market survey to look at both the determinants of the incidence of overeducation and the determinants of the entry into and exit from overeducation.

7.2 Survey of previous studies: a survey and meta-analysis of overeducation

Hartog (2000) presents a thorough review and discussion of the overeducation literature, while Groot and Maassen van den Brink (2000) provide a meta-analysis of the empirical outcomes of overeducation studies.

Four different ways of operationalizing overeducation can be distinguished in the literature: (A) based on job level or occupational classification system; (B) based on average years of education within occupation; (C) self-report on skill utilization; (D) based on self-report on skill requirements (for new workers) on the job. Hartog (2000) discusses the relative merits of the operationalization of the overeducation concept. He concludes that the job analysis approach based on a systematic evaluation by professional job analysts, who specify the required level of education for a specific job, is conceptually superior to the other methods. However, these measures are frequently not available or are costly to obtain. When these measures are available, then they are usually only for specific years. The worker's self-report on the quality of the match between actual and required schooling levels is therefore often the best available measure.

Hartog (2000) draws four conclusions from a survey of the empirical studies on overeducation:

1. Returns to years of schooling required are higher than returns to years of schooling actually acquired.
2. Returns to overeducation years are positive, but smaller than to required education.
3. Returns to undereducation years are negative, but in absolute terms smaller than returns to required education.
4. These conclusions are not sensitive to the measure of required education.

These conclusions are confirmed by the meta-analysis in Groot and Maassen van den Brink (2000). In this meta-analysis twenty-five studies on overeducation are analysed. From the twenty-five studies fifty estimates on the incidence of overeducation and thirty-six estimates for the incidence of undereducation are obtained. The unweighted average of the incidence of overeducation is 23.3% of the labour force (with a standard deviation of 9.9 percentage points), while the unweighted average incidence of undereducation is 14.4% (where the standard deviation is 8.2 percentage points). The average return to a year of actual education is 5.6%. The unweighted averages of the estimates of the returns to the different educational components are 7.8% for years of education required for the job, 3.0% for years of overeducation and −1.5% for years of undereducation. These averages imply that a worker with ten years of education, working in a job requiring ten years, would earn a return of 7.8% for every year of his education. In a job requiring only nine years, he would get 7.8% for the first (required) nine years and 3.0% for the last (overeducated) year. In a job requiring eleven years he gets a penalty of 1.5% on his missing year, and thus earns a return of 7.8% for the first ten years and $7.8 − 1.5 = 6.3\%$ on the last year.

The results show that the different definitions lead to large differences in the incidence of overeducation. Studies using the variation of years of education within occupations (definition B) yield the lowest estimate of overeducation, while studies based on self-reports on the educational requirements of the job for new workers (definition D) yield the highest estimate. The rate of overeducation varies from 13.1% among studies using definition B to 28.6% in studies based on definition D.

There appears to be less overeducation in European countries than in the United States. The average rate of overeducation among studies for the United States is 26.3%, while among European studies this is 21.5%. The same holds for the incidence of undereducation. The

Table 7.1 Average values by characteristics of the survey and characteristics of the sample used in the study (standard errors in brackets)

	Incidence of overeducation	Incidence of undereducation	Rate of return education attained	Rate of return education required	Rate of return overeducation	Rate of return undereducation
All studies	23.3% (9.9%)	14.4% (8.2%)	5.6% (1.0%)	7.8% (2.2%)	3.0% (4.7%)	−1.5% (5.8%)
Country						
United States	26.3% (11.1%)	15.6% (4.1%)	5.5% (2.4%)	8.1% (2.0%)	3.9% (4.8%)	−1.9% (3.8%)
Europe	21.5% (8.8%)	13.9% (9.4%)	5.6% (0.8%)	7.6% (2.4%)	2.1% (4.6%)	−1.2% (7.0%)
Year						
1970s	28.7% (10.8%)	16.0% (3.9%)	3.8% (0)	7.9% (2.3%)	4.6% (1.3%)	−2.9% (1.2%)
1980s	22.4% (8.2%)	14.9% (7.0%)	5.9% (1.1%)	7.4% (2.4%)	2.6% (5.7%)	−2.1% (4.3%)
1990s	21.0% (10.7%)	13.1% (10.8%)	5.7% (0.8%)	8.2% (2.1%)	1.4% (5.4%)	0.85% (9.6%)
Definition of overeducation *						
A	26.4% (9.2%)	30.2% (12.4%)		9.5% (2.4%)	3.8% (1.5%)	−5.3% (1.9%)
B	13.1% (3.5%)	9.6% (5.1%)	5.8% (0.9%)	7.4% (2.4%)	−1.5% (7.2%)	4.2% (8.5%)
C	24.8% (8.2%)	11.2% (3.3%)		3.3% (0)	1.9% (0)	−3.3% (0)
D	28.6% (8.6%)	15.5% (6.3%)	5.0% (1.4%)	7.9% (1.8%)	4.9% (1.5%)	−3.5% (2.1%)
Gender						
Male	21.0% (8.5%)	16.5% (11.0%)	5.7% (1.1%)	7.3% (1.9%)	2.8% (4.3%)	−1.3% (7.0%)
Female	24.0% (11.5%)	10.9% (6.3%)	5.5% (0.5%)	8.7% (2.4%)	4.2% (3.4%)	−0.7% (6.9%)

Table 7.1 (continued)

	Incidence of overeducation	Incidence of undereducation	Rate of return education attained	Rate of return education required	Rate of return overeducation	Rate of return undereducation
Combined sample	24.8% (10.1%)	15.4% (6.0%)	5.5% (1.7%)	7.4% (2.1%)	2.0% (5.9%)	−2.1% (4.4%)
Specification of the wage equation						
With actual education	11.2% (3.7%)	10.4% (7.9%)	6.2% (0.8%)		−8.4% (3.9%)	11.1% (6.4%)
With required education	24.4% (9.6%)	14.9% (8.2%)	5.4% (1.0%)	7.8% (2.2%)	4.5% (1.7%)	−3.5% (2.0%)

Note:
* Definition of over/undereducation: A based on job level or DOT classification; B based on average years of education within occupation; C self-report on skill utilization; D based on self-report on skill requirements (for new workers) on the job. Source: Groot and Maassen van den Brink (2000).

returns to overeducation are lower in studies using data for European countries than among studies using data for the United States. This is probably due to lower rates of return to education in general, as the average rate of return to a year of education required is somewhat lower among European studies as well.

The incidence of overeducation appears to have declined rather than increased over the past twenty years. Studies using data for the 1970s on average find that 28.7% of the workers are overeducated. Among studies using data for the 1990s the average incidence of overeducation is 21%. With the decline in the incidence of overeducation over time, the average rate of return to a year of overeducation has declined as well. In studies for the 1970s the pay-off to a year of overeducation was 4.6% on average. Studies for the 1990s find a rate of return of 1.4%. Both findings combined suggest that over time overeducation has become increasingly concentrated among lower-ability workers for whom the pay-off to a year of overeducation is low.

The incidence of undereducation appears to have declined from 16% in the 1970s to 13% in studies for the 1990s. The joint decline in overeducation and undereducation suggests that skill mismatches in the labour market have decreased since the 1970s.

Overeduction is more frequent among female workers than among male workers, while the opposite holds for undereducation. Among studies using data for male workers 21% are overeducated and 16.5% are undereducated. If data for female workers are used, the incidence of overeducation is 24% while 10.9% are undereducated.

To account for heterogeneity in the incidence of overeducation and undereducation, and the rates of return to years of education required, years of overeducation and years of undereducation regression equations were estimated. The estimates show that only the definition of overeducation based on within-occupation variation in years of education leads to a significantly lower measure of overeducation. Using definition B lowers the incidence of overeducation by 12 percentage points. Ignoring all insignificant variables the rate of overeducation is 26.2%. If definition B is used it is 14%.

The meta-analysis further shows that the definition of undereducation is more sensitive to the method of operationalization of the overeducation concept. Ignoring all other variations, the incidence of undereducation is 33.2% if definition A used, about 10% if definition B is used, 12% with definition C and 17% with definition D.

The year of data collection has an effect on the rate of return to years of education required. The point estimates of the coefficients indicate that the rate of return to a year of education required for the job was about 7.9% in the 1970s and 1980s and increased to almost 12% in the 1990s.

Few of the other covariates included in the equations for the rates of return to different education components are significantly different from zero. It appears therefore that there is little systematic variation between the estimated rates of return in the various studies in the meta-analysis. If we ignore all heterogeneity in the returns – i.e. heterogeneity stemming from the covariates included in the meta-analysis – the return to a year of overeducation is about 2.6%, while the rate of return to a year of undereducation is −4.9%. The latter coefficient is significantly different from zero at the 10% level only.

Rubb (2003b) replicates the meta-analysis by including only the studies that use the Duncan and Hoffman (1981) specification of the wage equation in which years of actual education are distinguished from years of education required: years of overeducation and years of undereducation. Furthermore, Rubb (2003b) includes fifty additional wage estimates in the meta-analysis. Rubb (2003b) finds somewhat larger estimates for the rates of return. The unweighted average returns to a year of education required is 9.5%, for a year of overeducation 5.2% and for a year of undereducation −4.8%.

An advantage of meta studies is that they enable us to include information on aggregate data in the analysis that cannot be included in the individual studies. In particular, it can be tested whether the incidence of, and returns to overeducation are determined by changes in the (aggregate) supply and demand for labour. If unemployment is high or the labour force is growing rapidly workers may have to do a job for which they are overeducated more frequently than in periods in which unemployment and the labour force growth rate are low. High unemployment and high labour force growth may further lower the rate of return to (over)education. To test these hypotheses Groot and Maassen van den Brink (2000) add information on the unemployment rate and the labour force growth rate to the equations. The data on unemployment and labour force growth refer to the period and the country in which the data for the original study are collected and are taken from various issues of the OECD *Employment Outlook*.

The results indicate that an increase in the labour force growth rate increases the incidence of overeducation. A one percentage point increase in the labour force growth rate increases the incidence of overeducation by about two percentage points. The results further show that the rate of return to education is negatively affected by the unemployment rate. A one percentage point increase in the unemployment rate decreases the rate of return to a year of education required by about 0.13 percentage points. This is in accordance with earlier studies on the wage curve that suggest that the unemployment elasticity of wages is about −0.1 (see Blanchflower and Oswald, 1994; Groot, Mekkelholt and Oosterbeek, 1992).

7.3 Our contribution: the dynamics of skill mismatches

Groot and Maassen van den Brink (2003) use data from the 1994 and 1996 waves of the Dutch OSA-Labour Market Survey to analyse the dynamics of skill mismatches. The respondents base overeducation on a self-report on skill mismatches. The descriptive statistics show that the incidence of overeducation is fairly stable over time: in both 1994 and 1996 around 10% of the workforce classified themselves as being overeducated.

Three conclusions emerge from the analyses. First, the dynamics in overeducation is high. Over a two-year period, the outflow rate of overeducation is about 40%, while the inflow rate is about 5%. Only 4% of the workers in the sample are classified as long-term or persistently overeducated. It appears that job-to-job mobility provides a way out of overeducation. Young workers are more likely to escape from overeducation than older workers. We also find that job mobility reduces the probability of persistent or long-term overeducation. Internal mobility does not seem to provide an escape from overeducation. However, we do find that the probability of *being* overeducated decreased with tenure at the current firm. So, although changing jobs from the current employer has no statistically significant effect on overeducation, the length of tenure has. A possible explanation for this – seemingly contradictory – finding is that workers perceive the match between their work and their education more positively the longer they are with their current employer and the longer the time since they left school. Alternatively, this may indicate a source of selection bias: good matches are not terminated by external mobility.

Secondly, we find evidence to support the hypothesis that overeducation is a compensation for lack of other productive skills. Contrary to some other studies, we find no gender differences in overeducation. We do, however, find a strong effect of hours of work. Part-time workers are more likely to be overeducated than full-time workers. And as more than two-thirds of all part-time workers are women, the gender difference found in earlier studies may simply be an artefact for hours of work. The negative effect of hours of work on the probability of being overeducated suggests that overeducation compensates for lack of (full-time equivalent) work experience and the lower productivity and higher employment costs of part-time workers.

A third conclusion we draw is that overeducated workers are almost three times as likely to search for work than workers who are not overeducated. Nearly 20% of the workers who are overeducated say they are actively searching for other work. This active search behaviour of overeducated workers does not appear to have a positive effect on their probability of job mobility. We find that overeducation does not have a statistically significant effect on internal or external mobility. So, although overeducation increases the likelihood of searching for other work, it does not improve the chance of actually finding another job. This may suggest that other employers perceive overeducated workers as less capable.

7.4 Conclusion and discussion

Whether overeducation is a cause for concern depends on whether for individual workers overeducation is a persistent phenomenon or rather a temporary state of affairs. Some workers stay in jobs for which they are overeducated for quite some years. However, for many workers overeducation is a temporary rather than a permanent phenomenon. Even if overeducation is part of an adjustment period in the labour market and disappears with years of experience, overeducation may be a permanent feature in western economies and create inefficiencies. Some workers experience an employment spell in which they bring more education to their job than they – at least initially – require for their work. This raises the issue of the optimal timing of educational investments. By the time the skills which are initially underutilized can be made productive, they may have become obsolete. Or these skills have been forgotten. When there are opportunities for lifelong learning, it may be argued that it is more efficient to train workers 'just in time'. Further, there is also the issue of the financing of these educational investments. Skills learned at school are usually (at least partly) publicly financed. If these skills are learned later on at the workplace, employers may pay part of the costs of these investments. If so, overeducation is in part a public subsidy for skill investments that would otherwise have been paid by firms. However, we have also found evidence for the hypothesis that overeducation compensates for lack of other productive skills, like experience. Rather than inefficiency, overeducation may even create a social benefit. If without this surplus education workers find it more difficult to find any employment and are more likely to be unemployed, overeducation may lead to savings in unemployment benefits and active labour market policies aimed at the insertion of workers in the labour market.

Twenty-five years of research on overeducation and its returns have yielded some interesting and relevant conclusions. Some of these have been summarized in this chapter. The question that arises then is: what remains to be done? Hartog (2000) presents some ideas for future work. Interestingly enough, most of these concern efforts to improve the estimation of the earnings function, such as accounting for measurement error and omitted variables in the equation. As noted by Hartog (2000), the most important problem is the lack of a coherent framework.

Within the current theoretical framework – or perhaps rather with a lack of a coherent framework – new empirical applications are unlikely to produce novel insights. All conclusions that can be drawn within the current approach to overeducation are adequately summarized in the four conclusions drawn in Hartog (2000) and the meta-analysis in Groot and Maassen van den Brink (2000). Our bet is that new estimations are unlikely to change these conclusions.

References

Blanchflower, D. and A. Oswald (1994). *The Wage Curve*. Cambridge, MA: MIT Press.

Büchel, F. and A. Mertens (2004). Overeducation, undereducation, and the theory of career mobility. *Applied Economics*, 36: 803–16.

Duncan, J. and S. Hoffman (1981). The incidence and wage effects of overeducation. *Economics of Education Review*, 1: 75–86.

Groeneveld, S. and J. Hartog (2004). Overeducation, wages and promotions within the firm. *Labour Economics*, 11: 701–14.

Groot, W. (1996). The incidence of, and returns to overeducation in the UK. *Applied Economics*, 28: 1345–50.

Groot, W. and H. Maassen van den Brink (1996). Overscholing en verdring-
  ing op de arbeidsmarkt. *Economisch Statistische Berichten*, 4042: 74–7.
  (2000). Overeducation in the labor market: a meta-analysis. *Economics of
  Education Review*, 19: 149–58.
  (2003). The dynamics of skill mismatches in the Dutch labor market, in
  F. Buchel, A. Mertens and A. Grip (eds.), *Overeducation in Europe*.
  Cheltenham: Edward Elgar Publishers, pp. 49–63.
Groot, W., E. Mekkelholt and H. Oosterbeek (1992). Further evidence on
  the wage curve. *Economics Letters*, 38: 355–59.
Hartog, J. (1993). On Human Capital and Individual Capabilities. Keynote
  speech to the European Association of Labour Economists, Maastricht,
  October.
  (1997). Wandering along the hills of ORU land, in J. A. M. Heijke,
  *Education Training and Employment in the Knowledge-Based
  Economy*. London: Macmillan.
  (2000). Over-education and earnings: where are we, where should we go?
  Economics of Education Review, 19: 131–47.
Hartog, J. and H. Oosterbeek (1988). Education, allocation and earnings in
  the Netherlands: overschooling? *Economics of Education Review*, 7 (2):
  185–94.
OECD (various years) *Employment Outlook*. Paris: Organization for Economic
  Cooperation and Development.
Rubb, S. (2003a). Overeducation: a short run or long run phenomenon for
  individuals? *Economics of Education Review*, 22: 389–94.
  (2003b). Overeducation in the labor market: a comment and re-analysis
  of a meta-analysis. *Economics of Education Review*, 22: 621–9.
Sicherman, N. (1991). 'Overeducation' in the labour market. *Journal of
  Labour Economics*, 9: 101–22.

8 | Underinvestment in training?

RANDOLPH SLOOF, JOEP SONNEMANS
AND HESSEL OOSTERBEEK

8.1 Introduction

When a newly hired employee enters a firm there are typically many
skills he has to acquire before becoming fully productive. A blue-collar
worker, for example, needs to get acquainted with the machines and
tools with which he is going to work, while white-collar workers
usually have to become familiar with, for example, the particular software package in place. Many of these skills are highly firm-specific,
i.e. they are of much lower value in other firms. Investing in firm-
specific skills is therefore a risky enterprise for the worker. Although
the employer may promise to reward the worker for skills acquisition,
for instance through a promotion or a wage increase, after the investment has been made she has an incentive to renege on this promise in
order to save on labour costs. Reneging is possible for the firm, because
the worker cannot collect the return to his newly obtained skills elsewhere (and because the labour contract is incomplete: see below).
Of course, workers will anticipate this opportunistic behaviour by the
firm and are unlikely to invest in the first place. Likewise, the firm has
not much of an incentive to make the investment. Once the worker has
obtained the skills, he will bargain for a wage increase or a promotion.
The firm is in a weak bargaining position, because the specific skills
required ensure that the worker cannot immediately be replaced by
another one. Part of the returns on investment are thus captured by the
worker, reducing the firm's initial incentives to invest.

In this chapter we focus on underinvestment in specific training. By
now there is a substantial theoretical literature that analyses underinvestment in firm-specific human capital: see Malcomson (1997,
1999) for overviews. The main focus is on factors that hinder efficient
investment in work-related training and on the assessment of potential
contractual remedies for these inefficiencies. It has been derived that, in
particular circumstances, well-designed contracts and/or other types of

113

arrangements may protect the specific investments made. Examples include the inclusion of payback clauses in the employment contract – for example, when the worker quits his job he has to reimburse part of the firm's training costs – and particular types of promotion policies like up-or-out: after a probation period a worker is either promoted or dismissed.

Underinvestment is predicted to occur when employers and workers behave selfishly. But in reality this is typically not always the case (cf. Bewley, 1999). The actual extent and importance of the under-investment problem is therefore ultimately an empirical issue. The same applies as to whether the proposed solutions do indeed work as theory predicts. By the very nature of the issues involved, however, it is difficult to gather field data to investigate this. First, underinvestment results from the fact that specific investments in human capital are not verifiable by a third party like a court. Enforceable agreements about who invests and how the returns and costs are divided therefore cannot be made at the time the worker signs the contract. But if a court cannot verify the acquisition of skills, why should the empirical researcher be able to do so? Indeed, in standard field data research the measurement of the amount of training is highly problematic; see section 3.3 for a clear and concise discussion of the conceptual and practical problems involved.

A second serious limitation of field data is that, even if it were possible to observe the level of investment in skills, it would be ex-tremely hard to determine the actual productivity of a worker and what he would have produced in alternative employment or without training. Yet this information is crucial for assessing both the extent of the underinvestment problem and the solutions to it. As explained in section 3.4, recovering this type of counterfactual information is *the* fundamental problem in estimating the wage returns to training (and thus in establishing underinvestment empirically).

With these kinds of data problems hampering the test of theoretical predictions, laboratory experiments offer an attractive alternative. In experiments almost everything is under the control of the researcher. In particular, the actual investment decision can be observed and the researcher fixes the economic value of the worker's productivity for every possible alternative. Exploiting these advantages, a number of controlled experiments have been run to verify the empirical relevance of the underinvestment problem and the performance of several contractual solutions to it. Although overall the results obtained are fairly mixed, two general conclusions can be drawn. First, underinvestment is typically much less of a problem than theory predicts it to be. As a result, the efficiency loss due to (less) underinvestment is much smaller than predicted. This finding is in line with the results reported in chapter 3 that the wage returns to training are fairly small.[1] Second, some of the theoretical solutions do indeed alleviate underinvestment, albeit to a lesser extent than predicted. One important reason is that subjects in our experiments behave less opportunistically than standard theory predicts. Other motivational factors like fairness and reciprocity play an important role. Taken together, these results do not indicate that government intervention is called for.

In the next section we discuss the results of one particular set of laboratory experiments in more detail. The set-up and the results of this experiment are representative of other experiments that are conducted within this research area. In the third section we provide a brief review of these other relevant experimental studies. The final section discusses both the limitations and the implications of the experimental results obtained.

8.2 Promotion rules and skill acquisition

A number of organizations make use of so-called *up-or-out* promotion policies. Examples include law firms, partnerships, the military and American universities. Up-or-out requires that, after a probationary period, an employee is either promoted or dismissed. By having such a harsh promotion policy, employees obtain strong incentives to invest in firm-specific skills. This holds because the more skills collected, the more likely it becomes that the employee will make the grade and get promotion. By boosting investment incentives, up-or-out may reduce underinvestment. Unfortunately, this promotion rule is not necessarily a free lunch and may come at potentially high economic costs: it may waste the acquired skills of those not promoted. For example, associates that appear unsuitable for becoming partners may still be very valuable employees for the current law firm; given the firm-specific knowledge they have collected it would result in an inefficient match if they were forced to leave the company and find employment elsewhere.

A well-known textbook on organizational economics formulates the above trade-off as follows (cf. Milgrom and Roberts, 1992: 364):

Promotions serve two roles in an organization. First, they help assign people to the roles where they can best contribute to the organization's performance and success. Second, promotions serve as incentives and rewards. These conceptually distinct roles are sometimes in conflict.

An alternative to up-or-out is to keep those valuable employees that are not promoted within the organization. This results in an *up-or-stay* promotion rule, under which non-promoted workers are offered some lower-level job. In the absence of a strong (and credible) threat of being fired, workers' investment incentives are now muted compared to up-or-out. This especially applies when firms use a no lay-off policy, such as large companies in Japan and US firms like IBM, Hewlett Packard and Lincoln Electric used to have (cf. Milgrom and Roberts, 1992).

The choice between up-or-out and up-or-stay represents the trade-off mentioned above between inefficient matching of workers to jobs and inefficient investments in skills acquisition. To what extent such a trade-off really exists, and whether up-or-out can indeed be used to strengthen investment incentives, is verified experimentally in Oosterbeek et al. (2006). A summary of this research project is given below. For brevity many of the details are left out; the reader interested in an in-depth discussion is referred to the original paper.

The economic environment

To facilitate internal validity and to keep full control, the laboratory experiment itself is very stylized. We first provide an exact description of the situation considered in the lab, before we provide an intuitive interpretation of what kind of real world situations are represented.

In the experiment a worker and an employer interact during two periods. In the first period the worker has the opportunity to make a relationship-specific investment at a cost of 25.[2] This investment increases the probability that he is of high productivity in the second period. Without investment this probability equals $1/4$; with investment it increases to $3/4$. Before the second period starts the employer has to offer the worker one of two possible job levels: an easy job or a difficult job. Alternatively she may decide to fire the worker. After the investment decision, but before the employer makes her job offer, the worker's actual productivity level is revealed to both parties. When the worker is of low productivity he produces 100 in the easy job and 0 if assigned to a difficult job. When the worker turns out to be of high productivity he produces 175 if he is assigned to the easy job and 220 in the difficult job. Independent of the productivity level within the firm, the worker's outside productivity equals 0.[3] When the worker is offered either the easy or the difficult job, he can accept or reject this offer. Rejection implies that the worker leaves the firm and obtains his outside wage of 0.

In this situation efficiency requires that low-productivity workers are assigned to the easy job and high-productivity workers to the difficult job. Moreover, making the investment is efficient, because the expected economic benefits of doing so (60) exceed the economic costs of 25. Here the expected benefits can be calculated as follows. The productivity advantage of a high-productivity worker over a low-productivity one equals $220 - 100 = 120$ points. Investment increases the probability of a high-productivity type by 50% (i.e. from $1/4$ to $3/4$), so on average the benefit of investment equals 50% of 120, i.e. 60.

Investment is efficient, but a priori it is not clear that the worker will indeed invest. Underinvestment may arise because parties can neither contract upon the worker's investment decision nor on his actual productivity. The employer can only attach wage levels to different job levels and can commit to these wages. We assume that the wage in the difficult job equals $w_d = 110$. Hence when the worker is of high productivity and assigned to the difficult job, the overall value of his productivity of 220 is divided equally; the employer gets 110 and the worker gets 110. The wage in the easy job w_e is used as a treatment variable, i.e. it is varied within the experiments, to account for the various types of promotion rules. Table 8.1 summarizes the number of points (gross pay-offs) the two parties obtain in each case, depending on the worker's level of productivity and his job assignment.

Table 8.1 Number of points (gross of investment costs) for employer and worker

Job:	Low-productivity worker		High-productivity worker	
	Employer	Worker	Employer	Worker
Difficult	-110	110	110	110
Easy	$100 - w_e$	w_e	$175 - w_e$	w_e
Out	0	0	0	0

One real world application the above situation represents is a law firm that recruits associates for junior positions. After a probationary period (period 1 in the experiment) the firm decides whether an associate is suitable for becoming a partner (i.e. is of high productivity). If so, the firm prefers to make him a partner (i.e. offer him the difficult job). If not, i.e. the associate is of low productivity, it would be best to keep him in the firm at the associate's position (i.e. in the easy job). Whether an associate is a suitable candidate for becoming a partner depends on personal characteristics, but also in part on the firm-specific skills obtained during the probationary period. In particular, associates that obtained more skills (i.e. made the investment) have higher chances of being a highly productive partner ($3/4 > 1/4$). The firm therefore would like to stimulate associates to invest in firm-specific skills. Unfortunately, however, both the associate's investment and his actual productivity are non-verifiable to a court and therefore cannot be part of the employment contract. The only thing the firm can do is to commit itself to certain wage levels belonging to different jobs, i.e. to a particular salary structure. As will be explained below, this de facto comes down to a particular type of promotion rule.

The experimental set-up may capture other situations as well. There actually need not be a big difference between the two different jobs, i.e. the firm may simply generate different 'job titles' for in essence the same type of tasks.[4] Think, for example, of junior and senior researchers, junior and senior managers, civil servants and so on. There is typically not much of a difference between the tasks of a junior employee and a senior employee. These different job titles are mainly generated to justify salary differences, which in turn can be used as an instrument for incentive purposes. Although the set-up in the experiment is highly simplified, it is thus able to capture the essential characteristics of promotion as an incentive device.

The different promotion rules

We return to the specifics of the experimental set-up. Recall that the wage in the difficult job is set equal to $w_d = 110$. The offered wage in the easy job (w_e) then determines the promotion and firing policies the employer will apply. In the experiment we consider three different values of w_e, namely, 110, 70 and 50. As will be explained in detail below, these three different wage levels correspond to the following three promotion rules:

1. Up-or-out promotion rule: $w_e = 110 \ (= w_d)$.
2. Up-or-stay promotion rule: $w_e = 70$.
3. Stay-or-stay promotion rule: $w_e = 50$.

To understand these promotion rules, assume that both the employer and the worker are only interested in the number of points they get themselves. In period 2 the worker then accepts any job offer, because both the easy and the difficult job yield him more than his outside option of 0. We thus can focus on the employer's job offer. Now consider first the up-or-out rule. With $w_e = 110$ the firm prefers to offer a high-productivity worker the difficult job. This yields the firm more than keeping him in the easy job ($110 > 175 - 110$) or firing him instead ($110 > 0$, cf. table 8.1). However, when a low-productivity worker is kept, the firm either obtains -110 (difficult job) or $100 - 110 = -10$ (easy job). So the firm is better off firing the low-productivity worker. Workers are thus either promoted or dismissed, explaining the term 'up-or-out'.

The predictions for the other two promotion rules follow similarly. Under up-or-stay the firm is best off assigning the high-productivity worker to the difficult job (because $110 > 175 - 70$) and the low-productivity worker to the easy job. The latter follows because the wage of $w_e = 70$ is now low enough for the firm to make a profit even when the worker is of low productivity. In the case of stay-or-stay ($w_e = 50$) the worker is always kept in the easy job, irrespective of his productivity. Here the additional wage costs ($110 - 50 = 60$) of promoting a high-productivity worker are simply too high compared to the productivity increase that results after promotion ($220 - 175 = 45$).

The promotion rules have different implications for the worker's investment incentives. Under stay-or-stay the worker will never invest, because the costly investment then yields him no private benefits at all. He will always be assigned the easy job and obtain $w_e = 50$. More generally, lacking any promotional prospects, workers have very weak incentives to invest in skills. Under up-or-stay the investment has some private benefits, because it increases the probability of getting the high wage of 110 rather than the low wage of 70 by 50%. Specifically, the worker's expected benefit of investment equals 50% of $(110 - 70)$, i.e. 20. Because this falls short of the investment costs of 25, the worker is still predicted not to invest. In this respect up-or-stay is

Table 8.2 Percentages of efficient decisions

		Up-or-out $(w_e = 110)$	Up-or-stay $(w_e = 70)$	Stay-or-stay $(w_e = 50)$
Investment:	Predicted	100%	0%	0%
	Actual	85%	46%[#]	43%[#]
Assignment:				
High → Difficult:	Predicted	100%	100%	0%
	Actual	100%	96%	69%
Low → Easy:	Predicted	0%	100%	100%
	Actual	19%	92%	97%

Remark. Within the rows labelled 'Actual' the observed percentages are significantly different (at the 5% level) between the three promotion rules, except for the comparison indicated by superscript # in the second row.

similar to stay-or-stay. The private benefits from investment are highest under the up-or-out promotion rule. The worker's expected return then equals 50% of $(110 - 0)$, i.e. 55, which induces him to invest.

Efficiency requires that the worker makes the investment and that the low- (high-)productivity worker is assigned to the easy (difficult) job. But theory predicts that none of the three promotion rules attains full efficiency.[5] Up-or-out wastes the skills/production of the low-productivity workers that are dismissed rather than kept in the easy job. Under up-or-stay job assignment is efficient, but the worker is predicted to refrain from efficient investment. Stay-or-stay is suboptimal with respect to both investment and assignment. The predicted percentages of efficient decisions are summarized in table 8.2, in the rows labelled 'Predicted'.

Experimental results

The theoretical predictions were tested in the CREED laboratory at the University of Amsterdam. Subjects could only communicate by means of a computer network and did not know with whom they were connected. Most of the 160 subjects that participated in the experiment were undergraduate students in economics (66%). The experiment started with on-line instructions. These instructions, and the experiment itself, were phrased neutrally; words like employer, worker and investment were avoided. Instead of using these value-laden terms we labelled the employer as the 'participant with role A' and the worker as the 'participant with role B'. The choice whether to invest or not was presented to the subjects as a choice between two different 'disks', with each of them representing visually the corresponding probability distribution of being of low ('blue') or high ('yellow') productivity.

Before the start of the first round all subjects received a message that informed them about their role. Subjects then played the strategic game described earlier 30 times (30 rounds). In particular, for a given promotion rule, workers first decided whether to invest or not. This determined their probability of being of high productivity. The computer then determined the individual worker's actual productivity on the basis of a random draw (using the appropriate probability distribution). Both the worker and the employer were informed about the outcome of this draw. Subsequently employers made their job offers, choosing between the difficult job, the easy job, or firing the worker. In the final stage the worker decided whether to accept the employer's job offer (if any) or not.

In each round subjects were paired with a different opponent. This was done in such a way as to keep the same matchings at a minimum. In particular, by using a rotating matching scheme that best preserved the one-shot nature of the strategic situation, we ruled out reputational considerations. After they had played 30 rounds, subjects filled out a short questionnaire. At the end of the experiment the earned experimental points were exchanged for money at a rate of 1 point = 1 eurocent. Subjects earned on average 22 euros in about one and a half hours.

The main results of the experiment are summarized in the rows labelled 'Actual' in table 8.2. These give, for each promotion rule respectively, the mean propensity to invest, the percentage of high-productivity workers that are efficiently promoted to the difficult job and the percentage of low-productivity workers that are efficiently kept in the easy job. Comparing the actually observed percentages across promotion rules by means of appropriate statistical tests, all differences are significant at the 5% level except for the insignificant difference in investment rates between up-or-stay and stay-or-stay.

We will discuss the outcomes for the three rules in detail below, but two main findings can already be noted from table 8.2. First, the predictions across the three different promotion rules are strongly supported by the data. In particular, (i) the propensity to invest is significantly higher under up-or-out than under up-or-stay and stay-or-stay (which do not differ in this respect), (ii) inefficient dismissals are significantly more likely under up-or-out and (iii) (efficient) promotions are significantly less likely under stay-or-stay. It thus holds true that up-or-out boosts investment incentives, at the cost of wasting the skills of those not promoted.

A second key finding is that in practice the promotion rules perform differently from what standard theory predicts. This especially holds true for the up-or-stay and stay-or-stay rules, which perform better than predicted. For the parameters chosen, this different performance even changes the efficiency ranking of the three promotion rules. The up-or-stay rule appears to perform best on efficiency grounds (evaluated at total surplus, see below), while standard theory predicts that up-or-out would be optimal. This result can be explained by the fact that the promotion rules differ in the extent to which they give scope to efficiency-enhancing reciprocity. Here reciprocity refers to the motivation to reward fair behaviour and to punish unfair behaviour, even though these rewards and punishments are costly to carry out. Below we discuss this in more detail, by first considering the three different promotion rules in isolation.

Up-or-out ($w_e = 110$)

The outcomes under up-or-out are closest to the theoretical predictions. The investment rate of 85% is fairly close to 100%, all high-productivity workers are assigned to the difficult job and low-productivity workers are typically not retained in the easy job. The assignment of low-productivity workers in fact varies with the actual investment made (this cannot be observed from table 8.2). After no investment 97% are laid off, while after investment only 73% of the low-productivity workers are fired. This assignment behaviour can be explained by positive reciprocity. The firm is sometimes willing to forgo some money in order to reward the worker for his unsuccessful investment. But, given that this channel to reciprocate is very cheap to the firm (it costs the employer 10 points to give a reward of 110 points to the worker), the fact that it is not observed in 73% of the cases suggests that this mechanism is not very strong. The impact in terms of overall efficiency is also rather minor; here efficiency is measured as the overall surplus realized, i.e. the worker's total productivity minus the actual investment outlays. There is a small efficiency gain because a small fraction of the low-productivity workers are kept rather than dismissed. Yet there is some extra efficiency loss because workers sometimes do not invest. The realized surplus is on average around 135 under the up-or-out contract, while 140 was predicted.

Up-or-stay ($w_e = 70$)

Here the mean propensity to invest equals 46%, while no investments are predicted. The actual assignment patterns can provide an explanation for the higher propensity to invest. Table 8.2 indicates that a very small fraction (4%) of high-productivity workers are not promoted and also that a small fraction (8%) of low-productivity workers are dismissed. What the table does not reveal is that these percentages actually vary with whether the worker made the investment or not. After investment both percentages are very low at 2%, while after no investment they both equal 9%. This assignment pattern can be interpreted as negative reciprocity, in the following way. There are workers who randomly (i.e. with probability $\frac{1}{4}$) turn out to be of high productivity without making the investment. They are not rewarded for their productivity but rather punished, as they made no effort. In particular, when non-investing workers appear to be of high productivity they are in 9% of the cases offered a less attractive job (easy) than corresponds with their productivity (difficult). The same applies to low-productivity workers who did not invest.

While only a small fraction of the non-investors are actually punished, this fraction is large enough to motivate workers' investment behaviour. Clearly, for this to be the case, workers have to anticipate the actual job offer patterns. Given these actual patterns the expected pay-off from investment equals 74 points, while the expected pay-off from not investing equals about the same. Hence, investment is not irrational at all when the up-or-stay contract applies, because the worker may correctly anticipate the negative reciprocal response of (a small fraction of) employers when he would not invest.

Because actual assignments do not exactly mimic the predicted efficient assignment rule, there are some additional efficiency losses under up-or-stay. The associated losses are, however, small in comparison with the efficiency gain resulting from the unexpectedly high (46%) investment rate. The realized social surplus under up-or-stay on average amounts to 140, where only 130 is predicted under this promotion rule. Up-or-stay thus performs better than up-or-out in terms of efficiency, although theory predicts this to be the other way round for the situation that we consider.

Stay-or-stay ($w_e = 50$)

Deviations from the theoretical predictions are the largest for the stay-or-stay rule. The actual investment rate is 43% whereas theory predicts a zero investment rate. In line with theoretical predictions, low-productivity workers are almost always assigned the easy job. However, 69% of the high-productivity workers are promoted, where it is predicted that such workers would also be kept in the easy job. In fact, assignment again depends on whether the worker made the investment or not. High-productivity workers that made the investment are promoted in 74% of the cases, those high productivity workers that did not invest (but simply turned out to be lucky) are promoted in only 55% of the cases. This points to the presence of a positive reciprocity mechanism. The employer considers investment a friendly action that justifies a reward in the form of promotion. This reciprocal reaction costs the employer 15 points and yields the worker a benefit of 60 points.

The presence of the positive reciprocity mechanism boosts both investment incentives and efficiency.[6] Given the actual assignment patterns, the expected pay-offs of investment equal 58.3 points and the expected pay-offs from not investing equal 58.25 points. These expected pay-offs are almost identical, explaining why on average workers are indifferent between investment and no investment. With respect to efficiency, under stay-or-stay there are actually efficiency gains on two accounts. One is due to the higher than predicted investment rate, the other to the higher than predicted promotion rate of high-productivity workers. On the other side of the balance sheet is a small loss due to the 3% low-productivity workers not assigned to the easy job. Taken together, the realized surplus is on average almost 126 while only 118¾ is predicted.

Promotion rules and the scope for reciprocity

From the above we conclude that the promotion rules differ in the extent to which they give scope to reciprocity. Theory predicts that under up-or-out the worker will invest. If he does so, there is no reason for the employer to give a reward, because investment is in the worker's self-interest. Consequently, there is no incentive to improve upon the predicted up-or-out assignment of workers, and hence there is no mechanism supporting low-productivity workers being kept within the firm.

In contrast, the up-or-stay and stay-or-stay promotion rules allow for reciprocity in a way that is efficiency enhancing. The theoretical prediction is that the worker will not invest. The two rules provide different incentives to reciprocate. Under up-or-stay the worker may decide to invest because he anticipates that the employer will punish non-investment by offering a less attractive job than corresponds with his productivity. This anticipated negative reciprocity mechanism does indeed operate. In case of stay-or-stay positive reciprocity plays a role. The worker may want to invest if he anticipates that the firm will reward that by offering a more attractive job. Also this mechanism appears to be present, thereby increasing investment levels and also improving assignment efficiency.

For employer reciprocity to have an impact on investment incentives, the worker must be able to anticipate this kind of behaviour. In the experiment workers could do so, because they had ample opportunities to experience employers' average behaviour during the 30 rounds that were played. However, because interaction was anonymous and the matching changed over the rounds, workers were not informed about the track records of individual employers. Clearly, in practice individual learning opportunities are different. On the one hand learning opportunities are more limited, because workers typically experience only a few different employers themselves. On the other hand, in reality the track record of individual employers can be identified; potential employees can learn from the experiences of former and current employees of a particular employer. Because the firm is a 'long-run' player with potentially many workers, it then has the opportunity (and the incentive) to build up a reputation for being reciprocal.

8.3 Overview of other experimental studies

The finding that in practice underinvestment appears less of a problem than theory predicts it to be is robust; it has been observed by various scholars and in a variety of experimental settings where underinvestment is predicted to play an important role.[7] These studies confirm that a partial solution to underinvestment is provided by reciprocity (and fairness) considerations. Because investment is typically considered to be fair behaviour, agents reward investors by granting them a higher than predicted return. Given the existence of this informal reciprocity mechanism, there is less scope for efficiency improvement than theory predicts.[8] The need for contractual solutions to underinvestment thus may be substantially less strong in practice.

Despite these findings, it is of interest to verify whether (contractual) solutions to underinvestment work as predicted and do have the (dis)advantages attributed to them by theory. In various related experiments we have considered a range of proposed solutions to underinvestment. Apart from the promotion policies discussed in section 8.2, these include elaborate contractual solutions based on restructuring of the ex post bargaining process, breach remedies, and disclosure rules and privacy rights. In the experiments the focus is typically on the *underlying mechanism* of the proposed solution. The idea is that when the underlying mechanism is not supported by the data, it is very unlikely that the solution based on it will work in practice. Moreover, this approach allows the use of tests based on comparative statics rather than on point predictions. This yields conclusions which are much more robust. We now briefly discuss some of the results obtained.

A large class of contractual solutions to underinvestment relies on the relationship between specific investments and the so-called *outside option principle*. The latter predicts that when two parties bargain over the division of a surplus, the party with an attractive (i.e. binding) outside option will get a share that exactly matches this outside option.[9] The other party then becomes residual claimant, creating efficient investment incentives. In Sloof et al. (2004) we find no support for the predicted comparative statics relationship. When outside options are binding underinvestment occurs, while it is less of a problem than predicted when the outside option is non-binding. The latter can partly be explained by a self-serving bias. Because non-investors have the outside option available, investors feel entitled to a larger return on investment than they can actually get out of the bargaining (and also larger than theoretically predicted). Overall these results suggest that contractual solutions that rely on the outside option principle are unlikely to solve underinvestment.

In practice labour contracts sometimes incorporate a remedy for breach of contract. In case the worker leaves, he has to pay a certain amount to reimburse the employer for the training expenses paid. In that way payback clauses can protect relationship-specific investments. In general there are various ways of calculating the amount of damages that has to be paid. In Sloof et al. (2003, 2006) we evaluate the breach remedies that are most commonly used in practice. These are: *liquidated damages* (the initial contract specifies the exact amount the worker has to pay), *expectation damages* (the worker compensates the employer such that the latter is equally well off as under contract performance) and *reliance damages* (the worker makes the employer equally well off as before the contract had been signed; in practice this implies that the worker pays back the direct costs of training).

Standard theory predicts that the above remedies are typically over-zealous in protecting specific investments, as they are expected to induce substantial overinvestment. Our experiments reveal that the predicted motives to overinvest are indeed present, although negative reciprocity acts as a minor counteractive force. We generally observe slightly less overinvestment than predicted. Breach remedies thus do appear to have the disadvantages ascribed to them in the theoretical literature. Moreover, there is much less need for sophisticated breach remedies than theory suggests. Parties are typically better off either by having no payback clause at all (because reciprocity mitigates underinvestment), or by adopting a contract that simply forbids unilateral separation (so-called specific performance contracts).

Finally, theory suggests that the underinvestment problem may disappear when the investor has private information about, for example, the actual return to investment or about the value of outside options. The underlying idea is that private information creates an informational rent in the ex post bargaining, boosting the ex ante investment incentives (when this rent is increasing in the investment made). In Sloof et al. (2002) we look at a situation in which the investor is privately informed about the actual returns to investment.[10] In line with theoretical predictions private information boosts investment incentives when there is limited scope for fairness and reciprocity. But with sufficient scope for these motivational factors, i.e. when the potential returns to investment are high relative to the costs of investment, unobservability does not affect specific investments. Hence only under a restricted set of circumstances can privacy rights be used as an effective instrument against underinvestment. Sloof (2003) considers the situation where parties are privately informed about their outside options. It is observed that the informal reciprocity mechanism that alleviates underinvestment also carries over to this more realistic case.

The general picture that emerges from all these findings is that some of the theoretically suggested solutions to underinvestment appear to work (e.g. breach remedies), while others do not (e.g. solutions that rely on the outside option principle). Moreover, the disadvantages theoretically attributed to some solutions to underinvestment (e.g. assignment inefficiency in the case of promotions, overinvestment in the case of breach remedies) are typically observed in the laboratory.

8.4 Conclusion and discussion

The typical objection raised against experimental results is that they are obtained in an artificial laboratory setting and that in reality people will behave differently. One criticism that is often made is that the stakes in laboratory experiments are usually rather low compared to those in the real world. Experiments that explicitly address this issue by increasing the stakes to economically highly significant amounts find only a weak effect on behaviour; higher stakes do not affect the main conclusions. In particular, motivational factors like fairness and reciprocity continue to play an important role; see Camerer (2003) for an overview.

Another usual criticism is that the experiments are typically conducted with students. This is problematic when the behaviour of student subjects is not representative of the behaviour of those taking investment decisions in the real world (i.e. actual workers and employers). Fehr and List (2004) explicitly address this issue in an experimental setting considering underinvestment. They do find some differences between students and a subject pool of chief executive officers, but not in a direction one a priori would expect; CEOs invest *more* and behave *more* reciprocally than student subjects. If anything, one would thus conclude that fairness and reciprocity motivations are even more important in practice.

A third potential criticism is that in the experiments reviewed in this chapter subjects were anonymously paired and could not communicate with each other. In reality interactions are typically not anonymous and parties are able to communicate. Ellingsen and Johannesson (2004b) explicitly investigate the impact of communication in a setting with potential underinvestment. In their experiment subjects could make non-binding promises and threats. Theoretically these cheap talk messages should not have an impact, yet it appears that these promises and threats do mitigate the underinvestment problem. It can similarly be expected that under repeated, non-anonymous interaction, as typically applies in practice, people are less likely to behave opportunistically. Economic agents might then build a reputation for trustworthy behaviour.

Notwithstanding the above remarks, it remains important to verify the external validity of the experimental results: do the findings obtained in the laboratory carry over to the real world? In the absence of information about this, conclusions from experiments remain premature. Compared to the existing studies future research thus should focus more on assessing external validity. Such an assessment entails that the insights obtained from experiments are incorporated into, and verified by means of field studies. This is far from easy, given the serious problems with obtaining field data that induced the use of the experimental method in the first place. Sometimes careful econometric techniques can provide a way out though. For example, as explained in the introduction, our first main conclusion that underinvestment is less of a problem than theory predicts is well in line with the small selectivity-corrected estimates of the wage returns to private sector training reported in chapter 3. Taking the results from both field and experimental data together, then, the empirical case for underinvestment in firm-specific human capital is rather weak. Recently some interesting results have also been obtained on the importance of reciprocity in practice, which we will briefly discuss (see also section 3.6).

In Leuven et al. (2005) we use a survey held in 2001 among a representative sample of the Dutch population aged 16–64. Besides background characteristics like formal education, age and gender, this dataset also contains information about participation in work-related training and who (employer or worker) paid for this training. By incorporating an additional survey question, we try to measure the reciprocal attitude of employees. In particular, we ask them: 'If someone does something that is beneficial to you, would you be prepared to return a favour, even when this was not agreed upon in advance?' The answers given enable a classification of employees into three different categories, i.e. employees having either weak, intermediate or strong reciprocal motivations. If reciprocity really matters one would expect, based on the existing experimental findings, that the more reciprocal workers are more likely to obtain firm-sponsored training. And this is exactly what we observe. Workers with a high sensitivity to reciprocity have a 15 percentage points higher firm-sponsored training rate than those with a low sensitivity to reciprocity. This result is robust to differences in background characteristics between workers. Interestingly, participation in training that is fully paid for by the worker her/himself is unrelated to her/his reciprocity type, as one would expect. All in all the key role of reciprocity for underinvestment thus appears to carry over to the real world and employers seem to actively rely on reciprocity as an informal enforcement mechanism.

The results reported in Leuven et al. (2005) are promising, because they indicate that some important insights obtained from experiments are indeed highly relevant in practice. More work should be done though, before we can convincingly translate the findings into valuable policy implications. Yet the results up till now do suggest that there does not seem much need for government intervention, nor for firms to change their HRM policy. Underinvestment is much less of a problem than it is predicted to be. And, besides that, employers seem to actively rely on (informal) mechanisms against it.

Notes

1. Small wage returns indicate that the marginal returns to additional investments are small, and thus provide no evidence for substantial efficiency losses due to underinvestment.
2. In the experiment subjects earn points on the basis of the *actual* choices they make. At the end of the experiment these points are converted into euros. The experimental points reflect the economic costs and benefits of the various decisions. The numbers mentioned in the main text are the ones used in the experiment.
3. The worker's outside productivity is taken as the benchmark and normalized to zero. Productivities within the firm are specified in comparison to productivity elsewhere. The important point to note is that the worker's productivity within the firm is always higher than elsewhere.
4. The difference between 220 (i.e. productivity of a high type of worker in the difficult job) and 175 (productivity of a high type of worker in the easy job) can be interpreted as the extent to which the two jobs really differ. When these numbers become very close, the firm is simply generating job titles. Although in the experiment we keep the various productivity levels

fixed (as in table 8.1), the stylized setting with only two different jobs can thus capture various types of job designs within firms.

5. In fact it can be shown that no wage combination (w_d, w_e) does so in the setting that we consider. Theory thus predicts that the trade-off between inefficient investment and inefficient matching is unavoidable.

6. Positive reciprocity obviously only applies to workers who did make the investment. The 55% promotion rate amongst the high-productivity workers who did not invest can be explained by anticipated negative reciprocity. A high-productivity worker who is not promoted may feel mistreated. He may then punish the employer by not accepting the easy job offered. As reported in Oosterbeek et al. (2006), 46% of the high-productivity workers who are offered the easy job do not accept this offer and quit. Employers that anticipate this reciprocal response are indeed better off by granting the worker promotion. In fact, an additional treatment in which the worker has private information about the investment made reveals that anticipated negative reciprocity is (in this setting) a stronger mechanism than positive reciprocity.

7. See, for example, Berg et al. (1995), Ellingsen and Johannesson (2004a, 2004b), Gantner et al. (2001), Hackett (1993, 1994), Königstein (2000), Oosterbeek et al. (2001, 2003), Sloof et al. (2002, 2006) and Sonnemans et al. (2001).

8. Other recent experimental studies reveal that reciprocity also has an impact on contractual choices (Bohnet et al. 2001; Fehr et al. 2004; Fehr and Schmidt 2000). The main result of these papers is that many contracts are deliberately left incomplete in order to rely on reciprocity as the more powerful enforcement device (see also Fehr et al., 1997).

9. Here the term 'outside option' should not be taken literally; it in fact refers to any option that, if taken, effectively puts an end to the bargaining. In the proposed solutions such 'outside options' are *endogenously* created through the design of the initial contract. One could, for example, think of a one-sided option to extend the contract for some additional period of time; this kind of provision is not uncommon in contracts of soccer players.

10. In the experiment described in section 8.2 this would correspond to a situation in which only the worker knows his own productivity.

References

Berg, J., J. Dickhaut and K. McCabe (1995). Trust, reciprocity, and social history. *Games and Economic Behavior*, 10: 122–42.

Bewley, T. F. (1999). *Why Wages Don't Fall during a Recession*. Cambridge, MA: Harvard University Press.

Bohnet, I., B. S. Frey and S. Huck (2001). More order with less law: on contract enforcement, trust and crowding. *American Political Science Review*, 95: 131–44.

Camerer, C. F. (2003). *Behavioral Game Theory. Experiments in Strategic Interaction*. Princeton, NJ: Princeton University Press.

Ellingsen, T. and M. Johannesson (2004a). Is there a hold-up problem? *Scandinavian Journal of Economics*, 106: 475–94.

   (2004b). Promises, threats and fairness. *Economic Journal*, 114: 397–420.

Fehr, E. and J. A. List (2004). The hidden costs and returns of incentives – trust and trustworthiness among CEOs. *Journal of the European Economic Association*, 2: 743–71.

Fehr, E. and K. Schmidt (2000). Fairness, incentives, and contractual choices. *European Economic Review*, 44: 1057–68.

Fehr, E., S. Gächter and G. Kirchsteiger (1997). Reciprocity as a contract enforcement device: experimental evidence. *Econometrica*, 65: 833–60.

Fehr, E., A. Klein and K. Schmidt (2004). Fairness, contracts and incentives. CEPR Discussion Paper 4464.

Gantner, A., W. Güth and M. Königstein (2001). Equitable choices in bargaining games with advance production. *Journal of Economic Behavior and Organisation*, 46: 209–25.

Hackett, S. (1993). Incomplete contracting. A laboratory experimental analysis. *Economic Inquiry*, 31: 274–97.

   (1994). Is relational exchange possible in the absence of reputations and repeated contract? *Journal of Law, Economics and Organization*, 10: 360–89.

Königstein, M. (2000). *Equity, Efficiency and Evolutionary Stability in Bargaining Games with Joint Production*. Berlin: Springer Verlag.

Leuven, E., H. Oosterbeek, R. Sloof and C. van Klaveren (2005). Worker reciprocity and employer investment in training. *Economica*, 72: 137–49.

Malcomson, J. M. (1997). Contracts, holdup, and labor markets. *Journal of Economic Literature*, 35: 1916–57.

   (1999). Individual employment contracts, in, O. Ashenfelter and D. Card (eds.), *Handbook of Labor Economics*, vol. IIIB. Amsterdam: North-Holland, pp. 2292–2372.

Milgrom, P. and J. Roberts (1992). *Economics, Organization and Management*. Prentice-Hall: Englewood Cliffs, NJ.

Oosterbeek, H., R. Sloof and J. Sonnemans (2001). Who should invest in specific training? forthcoming in *Journal of Population Economics*.

   (2006). Promotion rules and skill acquisition: an experimental study. *Economica*, forthcoming.

Oosterbeek, H., J. Sonnemans and S. van Velzen (2003). The need for marriage contracts: an experimental study. *Journal of Population Economics*, 16: 431–53.

Sloof, R. (2003). Price setting power versus private information: an experimental evaluation of their impact on holdup. SCHOLAR Working Paper Series WP 42/04, Amsterdam.

Sloof, R., H. Oosterbeek and J. Sonnemans (2002). Does making investments unobservable boost investment incentives? Amsterdam. Forthcoming in *Journal of Economics and Management Strategy*.

Sloof, R., E. Leuven, H. Oosterbeek and J. Sonnemans (2003). An experimental comparison of reliance levels under alternative breach remedies. *RAND Journal of Economics*, 34: 205–22.

Sloof, R., J. Sonnemans and H. Oosterbeek (2004). Specific investments, holdup, and the outside option principle: an experimental study. *European Economic Review*, 48: 1399–1410.

Sloof, R., H. Oosterbeek, A. Riedl and J. Sonnemans (2006). Breach remedies, reliance and renegotiation. *International Review of Law and Economics*, forthcoming.

Sonnemans, J., H. Oosterbeek and R. Sloof (2001). On the relation between asset ownership and specific investments. *Economic Journal*, 111: 791–820.

9 | *Human capital and risk*

JOOP HARTOG AND SIMONA
MARIA BAJDECHI

9.1 The risks of human capital investments

Schooling decisions involve far more than just choosing the optimum number of school years. Most schooling systems confront students with an increasing array of choices as they advance in their schooling career. Whereas at the elementary level the curriculum is usually fixed and identical for all pupils, at some point after basic education students have to decide on the type of school they will attend next and on the type of curriculum within those schools. After completing secondary school, they may attend university education, where the number of options between disciplines, and curricula within the disciplines, is even larger.

The uncertainties surrounding these choices can be grouped into three main categories. First, students seldom have a clear perception of the precise content of a schooling programme. They will also be unsure about their ability to complete it. The programme may turn out to be more difficult or less interesting than anticipated and the individual may discover that he lacks the ability or perseverance to fulfil the requirements. Second, after completing education for a particular trade or profession, the graduate may still lack the ability to become a successful practitioner. There may be a wide dispersion of performance or productivity in the job and the individual may not know her true competence when entering the trade. Adam Smith, as far back as 1776, was well aware of this: 'The probability that any particular person shall ever be qualified for the employment to which he is educated is very different in different occupations. Put your son apprentice to a shoemaker, there is little doubt to his learning to make a pair of shoes; but send him to study the law, it is at least twenty to five if ever he makes such proficiency as will enable him to live by the business' (Smith, 1776: 208). On top of uncertainty about a future position within a particular occupation, there is, third, uncertainty about future market value of the entire occupation. There may be cyclical fluctuations, as for *chefs de cuisine*, and there may be structural fluctuations, as witnessed by jobs moving to the world's low-wage regions or the emergence of completely new jobs. No doubt students making their choices have at least some minimal awareness of these risks, and will take these into account when comparing the alternatives.

Kodde (1985: 56) surveyed secondary school graduates and asked for their expected earnings from pursuing a university education, and the maximum and the minimum they anticipated. The gap between average maximum and average minimum earnings was 65% of expected mean earnings, with a standard deviation of 32%. Dominitz and Manski (1996) extracted the variance in an individual's anticipated earnings distribution, and found that Wisconsin high school students on average anticipated dispersion after taking a college education that was larger than the actual dispersion for college graduates. Investing in human capital is risky and students are well aware of it.

Considering the pervasiveness of risk in schooling decisions, it is remarkable that standard human capital analysis has for so long mostly ignored the issues. The existence of risk has implications for schooling choices, for impact of differences in curricula, and for the operation of the markets for educated labour. There are important policy consequences for the design of schooling systems and for financing education, and in particular for financial support for low-income students. Only recently has academic research begun to respond to the challenges. We will summarize the literature, and highlight our own contributions, on four issues: educational choice under risk, information on risk by education (earnings variance), dispersion in rates of return and risk compensation in wages.[1] After outlining the agenda for further research we will consider the policy implications of what we know and what we do not know.

9.2 Educational choice under risk

The literature starts with Levhari and Weiss (1974), with Eaton and Rosen (1980), Kodde (1985) and Jacobs (2002) building on their model (see also chapter 13). Levhari and Weiss introduce a two-period model, with work in period 2 and a choice between time devoted to school or to work in period 1. Risk is defined as uncertain returns to time spent in school, either because the production of skills in school is uncertain, or because the return to these skills is not known with certainty. The return is revealed at the beginning of period 2. Increasing risk (increasing variance in the returns to school time) reduces investment in education if good states of the world generate higher marginal returns to education.

Williams (1979) moves away from the single up-front decision-making and uses stochastic dynamic programming, where individuals respond to new information on the stochastic variables. The production of human capital, the depreciation of human capital and future wages are each stochastic. Higher risk, as larger variance in the production of human capital from given inputs, reduces investment in schooling, unless risk aversion is very strong and the covariance between depreciation and production of human capital is highly negative. Belzil and Hansen (2002) estimate a stochastic dynamic programming model on American longitudinal data for the years 1979–90, assuming all individuals have identical risk aversion (the required compensation for additional risk is a constant percentage of income). They conclude from their estimates that an increase in risk (variance of labour earnings) increases schooling length. This happens because increased risk in the labour market makes schooling more attractive as this comes with receiving more riskless parental income support. Intuitively, this is not very appealing. The elasticity, at 0.07, is quite small though.

Groot and Oosterbeek (1992) extend the basic human capital model with the possibility of unemployment (and unemployment risk sensitive to length of education) and with a wage offer distribution rather than a given post-school wage. Under the assumption that individuals aim for maximum expected lifetime earnings (and hence are risk neutral), their model implies that an increase in the dispersion of earnings by schooling level leads to a decrease in desired schooling length.

Hogan and Walker (2001) construct a stochastic dynamic programming model where being in school has utility value, and the wage that can be realized when leaving school follows a stochastic process. Once the student leaves school, this wage becomes fixed for the entire working life. Increasing risk, as an increase in variance of the post-school wage, implies an increase in the upside risk, the probability of obtaining a high wage, while the increase in downside risk remains ineffective, because at a low wage students stay in school anyway. As a result, individuals react by staying in school longer as risk increases. The model ignores all risk once individuals have left school. As individuals can permanently monitor the wage they may get if they were to quit school, one may be tempted to see this wage as the given reward for stochastic production of skills while in school (production of skills is uncertain but the price per unit of skill is fixed). If one then also assumes that less able individuals face greater risk in their production of skills, the model implies that less able students will stay in school longer, which is certainly at variance with reality.

In Hartog and Diaz Serrano (2002), we develop a very simple model of investing in education under uncertainty about the benefits, and derive an explicit relation for optimum length of schooling and key parameters: the expected return to the investment, the gradient of risk (i.e. the relation between earnings variance and schooling length) and the individual's risk attitude. If risk increases with the length of schooling, optimum schooling length falls; if risk aversion is lower, the negative effect of risk on schooling length is diminished. This is, of course, what one would intuitively have expected. We test the model with Spanish data on participation in university education, where variation in returns (risk) is measured from observations on provinces. We find strong support for the model: in provinces where the difference in earnings risk between university and secondary education is greater, individuals are less inclined to participate in university education. And, indeed, the sensitivity to risk is reduced if the degree of risk aversion in the household is lower.

9.3 Earnings variance by education

Earnings distributions by education can tell us whether schooling moves individuals to distributions with different variances. Earnings variance by education reflects differences between individuals in abilities, quality and effectiveness of schooling as well as the uncertainties of the rewards in the labour market. If individuals cannot disentangle the influence of these factors, and cannot single out distributions for individuals with qualities similar to their own, such overall distributions provide individuals with a crude indication of differences in risk by education.

There are not many studies that deliberately focus on differences in earnings variance by education, but often the information just happens to be available. In Hartog, Van Ophem and Bajdechi (2004a), we surveyed such studies, without attempting to be exhaustive, and found that internationally there is no unequivocal pattern of earnings dispersion by education level or by experience. There are very few robust 'stylized facts', and earnings variance apparently may increase, decrease or have no relation at all with education. (A similar conclusion holds for the relation with experience.) In Hartog, Van Ophem and Bajdechi (2004b), we made a targeted investigation of the data from the Luxembourg Income Studies (LIS), for eight OECD countries and Poland. We tested for systematic patterns by estimating a general quadratic relationship of residual earnings variance (variance remaining after allowing for school years and age with a Mincer earnings equation; see chapter 1) with education and age. Again, we found no evidence of simple relationships that are stable across countries. School systems differ in extent and nature of differentiation, school admission rules and curriculum structures (e.g. broad versus specialized types of education). This leads to different segmentations of the labour force. The results also suggest that the risk structure by education may be quite different between countries.

While students face substantial uncertainty about their individual position in post-school earnings distributions, they are not wholly ignorant on the relevant structure of pay. In Webbink and Hartog (2000), we used a Dutch longitudinal survey of students, who in their first year in higher education (university and higher vocational) reported their expected starting salaries, to compare these with actual starting salaries in 1995. We found that individual expectations quite accurately mimic the differences in starting salaries by field of study and by various individual characteristics (gender, repeating class). But there is no correlation between individual errors in the regression equation for expected earnings and the equation for realized earnings. This implies that individuals can predict the mean wage by field of study, but they cannot predict their own position within that distribution.

9.4 Dispersion in rates of return

Earnings risk may indeed be characterized by the variance of earnings in alternative options. As human capital theory has focused on comparing earnings flows in the alternatives (schooling–no schooling, to go to university or not) as expressed in an internal rate of return, we may also look at the dispersion in the rate of return, just as in financial analyses both the mean and the variance of the rate return are considered. To get some idea of the range within which returns may fluctuate, we considered the variation of rates of return that have been found in empirical studies (Hartog, Van Ophem and Bajdechi, 2004a).

The Mincerian rate of return (see chapter 1) in one country may easily be two to three times the rate in another country. Across countries, the coefficient of variation (standard deviation divided by mean) may be something like 0.5. Within countries, there is generally a fair amount of stability over several decades. Large changes in the Netherlands between the early 1960s and the early 1980s and for black men in the United States over several decades seem exceptional (chapter 1; Heckman et al., 2003). Within countries the differences between the minimum and the maximum rate, over time, seem generally perhaps no more than a third of the minimum rate. On differences in returns between individuals there is even less information. Available studies suggest a coefficient of variation between 0.4 and 0.6.

In Hartog, Van Ophem and Bajdechi (2004a), we develop a simulation model where individuals face random lifetime earnings profiles for two levels of education (we extend a standard experience-earnings profile with annual random shocks), solve for the internal rate of return for each set of draws for lifetime earnings shocks, and repeat this 100,000 times. Thus, we calculate rates of return, as in chapter 1, for earnings profiles that are subject to risk. Parameters are chosen from existing empirical studies. The simulations reveal that the distribution of the internal rate of return is skewed to the right, with an elongated upper tail. We conclude that an ex ante coefficient of variation of about 0.3 is a reasonable guess. This makes investment in a college education as risky as investing in the New York stock market, with a portfolio of some thirty randomly selected stocks (Fisher and Lorie, 1970).

The standard deviation of the rate of return is of course sensitive to the magnitudes of the shocks in the earnings profiles. It turns out that what counts is the sum of the variances of the two earnings profiles and the correlation in the shocks across the schooling levels. If the standard deviations in the earnings dispersions innovations increase from their joint low of 0.25 to their joint high of 0.65, the standard deviation of the rate of return increases fourfold. If shocks in the two income streams correlate positively, a higher than average income in some year in the chosen option (e.g. university education) would tend to be associated with a higher than average income in the option that has not been chosen (secondary education only), thus limiting the impact of the shocks on the rate of return. The converse holds for negative correlation. Indeed, if the correlation decreases from $+1$ to -1, the standard deviation increases more than threefold.

Unintentionally, we have found substantial effects on the expected rate of return from differential growth rates of earnings with experience (cf. chapter 1). Steeper earnings growth for more highly educated people is well documented, and such differences can easily bring an extra 4% return. While obvious, this effect is routinely overlooked. Less obvious, just introducing stochastic components in earnings profiles has a marked effect on the expected rate of return. With our baseline parameters, in the riskless Mincer world the rate of return would be 0.065; in our reference case with uncertainty it has an expected value of 0.071. With increasing differences in shock distributions between the alternatives, the gap with the riskless world can easily increase to several percentage points.

9.5 Risk compensation in wages

Adam Smith not only observed that different types of education (and occupations) provide different probabilities of success, but also considered that the labour market may compensate for these risks. If compensation were to work as a fair lottery, he notes, 'those who draw the prizes ought to gain all that is lost by those who draw the blanks'. That is a nice way of saying that risk-neutral individuals will only enter education if the earnings they can expect are high enough to compensate for the possibility of failure.[2] When risk-averse, individuals want more than just what the losers lose.

Weiss (1972) noted that estimated rates of return to education may contain a compensation for risk, and corrected them by assuming different magnitudes for the parameter of risk aversion. Modest degrees of risk aversion can easily swamp the observed returns. That would imply that higher earnings associated with extended education are not compensation for postponing earnings but for risk (Groot and Oosterbeek (1992) reach the same conclusion in their empirical analysis). However, Hause (1974) has pointed out that Weiss's correction confounds risk aversion and time preference and is in fact mostly sensitive to postponement of obtaining an income, rather than risk aversion.

The effect of risk on wages has been tested empirically in several studies. The problem is to find a proper measure of risk. The basic approach is to consider variation in wages around the mean in the alternatives. Means are predicted from a Mincer regression: individual wages regressed on years of schooling, experience and perhaps some other variables. Risk is then measured as the variance around the mean in the particular group to which the individual belongs: education, occupation, gender. The argument is that individuals can foresee average wages for alternative types of education and occupations (and allow for the effect of experience) by just looking at the average wages for individuals who have selected that alternative and who are already in the labour market. The variance around the mean, within schooling-occupation groups, is a measure of ignorance of the unpredictability of wages and hence of risk. It is included in a second-round wage regression, to see if wages are related to the risk in the individuals' chosen alternative. We call this second-round regression equation the *Risk Augmented Mincer equation*.

Measuring risk in this way is critical and open for debate. Essentially, it assumes that individuals cannot make better predictions of their future wages in a given education than by looking at the wage distribution of graduates, just as the researcher can, with only an allowance for the effect of experience. The residual distribution will also contain the effects of differences between individuals in abilities and motivation. One might think that individuals have information on these variables that allow them to make better predictions on their future position in the wage distribution, and thus have better information on their risk. But the failure to predict starting salaries four years ahead (Webbink and Hartog, 2000; see section 9.3 above) does not support this supposition. The issue is quite important. If risk differs across individuals, and individuals react to this when selecting an education, observed variance gives a distorted picture: it is the variance for those individuals who have chosen the education, not the risk facing an individual considering starting that education. Selectivity would then be a problem (cf. chapters 1 and 3). Even if one believes that potential students are not much better informed than by what the earnings distribution of graduates reveals, the issue requires substantial empirical testing. Not much has been accomplished in this area, however.

McGoldrick and Robst (1996) discuss several studies, with the common finding that risk is indeed compensated in individual wages. Both general observation and economic theory suggest that skewness of an earnings distribution is also relevant. Just as expected wages for some education should increase with the variance because individuals dislike risk, the expected wages may be lowered for positive asymmetry in the distribution: individuals appreciate a long upper tail of the distribution as it gives them chances of large gains, and they are willing to pay for it by accepting lower wages. Indeed, King (1974) and McGoldrick (1995) found mean income in an occupation to be positively related to the standard deviation and negatively to the skewness. King's results also hold when adding mean ability levels in the occupation. McGoldrick and Robst (1996) extend the basic framework with worker mobility. They argue that compensation for risk should be lower if mobility is higher (as individuals have an escape from bad draws) and that the probability of mobility will be higher if risk is higher, and they find support for their argument. Feinberg (1981) uses an index of risk aversion developed in the Michigan PSID data, a combination of data on insurance behaviour, use of seat belts and drinking and smoking behaviour and finds more risk-averse individuals get a higher compensation for risk.

Olsen, White and Shefrin (1979) model the situation for American students considering college training after finishing high school, including details of the student loan programme. They find that accounting for risk actually increases the return to college education, but the effect is very modest.

Low and Ormiston (1991) focus on the structure of the residuals in the earnings function, and thus explicitly model the structure of risk. Just like Weiss they conclude that risk adjustment on the estimated rate of return may be substantial, but of course it is entirely dependent on the assumed degree of risk aversion. However, their model implies that absolute risk aversion will increase with income, a very implausible assumption.

One of our prime contributions has been to provide extensive evidence on compensation for earnings risk, by estimating the Risk Augmented Mincer earnings function on a variety of samples. When we apply the straightforward approach outlined above to data for the Netherlands, Germany, Portugal and Spain, we find that wages indeed increase with risk (variance) and decrease with skewness. The elasticity of risk is mostly in the interval 0.1–0.3: an increase in variance by 10% is associated with an increase in wages of 1 to 3%. The elasticity for skewness is much smaller, smaller than zero as predicted, and usually in absolute magnitude substantially below the upper threshold of −0.15. The values found by McGoldrick for the United States also fit in these ranges.

With data for the second half of the 1990s in the United States we reproduce the basic results of risk compensation (Hartog and Vijverberg, 2002). We can also establish that our results are not due to ignoring compensation for other variables that affect the attractiveness of jobs. If we include variables measuring job amenities and disamenities (job hazards, uncomfortable working conditions, extreme physical demands, etc.), our basic results are unchanged. For men we find that wages on average would be some 8 to 16% lower if workers experienced no earnings risk rather than the average risk. Their average wage would be 11 to 15% higher if their earnings distribution was symmetric rather than exhibiting the average skew across occupations and time. For women, the compensation for risk is statistically not significant (and the coefficient is very small). Eliminating skew from the average value, would increase their average wage by 8 to 10%. From the American data we learn mostly that results are quite sensitive to the measures of risk and skew. Generally, annual values are measured with substantial error; because of small numbers of observations, the outcomes are very sensitive to outliers. We get statistically more reliable results if we measure risk and skewness over a number of years (and use the median value), rather than using annual observations.

In the American dataset we test for risk compensation in wages by calculating risk (and skew) for education-occupation cells. We do so to generate sufficient observations on the measures of risk and skew. This is inappropriate to the extent that occupational attachment is not fixed. In case of bad outcomes, individuals may switch occupation (cf. McGoldrick and Robst, 1996), thus leaving us with an underestimate of the bad risks. With a large Danish dataset we can use measures based on education only (Diaz Serrano, Hartog and Skyt Nielsen, 2004). We use observations on seventy-five types of education (as an aggregate of some 1,750 types of education) with seventeen years of earnings for a 10% sample of the Danish labour force. Using annual data, we find solid evidence of positive compensation for risk and negative compensation for skew in every single year. Because these data are longitudinal, we can distinguish between 'permanent risk', associated with variance between individuals, and 'temporary risk', as the variance in earnings over time for given individuals. The earnings variance between individuals measures risk if individuals at the time of deciding on their education do not know what type they are in terms of earnings capacity with the given education. Compensation for temporary risk is larger than for permanent risk, which is compatible with the thesis that individuals are better informed on these permanent effects than on the transitory effects. If the permanent effect reflects differences between individuals that they are well aware of at the time of decision (as they know their abilities and motivation), this would involve no risk and would require no compensation. This interpretation conflicts, however, with our finding that individuals at the beginning of their studies cannot predict their starting salary with any precision. The Danish data also allow for different measurements of earnings risk. Instead of calculating variance and skew of the distribution of earnings, we can calculate measures for the probability of moving up or down in the educational earnings distribution over time (e.g. the probability of moving up one or more deciles from one year to the next). The tests indicate that when risk is measured differently, we still find the compensation in expected wages. Clearly, empirical support for risk compensation is not dependent on measuring risk as residual variance.

We have also used a large Dutch dataset to measure risk by education, with similar results (Hartog and Webbink, 2004). Distinguishing some fifty different types of education we find solid support for positive compensation for risk and negative compensation for skew. There can be no doubt that this is a very robust relation, across time, place and datasets. In table 9.1 we have collected the estimates that are now available, as far as we can see a complete overview. The results are presented as effects on expected income when risk or skew are completely eliminated, i.e. reduced from their sample means to zero. The outcomes fluctuate within a reasonable range, apart from some outliers. The impact of risk is larger than the impact of skew in twenty out of the twenty-five estimates. The modal value is 11.4% change in income for risk elimination and 3.2% for skew elimination.

9.6 Research agenda

A foremost problem in testing for risk compensation in wages is the distinction between individual heterogeneity and risk. The variance in (residual) earnings will reflect effects of unobserved differences between individual abilities and motivation and labour market risk.

Table 9.1 *Percentage change in income[a] if risk and skew are reduced from sample mean values to zero*

	Risk (R)	Skew (K)
USA, education/occupation[b]		
Men	−10.6	+12.5
Women	0.0	+8.7
USA, occupation[d]		
Men	−23.1	+3.5
Women	−15.0	+1.8
Spain, occupation[c]		
Full sample	−2.0	+1.0
Men	−2.5	+1.6
Women	−3.6	+10.1
Public sector	−8.6	+9.0
Private sector	−1.8	+1.2
Spain, occupation[d]		
Men	−29.0	+1.6
Women	−9.5	+2.0
West Germany, occupation[d]		
Men	−11.4	+2.0
Women	−24.6	+5.3
East Germany, occupation[d]		
Men	−12.0	+1.1
Women	−8.4	+1.5
Portugal, 1992, occupation[d]		
Men	−36.6	+16.6
Women	−76.2	+3.2
Netherlands, occupation[d]		
Men	−17.6	+4.6
Women	−15.3	+6.2
Netherlands, education[e]		
Men	−35.6	+8.9
Women	−2.9	+1.5
Immigrants	−25.0	+6.5
Natives	−22.7	+6.7
Denmark, education,[f] men		
Permanent shocks	−1.0	+0.0
Transitory shocks	−10.7	+0.3

Notes:
[a] more precisely, change in Ln income.
[b] Hartog and Vijverberg (2002), NBER-CPS, table 4.
[c] Diaz Serrano (2000), table 7.3, p. 144.
[d] Hartog, Plug, Diaz Serrano and Vieira (2003), table 2.
[e] Hartog and Webbink (2004), table 1 and means given in the text.
[f] Diaz Serrano, Hartog and Skyt Nielsen (2004), table 5.

To the extent that individuals know their own scores on abilities and motivation, and know their impact on future earnings, this component does not reflect risk, and should be eliminated from the risk measure used for testing compensation.[3] The analysis in Jacobs, Hartog and Vijverberg (2005) shows that if ability and risk are independent, the effect of risk on wages will be underestimated if ability is not controlled for. This is because residual earnings variance is an overestimate of risk if it also includes the effect of ability; with risk overestimated, the coefficient for risk compensation is underestimated. If ability and risk are correlated, the direction of the bias cannot be predicted. In Berkhout, Hartog and Webbink (2006), we find that our key results on risk compensation survive if we control for ability as measured by secondary school exam grades. But we also found, in the Danish data, that permanent risk gets less compensation than transitory risk, which might reflect that individuals are better informed on the former than on the latter, and that it might reflect individual heterogeneity known to the individuals themselves. This is an issue that definitely calls for more work. Cunha et al. (2005) conclude that about 60% of the variation in returns to schooling can be forecasted. The conclusion is based on an ingenious model that tests whether information that becomes available to the researcher during an individual's career (in long panel data) can improve the prediction of schooling choice. We hope to extend our contribution by studying actually held expectations in greater detail, as Dominitz and Manski (1996) did.

The issues of heterogeneity and selectivity will be intertwined with differences in risk attitude between individuals. High-risk types of education may be chosen by individuals with low risk aversion. This would imply that risk compensation is not a constant across all options. Not much is known empirically about risk attitudes (Hartog, Ferrer-i-Carbonell and Jonker, 2002) and here also more work is needed.

We have noted that the variance of earnings reacts differently to levels of education in different countries. There was no evidence of stylized facts that hold in every country. This is a result that calls for an explanation. It suggests that education as a system to sort and segment the labour force works out differently in different countries, which may also impact on risk by level of education. As yet, it is not clear how exactly this comes about. Perhaps the degree of selectivity in access to schools plays a role here.

The demand side of the labour market so far has been completely neglected. It would no doubt be useful to investigate the sources of risk and alternative methods of providing insurance to employees. Various types of institutional arrangements can be considered, such as job tenure, promotion ladders, wage guarantees, etc. In fact, the whole set of instruments available in internal labour markets may interact with risk compensation in wages.

9.7 Conclusions and discussion

Should we worry about risk? The effect of risk and risk attitudes on schooling participation decisions is quite important from the perspective of barriers that may hold back children from lower social backgrounds. Higher aversion to take risks is often stated as a possible explanation for lower schooling participation from these backgrounds. Unfortunately, we do not have much empirical evidence on these issues. Adam Smith thought that risk would be under-recompensed, but judged that supply would still be forthcoming because of the great prestige associated with professional occupations and the inclination of youth to overestimate their probability of success. Our result allows some illustrative exercises.

The simulations indicate a coefficient of variation in returns of about 0.3. If we take a reference return of 6% (see chapter 1), then with a standard deviation of 1.8, 95% of individuals would have a return between 2.4 and 9.6%, and 99.7% would be between 0.6 and 11.4%. In this case, risk would not be a very big issue, as returns are mostly attractive and seldom negative. The latter result matches the empirical finding in Harmon, Hogan and Walker (2003) that only 4.5% of men and 1.7% of women in the UK have negative returns. Maier, Pfeiffer and Pohlmeier (2004), however, report larger shares of negative returns in Germany.

The results in table 9.1 indicate low elasticity of earnings with respect to risk, at a modal value of 0.114. Although this would indeed suggest that risk is under-recompensed, the true test is in the comparison with the individual's reservation price of risk. Evidence on this is very scant. Our analysis of schooling decisions in Spain, exploiting variation in risk across regions, indicates that, with 10% higher risk, 2% compensation in expected earnings is required to keep the probability of university attendance constant. If we boldly (if not blindly) pool all the international evidence, that would suggest that in most cases actual risk compensation falls short of required compensation: only a few estimates in table 9.1 surpass the threshold value of 20%. These are obviously very crude calculations and the need for refined measurement duly reflecting heterogeneity is obvious. Heterogeneity on required risk premiums for earnings risk in the labour market is also hidden in clouds of ignorance. In Hartog, Ferrer-i-Carbonell and Jonker (2002), we estimated the individual coefficient of absolute risk aversion from a survey question on willingness to pay for a specified lottery ticket. For an individual's own income we estimated that an increase in income by 10% would reduce the required compensation for a given risk by 12.9%. If we applied that ratio to the effect of parental income on children's schooling with respect to risk, it would point to substantial effects of socio-economic background on schooling participation, as low-income households would be strongly put off by the risk of the investment in schooling. Differences in background may even have lasting effects. In one sample we estimated that the reservation price for earnings risk would be 4% higher for respondents whose father had a low-level job rather than a high-level job. In another dataset the difference in low or high father's education translated into a 1% higher reservation price, while the same difference for mother's education translated into a 5% difference in reservation price for risk. The potential policy implications for promoting efficient decisions on schooling participation of these results are obvious (see also chapter 13), but we should hasten to add that the numbers we report are no more than first indications of very relevant parameters. With proper information on empirical magnitudes, we would be better able to formulate specific recommendations on financial aid to students and the differentiation by family background. Already the finding that the financial risk of an education finds compensation in mean earnings implies a mitigation of financial risk as a deterrent to participation in extended education. If the more highly educated are under-recompensed, as Adam Smith claimed long ago, financial aid might acknowledge this and provide additional insurance (or equity participation; see chapter 13). If the market compensates sufficiently, students will not be deterred from starting a risky education as the ex ante reward is high enough, even though some will ex post find that they have drawn a blank.

Notes

1. The risk of dropping out of school before obtaining a diploma is also relevant and there is a literature dealing with it (see Montmarquette et al.,

2001; Oosterbeek, 1992). However, as we have made no new contributions, we will not dwell on the issue.

2. Suppose one opted for training as a teacher and earned, riskless, 50,000 euros annually. Or one might enter a business school and face an 80% chance of ending up with 40,000 euros and a 20% chance of ending up with 90,000 euros annually. Expected earnings from the business school are 50,000 euros, equal to being a teacher (no risk premium). From 100 students entering business school, 80 'fail' and lose 80*(50,000 − 40,000) = 800,000 euros and 20 'succeed' and gain 20*(90,000 − 50,000) = 800,000 euros.

3. In Diaz Serrano and Hartog (2006) we have corrected for the fact that risk is a generated regressor (estimated in a regression), but this has no effect at all on the results.

References

Belzil, C. and J. Hansen (2002). Earnings dispersion, risk aversion and education. IZA Discussion Paper 513, Bonn.

Berkhout, P., J. Hartog and D. Webbink (2006). Compensation for earnings risk under worker heterogeneity. Working Paper, University of Amsterdam.

Cunha, F., J. Heckman and S. Navarro (2005). Separating uncertainty from heterogeneity in lifecycle earnings. *Oxford Economic Papers*, 57: 191–261.

Diaz Serrano, L. (2000). Human Capital, Progressive Taxation and Risk Aversion. PhD thesis, Universita Rovira i Virgili, Spain.

Diaz Serrano, L. and J. Hartog (2006). Is there a risk-return trade-off across educations? Evidence from Spain. *Investigaciones Economicas*, 30 (2): 353–80.

Diaz Serrano, L., J. Hartog and H. Skyt Nielsen (2004). Compensating wage differentials for schooling risk in Denmark. Discussion Paper Maynooth/Amsterdam/Aarhus.

Dominitz, J. and C. Manski (1996). Eliciting student expectations of the return to schooling. *Journal of Human Resources*, 31 (1): 1–26.

Eaton, J. and H. S. Rosen (1980). Taxation, human capital and uncertainty. *American Economic Review*, 70 (4): 705–15.

Feinberg, R. M. (1981). Earnings-risk as a compensating differential. *Southern Economic Journal*, 48: 156–63.

Fisher, L. and J. Lorie (1970). Some studies of variability of returns on investments in common stocks. *Journal of Business*, 43 (2): 99–134.

Groot, W. and H. Oosterbeek (1992). Optimal investment in human capital under uncertainty. *Economics of Education Review*, 11 (1): 41–9.

Harmon, C., V. Hogan and I. Walker (2003). Dispersion in the economic return to schooling. *Labour Economics*, 10 (2): 205–14.

Hartog, J. and L. Diaz Serrano (2002). Earnings risk and demand for higher education: a cross-section test for Spain. IZA Discussion Paper 641, Bonn.

Hartog, J. and W. Vijverberg (2002). On compensation for risk aversion and skewness affection in wages. Discussion Paper, Amsterdam/Dallas; revision of IZA DP 426, 2002.

Hartog, J. and D. Webbink (2004). Schooling, earnings and earnings risk in the Netherlands. Discussion Paper, Amsterdam.

Hartog, J., A. Ferrer-i-Carbonell and N. Jonker (2002). Linking measured risk aversion to individual characteristics. *Kyklos*, 55 (1): 3–26.

Hartog, J., E. Plug, L. Diaz Serrano and J. Vieira (2003). Risk compensation in wages, a replication. *Empirical Economics*, 28: 639–47.

Hartog, J., H. van Ophem and S. Bajdechi (2004a). How risky is investment in human capital? CESifo Working Paper 1261, Munich.

(2004b). Investment in education in seven nations – return and risk. Discussion Paper, Amsterdam.

Hause, J. C. (1974). The risk element in occupational and educational choices: comment. *Journal of Political Economy*, 82 (4): 803–7.

Heckman, J., L. Lochner and P. Todd (2003). Fifty years of Mincer earnings regressions. IZA Discussion Paper 775, Bonn.

Hogan, V. and I. Walker (2001). Education choice under uncertainty. Working Paper, University College Dublin/University of Warwick.

Jacobs, B. (2002). Public Finance and Human Capital. PhD thesis, Tinbergen Institute, Amsterdam.

Jacobs, B., J. Hartog and W. Vijverberg (2005). Self-selection bias in estimated wage premiums for earnings risk. Working Paper, University of Amsterdam.

King, A. G. (1974). Occupational choice, risk aversion and wealth. *Industrial and Labor Relations Review*, 27 (4): 586–96.

Kodde, D. (1985). Microeconomic Analysis of Demand for Education. PhD thesis, Erasmus University, Rotterdam.

Levhari, D. and Y. Weiss (1974). The effect of risk on the investment in human capital. *American Economic Review*, 64 (6): 950–63.

Low, S. and M. B. Ormiston (1991). Stochastic earnings functions, risk and the rate of return to schooling. *Southern Economic Journal*, 57 (4): 1124–32.

Maier, M., F. Pfeiffer and W. Pohlmeier (2004). Returns to education and individual heterogeneity. ZEW Discussion Paper 04–34, Mannheim.

McGoldrick, K. (1995). Do women receive compensating wages for earnings risk? *Southern Economic Journal*, 62: 210–22.

McGoldrick, K. and J. Robst (1996). The effect of worker mobility on compensating wages for earnings risk. *Applied Economics*, 28: 221–32.

Montmarquette, C., S. Mahseredjian and R. Houle (2001). The determinants of university dropouts: a bivariate probability model with sample selection. *Economics of Education Review*, 20 (5): 475–84.

Olsen, L., H. White and H. M. Shefrin (1979). Optimal investment in schooling when incomes are risky. *Journal of Political Economy*, 87 (3): 522–39.

Oosterbeek, H. (1992). Essays on Human Capital Theory. PhD dissertation, University of Amsterdam.

Smith, Adam (1776/1976). *The Wealth of Nations*. Harmondsworth: Penguin.

Webbink, D. and J. Hartog (2000). Can students predict their starting salary? Yes! *Economics of Education Review*, 23 (2): 103–13.

Weiss, Y. (1972). The risk element in occupational and educational choices. *Journal of Political Economy*, 80 (6): 1203–13.

Williams, J. (1979). Uncertainty and the accumulation of human capital over the lifecycle. *Journal of Business*, 52: 521–48.

PART III

Policy interventions

10 | Using (quasi-)experiments to evaluate education interventions

HESSEL OOSTERBEEK

> '... Can you name the two forces underlying all life in
> this world?'
> 'Uh – wealth and poverty?'
> 'Not wealth and poverty.'
> 'Good and evil?'
> 'No – *cause* and *effect*. ...'
>
> From *Vernon God Little* by D. B. C. Pierre (2003)

10.1 Introduction

The key question in any evaluation study is how to assess what would have happened in the absence of the policy that is investigated. Simply comparing the average outcomes for participants and non-participants will in general provide an incorrect estimate of the policy's effect. Correcting the estimates for differences in observed characteristics, as is done in a regression framework or with matching methods, may solve the problem partially but not entirely.

Consider the following three examples. First, when we are interested in the effect of class size reduction on pupils' achievement, we might want to compare the average achievement of pupils who attend small classes with the average achievement of pupils who attend large classes. But if we do that in the Dutch context we are basically comparing pupils from disadvantaged backgrounds (who are typically placed in small classes to compensate for their disadvantage) with non-disadvantaged pupils. We therefore need to control for social background. But even if we do so, some parents may want to have their children placed in small classes while others do not care. If parents with a preference for small classes differ from other parents, for instance in how much they care about their children's performance, then we are not only comparing children who are placed in small and large classes, but also children who have parents with different preferences and interests in their children's performance (for more on this, see Krueger, 1999; Angrist and Lavy, 1999; Dobbelsteen, Levin and Oosterbeek, 2002).

A second example relates to the effect of the presence of children on the probability that a couple divorces. Couples with children have lower divorce rates than couples without children. Simply comparing these divorce rates and attributing the difference to the presence of children ignores the fact that couples that have a better relationship may be more inclined to have children. This implies that one needs to take into account differences in the quality of the relationship before the first child is born. This is difficult to measure.

A final example relates to the effect of years of schooling on earnings. People with more education generally earn more than less well educated people. Attributing the difference in average earnings of better- and less well educated people entirely to the difference in education ignores the fact that better-educated people are probably also smarter and more motivated than less well educated people (see chapters 1 and 4.

In all these examples the important issue is how to get rid of systematic (but unobserved) differences between the group that participated in the programme and the group that did not participate. Probably the most convincing way to achieve this is by means of an experiment in which people are randomly assigned to treatment and control groups. Experiments with random assignment are sometimes referred to as the gold standard in evaluation research (e.g. Currie, 2001). But while this form of evaluation is fairly standard in the field of medicine, it is quite uncommon in the social sciences. It is often argued that field experiments in the social sciences are too expensive, require too much time and are unethical. There is surely some truth in each of these arguments but they seem equally as applicable to medical research as to research in the social sciences. Moreover, the fact that some field experiments have been conducted indicates that occasionally less weight is attached to these problems.

For researchers the problems mentioned above almost always work as a constraint. Even if the researchers themselves are convinced that a field experiment with random assignment is the preferable research method to address a particular question, they need to convince others of this. This will often be impossible. It is probably for this reason that researchers have been looking for alternative research designs that are easier to implement but are in the same spirit as real randomized experiments, namely by treating very similar cases very differently. Such second-best research designs are classified under the heading of quasi-experiments (cf. Meyer, 1995; Shadish et al., 2002). Quasi-experimental designs typically exploit some feature that almost randomly sorts people who are almost identical to different treatments.

In recent years economists in different countries have applied (quasi-) experimental methods to evaluate the effects of education policies. The next section discusses briefly two papers that were important for these recent developments. After that we give more detailed summaries of some of the evaluation studies that have been conducted within the SCHOLAR research. These evaluations deal with the following policy measures/interventions:

- providing university students with a financial incentive for higher achievement;
- a policy which offers firms an extra tax deduction for training older workers;
- a scheme that gives extra funding for personnel to primary schools with a high proportion of minority pupils;
- a scheme that gives extra funding for computers to primary schools with a high proportion of disadvantaged pupils;
- changes in the age at which young children are allowed to attend school.

For further information about these studies we refer the reader to the respective research papers. The aim of this chapter is twofold: first to give the reader some insight into the research design of 'state-of-the-art' evaluation studies in the economics of education; and second to present a number of interesting and policy-relevant research outcomes.

10.2 Review of related studies

For a long while the common wisdom among economists about the effectiveness of education interventions was only based on Hanushek's (1986) influential review article. Hanushek summarized the results from many evaluation studies and based on that he concluded that there was no clear relation between inputs and student outcomes. Only recently Hanushek's findings have been challenged by economists conducting their own evaluation studies. Important contributions are Krueger (1999) and Angrist and Lavy (1999).

In the mid 1980s a field experiment was organized in the state of Tennessee in which pupils and their teachers in kindergarten through third grade were randomly assigned to classes of different sizes. A careful analysis of the results is reported in Krueger (1999). The main finding is that pupils who have been assigned to smaller classes perform better than the pupils placed in larger classes, both in terms of short-term outcomes and in terms of longer-term outcomes. Especially pupils from disadvantaged backgrounds seem to benefit from being placed in smaller classes. From the perspective of the current chapter, Krueger's study is important for two reasons. First, it shows that a large-scale field experiment in education is feasible. Second, the finding that class-size reduction has a beneficial effect on pupils' achievement challenges the conclusion from Hanushek's review article.

Although field experiments with random assignment are seen as the gold standard in evaluation research, a legitimate concern is that teachers are aware of their assignment to the treatment or control group and this may have a separate impact on their behaviour (cf. Hoxby, 2000). A study that does not suffer from this concern is Angrist and Lavy (1999). That paper uses a regression discontinuity design resulting from specific features of the funding rules applying to primary schools in Israel. According to the so-called Maimonides' rule, an extra teacher is added to a grade level as soon as the number of pupils at the grade level exceeds a multiple of 40. Therefore average class size is expected to equal 40 when the school has 40 pupils at the grade level, while it is expected to equal 20½ when the school has 41 pupils at the grade level. By comparing the achievement of pupils in schools just above and just below the cut-offs, a credible estimate of the causal effect of class size on achievement is obtained. The identifying assumptions are that parents cannot choose schools based on their position around the cut-off, and that no other special events happen precisely at the grade level size of 40. Like Krueger (1999), Angrist and Lavy find positive effects of smaller classes, and effects are larger at schools with higher proportions of disadvantaged pupils. An interesting element of Angrist and Lavy's study is that they find completely opposite results when they run a simple regression of achievement on class size. This shows that correcting for endogeneity may lead to qualitatively very different results.

10.3 Summary of SCHOLAR evaluation studies

10.3.1 The effect of financial incentives on students' achievement

In the first trimester of academic year 2001/2 a real field experiment was carried out among first-year students in economics at the University of Amsterdam (cf. Leuven et al., 2004c). Two hundred and forty-nine participants were randomly assigned to three equally sized groups. Those assigned to the first group were promised a financial reward of 1,500 guilders[1] upon fulfilling all requirements of the first study year before the second study year started (September 2002). Those assigned to the second group were promised a financial reward of 500 guilders for the same achievement. Those assigned to the third group could not earn a reward.

The motivation for this intervention is that before the implementation of the experiment only 20% of each annual cohort passed the first year within its nominal duration. This low pass rate occurred despite various other interventions aimed at improving achievement, such as tutoring by older students, increased teaching hours and more intensive courses. A widely accepted explanation for the ineffectiveness of these other interventions is that they failed to increase students' effort. An indication that financial incentives to students in the form of performance rewards are effective comes from a pilot study conducted some years ago amongst first-year students in econometrics, also at the University of Amsterdam. Halfway through the first study year these students were promised a reward of 1,000 guilders upon fulfilling all requirements of the first study year before the second study year started. In that particular year 50% of the students passed the first year before the start of the second year. In previous years this pass rate was around 0.25. The high pass rate in the year of the reward certainly suggests the effectiveness of financial incentives. It cannot be ruled out, however, that the high pass rate was due to other changes, such as less demanding exams, different grading behaviour or the inflow of a more able or more motivated cohort. An experiment with random assignment could provide more clear-cut and more convincing evidence. The results of the experiment are also informative about the effectiveness of features of the national financial aid scheme in the Netherlands, which includes elements of financial incentives.

The key finding of the study is that the pass rates are not significantly different across the three groups. In the high-reward group the pass rate was 0.23; in the low-reward group and in the control group it was 0.20. This indicates no (or only very small) effects for the reward scheme. This is confirmed by the finding that the numbers of collected credit points were equal in the three groups. The same holds for reported study effort (average number of study hours per week). The study does, however, report some indication that better students (defined by their grades for maths in secondary school) respond to the rewards. This is, however, not the most interesting group because they are already close to fulfilling requirements.

10.3.2 *The effect of a tax deduction of training costs on training participation of older workers*

The previous subsection reported a real field experiment. This subsection turns to the first example of a quasi-experimental design (see Leuven and Oosterbeek, 2004). In an attempt to stimulate participation in the training of workers, in 1998 the Dutch government decided to allow firms an extra tax deduction from their training costs. (Training costs can already normally be deducted from tax.) On top of the extra tax deduction, an additional ('extra extra') deduction was allowed for costs pertaining to the training of employees who were at least 40 years old. This additional deduction made it 14% cheaper to train an employee of age 40 than to train an employee of age 39. This gave two groups: employees who were 40 years old or slightly older and employees who were just under 40. Assuming that in the absence of the additional age-dependent tax deduction nothing special happened that affected training participation at the age of 40, this policy was like an experiment that assigned employees almost randomly to the two groups. The crucial feature was that employees who were almost identical were treated rather differently. Moreover, it was known on the basis of which criterion employees were assigned to different groups. The study also controlled for the direct effect of age on training participation.

The key result of this study is shown in figure 10.1. This figure shows the relation between training rates and age in 1999 and in 1994. The year 1999 was after the policy was put into place, 1994 was a pre-intervention year. For 1999 we observe that the training rate among

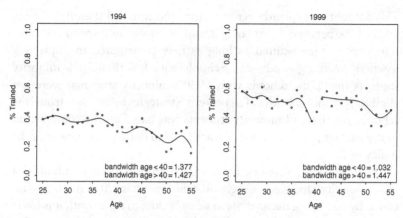

Figure 10.1. Relation between age and training participation

employees just over 40 is substantially greater than the training rate of employees just under 40; the difference is 15 percentage points. Without further information this difference suggests that the policy is very effective. Closer inspection of the training profiles for the two years, however, indicates that this is probably not the case. The 1999 profile reveals a sharp drop in the training rate of employees of 38 and 39 years old. Such a drop is absent in the pre-intervention profile of 1994. This suggests that the additional tax deduction for the training of older workers led to a delay in training workers of just under 40. The study reports a more detailed statistical analysis and concludes that the training rate of the employees between 40 and 45 years old has not increased as a result of the additional tax deduction. Instead of stimulating additional training (the aim of the intervention) the tax deduction led to postponement of training by employees just under 40.

10.3.3 Effects of extra funding for personnel for schools with minority students

This subsection reports on another study that exploits an abrupt change in how different units are treated (see Leuven et al., 2004a). In an attempt to boost the performance of schools with a large share of minority students, the Dutch Ministry of Education decided to give extra funding to primary schools that had a share of at least 70% minority students. All schools with at least 70% minority students received the same extra funding of about 13,000 guilders per teacher.

This amount was spread over two years and equalled slightly less than 10% of the personnel costs of a 'school. Schools could spend the extra resources as they wanted as long as they contributed to improving teachers' working conditions. Schools with less than 70% minority students (including schools with 69.9% minority students) were not eligible for the subsidy. To prevent strategic behaviour from the schools, the share of minority students was based on the composition of the student population some years prior to the announcement of the policy in 2000.

This policy design created two different groups: schools with at least 70% minority students and schools with less than 70% minority students. By restricting the analysis to schools close to the cut-off, it is likely that there were no systematic differences between the two groups. The study restricts the analysis to schools with at least 60% and at most 80% minority students. This choice of bandwidth balances having more comparable schools and having more observations. Again assuming that there was no systematic difference just at the cut-off point, this subsidy scheme was like an experiment that assigned schools almost randomly to the two groups. The empirical analysis also controlled for the direct effect of the share of minority students on achievement. Again, this is an example of a policy that treats almost identical cases very differently.

As outcome measure the study took the scores of students in eighth grade for language, arithmetic and information processing at the so-called CITO final test. In the Netherlands 80% of primary schools participate in this test, and it is considered to be quite important. Results are used to allot students to different levels of secondary schools, and higher-level secondary schools require specific minimum levels of performance. Moreover, the students' average score on this test is used in the assessment of the school's performance. This all implies that doing well on the CITO final test is important for both students and schools. Outcome measures are available for 1999, 2000, 2002 and 2003. The first two are pre-intervention measures; the last two are post-intervention measures. As a result the study focuses on changes in achievement rather than levels of achievement.

Between the first and last payments of the subsidy a research bureau interviewed schools' headteachers about the subsidy. The results of these interviews show that around 90% of the extra funding schools received is spent in accordance with the ministry's intentions. Hiring and recruitment of extra personnel, extra payments to personnel and extra facilities appear to be the main components. Of the extra funding 10% was not spent immediately but was added to schools' reserves. The study's choice of achievement as a relevant outcome measure reflects the view that ultimately extra personnel, extra payments and extra facilities should translate into higher test scores for students. This seems a reasonable view given that the extra resources were directed to schools with large shares of disadvantaged students; these students are regarded as disadvantaged because they perform worse (especially on the CITO final test).

The estimation results reported in the study are not significantly different from zero. The reported estimates are quite precise so that even modest positive effects can be excluded. For instance, for language the study can rule out effects in excess of 3% of a standard deviation with a 95% probability. For the interpretation of this result it is important to realize that the main funding scheme for primary schools in the Netherlands already channels a substantial amount of compensatory resources to schools with large shares of disadvantaged students. In this main funding scheme minority students enter with a weight of 1.9 relative to a unit weight for a non-disadvantaged student. This implies that schools with at least 70% minority students already receive over 50% more resources than a school with no disadvantaged students. The results from the evaluation study suggest that an adequate level of resource has already been reached (or surpassed). The results also indicate that a substantial amount was spent without a noticeable effect on students' achievements.

10.3.4 *Effect of extra funding for ICT for schools with disadvantaged students*

An intervention similar to the one in the previous subsection is a subsidy scheme that provided a fixed amount of 209 guilders per student to all schools with a share of at least 70% disadvantaged students (cf. Leuven et al., 2004a). Disadvantaged students cover minority students and students with less well educated parents as the two main categories. Schools with less than 70% disadvantaged students (including schools with 69.9% disadvantaged students) were not eligible for the subsidy. To prevent strategic behaviour from the schools, the share of minority students was based on the composition of the student population some years prior to the announcement of the policy in 2000.

This policy design created two different groups: schools with 70% or more disadvantaged students and schools with less than 70% disadvantaged students. The study again restricted the analysis to schools with at least 60% and at most 80% of the targeted type of students. Again assuming that there was no systematic difference just at the cut-off point, this subsidy scheme was like an experiment that assigned schools almost randomly to the two groups. The empirical analysis also controlled for the direct effect of the share of disadvantaged students on achievement. As before, very similar cases were treated very dissimilarly.

Outcome measures were again the scores of students in eighth grade for language, arithmetic and information processing at the CITO final test. Test results are available for 1999, 2000, 2002 and 2003. The first two are pre-intervention measures; the last two are post-intervention measures. As a result the study focuses on changes in achievement rather than levels of achievement.

All estimation results reported in the study are negative and in some cases even significantly different from zero. This holds especially for language and arithmetic. The extra funding for ICT seems to have adverse effects on students' achievement. The study also reports results from a questionnaire sent to schools in the 65 to 75% interval. The questionnaire included items concerning the computer/student ratio, the 'age' of the computers and the intensity of computer use in general and for language and arithmetic in particular. The results reveal no significant differences in computer/student ratio and age of computers. In both the treatment and control schools this ratio is on average 1:5, which is high when compared to the standard of 1:10 in primary schools. There is, however, a significant difference in the amount of school-time students use a computer. Students in the treated schools spend on average 50 minutes per week more using a computer than students in the control group. Part of this extra time is used for computer-based language and arithmetic instruction. Hence, extra resources for computers and software increase school-time using a computer but reduce test scores.

The finding that computer usage did not improve test scores in this Dutch study are consistent with findings from two other recent studies. Angrist and Lavy (2002) evaluate the effects of a programme in which the Israeli State Lottery funded new computers in elementary and middle schools in Israel. They used several estimation strategies and found 'a consistently and marginally significant relationship between the program-induced use of computers and the 4th grade Math scores'. For eighth graders and for scores on Hebrew, the estimated effects were mostly negative although not significantly different from zero. Rouse et al. (2004) study the effects of the instructional computer program Fast ForWord (FFW). They find no evidence that the use of FFW results in gains in language acquisition or actual reading skills. Interestingly, the time spent using FFW was in addition to the amount of time spent in regular reading instruction. Although Rouse et al. (2004) do not find negative effects, the broader use of computers in instruction is likely to substitute regular instruction. If computer-based learning is less effective than more traditional forms of classroom teaching, negative effects cannot be ruled out.

10.3.5 *Effect of extra time in school on early test scores*

The final study summarized here exploits two specific features of the Dutch regulations with regard to primary school enrolment (cf. Leuven et al., 2004b). The first feature is that a child is allowed to enrol in school immediately after his/her fourth birthday. This is different from the situation in most other countries where typically all children born before a certain date start on the same day. The second feature is that a school year cohort consists of the children born between 1 October of one year and 30 September of the next year. As a result, children turning age 4 before, in and after the summer holiday are placed in the same class.

Together these two features generate – conditional on age – variation in the maximum number of schooldays a child can get at any given date during its school career. Consider, for example, a child having its birthday at the beginning of a six-week summer holiday period. When this child turns 4 years and 10 weeks, it will have four potential weeks in school. On the other hand, when a child having its fourth birthday at the end of the summer holiday reaches this age of 4 years and 10 weeks, it will have a maximum number of schooldays equal to 10 weeks.

The evaluation study reports significantly positive effects of extra time in school on language and arithmetic scores in grade 2 for disadvantaged pupils. Both minority students and students with poorly educated parents benefit from the opportunity to spend more time in school. The effect is quite substantial; one more month of potential school enrolment increases early test scores by 6% of a standard deviation. To illustrate, the difference in average test scores of a school without any disadvantaged students and a school with only minority students amounts to one standard deviation. Non-disadvantaged pupils do not benefit from the opportunity of extra time in school at a young age.

The study also reports results showing an almost one-to-one relation between potential time in school and actual time in school. Students that are given an extra month of potential time in school on average realize an extra month in school. The reported effect of extra potential time in school can therefore also be interpreted as the effect of extra actual time in school. This implies that we may also expect beneficial effects from lowering the compulsory school attendance age for children with disadvantaged backgrounds. This last result is interesting in light of recent policy discussions in the Netherlands. At some stage the deputy Minister of Education proposed lowering the compulsory school attendance age from 5 years to 4 years. But when the cabinet to which this deputy minister belonged was replaced by a new cabinet after the elections, one of the first actions of the new Minister of Education was to withdraw this proposal.

10.4 Conclusion and discussion

The previous section summarized the results from evaluation studies of five different education interventions. One evaluation used an experimental design with random assignment; the others were based on some quasi-experimental designs. These designs produced results which had a high degree of internal validity. That is, one could validly conclude from these studies that the differences in outcomes were caused by the differences in treatment (cf. Meyer, 1995: 152). The possibility that the findings are corrupted by one of the usual threats to internal validity like omitted variables, trends in outcomes, simultaneity, selection or attrition seems negligible.

An important limitation of the results is, however, the extent to which they generalize to other contexts. For instance, the fact that there is no effect of financial rewards up to 1,500 guilders among first-year students in economics in Amsterdam does not prove that financial rewards of, say, 15,000 guilders would not have any effect, or that students from other fields or in other cities would be equally unresponsive. Likewise, the fact that Dutch primary schools with around 70% of disadvantaged students fail to transform extra resources for computers into higher test scores does not prove that extra resources for computers would have no effect at schools without disadvantaged students. The Dutch findings about the negative effects of extra resources for computers are given, however, more weight when complemented with the other recent findings from other countries and in other contexts. At the same time the Dutch findings give more weight to these other studies as well.

When we limit attention to the Dutch context, the evaluations of the five interventions paint a clear picture. Extra resources, for personnel or for computers, for schools with a high share of disadvantaged students have no impact on students' achievements. Financial rewards for higher education students are unlikely to reduce their study delay. Likewise, firms seem not to increase training participation in response to a cost reduction. The only intervention that has a clear beneficial effect is allowing (or requiring) young children from disadvantaged families to attend school at a younger age. This policy recommendation concurs with Heckman's (1999) advice to start investing in human capital at a young age.

The summary of findings has also an important methodological edge. Three of the five interventions could be evaluated with a convincing approach due to specific features of the implemented policy. The additional age-dependent tax deduction makes an abrupt distinction between employees aged 40 or older and employees under 40. The personnel subsidy for primary schools treats schools with at least 70% minority students very differently from schools with less than 70% minority students. Finally, the computer subsidy for primary schools treats schools with at least 70% disadvantaged students very differently from schools with less than 70% disadvantaged students. In all three cases the specific design of the policy offers a neat research design, but in all three cases this was not intentional. The policy-makers were not aware of the nice evaluation opportunities they created. This gives rise to two recommendations. First, it seems not unlikely that more policies with discontinuous treatments have been implemented without the intention of using them for evaluation. Researchers should utilize these features whenever possible. Second, the three examples show that it is possible to implement policies that treat very similar cases rather differently. Policy-makers should take advantage of this by including such features in the designs of new programmes. These features can then be exploited to evaluate the policy.

Note

1. Guilders were changed into euros at the rate of 1 guilder to 0.45 euro.

References

Angrist, J. D. and V. Lavy (1999). Using Maimonides' rule to estimate the effect of class size on scholastic achievement. *Quarterly Journal of Economics*, 114: 533–75.

(2002). New evidence on classroom computers and pupil learning. *Economic Journal*, 112: 735–65.

Currie, J. (2001). Early childhood interventions. *Journal of Economic Perspectives*, 15: 213–38.

Dobbelsteen, S., J. Levin and H. Oosterbeek (2002). The causal effect of class size on scholastic achievement: distinguishing the pure class size effect from the effect of changes in class composition. *Oxford Bulletin of Economics and Statistics*, 64: 17–38.

Hanushek, E. (1986). The economics of schooling: production and efficiency in public schools. *Journal of Economic Literature*, 49: 1141–77.

Heckman, J. J. (1999). Policies to foster human capital. NBER Working Paper 7288, Boston.

Hoxby, C. M. (2000). The effects of class size on student achievement: new evidence from population variation. *Quarterly Journal of Economics*, 115: 1239–85.

Krueger, A. B. (1999). Experimental estimates of education production functions. *Quarterly Journal of Economics*, 115: 1239–85.

Leuven, E. and H. Oosterbeek (2004). Evaluating the effects of a tax deduction on training. *Journal of Labor Economics*, 22: 461–88.

Leuven, E., M. Lindahl, H. Oosterbeek and D. Webbink (2004a). The effect of extra funding for disadvantaged pupils on achievement. *Review of Economics and Statistics*, forthcoming.

(2004b). The effect of potential time in school on early test scores. Working Paper.

Leuven, E., H. Oosterbeek and B. van der Klaauw (2004c). The effect of financial rewards on students' achievement: evidence from a randomized experiment. Working Paper.

Meyer, B. D. (1995). Natural and quasi-experiments in economics. *Journal of Business and Economics Statistics*, 13: 151–61.

Pierre, D. B. C. (2003). *Vernon God Little*. London: Faber and Faber.

Rouse, C. E., A. B. Krueger and L. Markman (2004). Putting computerized instruction to the test: a randomized evaluation of a 'scientifically-based' reading program. *Economics of Education Review*, 23: 323–38.

Shadish, W. R., T. D. Cook and D. T. Campbell (2002). *Experimental and Quasi-Experimental Designs for Generalized Causal Inference*. Boston: Houghton Mifflin.

11 | *Unemployment duration: policies to prevent human capital depreciation*

BAS VAN DER KLAAUW

11.1 Introduction

European labour markets traditionally display a low inflow into unemployment and a high average duration of unemployment. Therefore, these labour markets suffer from a relatively large share of long-term unemployed workers, which is one of the main problems of European economies. Being unemployed causes loss of human capital and demotivates and stigmatizes workers, which reduces re-employment probabilities (see Frijters and Van der Klaauw, 2006; Machin and Manning, 1999). Therefore, unemployment has been an important issue for policy in the past decades.

The recession at the beginning of the 1990s induced the introduction of a large range of policy measures to help unemployed workers in finding work and to increase their human capital. In the past few years the OECD has strongly advocated active labour market programmes and the European Union adopted this as a cornerstone of macroeconomic policy in 1997. According to the OECD (2003) the total spending on active labour market policies in the European Union increased from 0.8% of GDP in 1995 to over 1% in 2001. In the Netherlands, the costs of active labour market policies are currently around 5 billion euros. Examples of these policies are training and schooling programmes, subsidized employment for youth and long-term unemployed workers, counselling and monitoring, and punitive benefit reductions. Machin and Manning (1999) argue that knowledge about the underlying unemployment dynamics is crucial in targeting active labour market programmes. In particular, programmes should be aimed at periods in which duration dependence is most pronounced. Frijters and Van der Klaauw (2006) show that unemployed workers already start losing human capital early in the spell of unemployment. Keese and Martin (2002) therefore advocate early and sustained interventions, in particular for young unemployed workers, to avoid human capital depreciation.

Programmes aimed at directly improving the human capital of unemployed workers are not very often found to be effective (see Heckman, LaLonde and Smith, 1999). Training and schooling programmes might increase the skills of individuals who have been out of the labour force for some time, but are generally not found to improve the labour market prospects of (long-term) unemployed workers. It is therefore ill advised to concentrate resources on programmes to accumulate human capital for the unemployed: it would be much more effective to spend resources on preventing loss of human capital, by stimulating a quick return to work. Rather than investing in schooling and training of the unemployed, one might expect more from job search assistance programmes and financial incentives such as bonuses and punitive benefit reductions.

The aim of this chapter is twofold. First, we provide insight into the mechanisms underlying unemployment dynamics. In particular, we consider the inflow to unemployment, the outflow from unemployment and the composition of unemployed workers. We pay particular attention to the business cycle as the inflow, outflow and composition of unemployed workers are all sensitive to business cycle fluctuations. The second aim of the chapter is to discuss the evaluation of active labour market programmes. Many active labour market policies have not been evaluated properly.

Economic theory can be very useful in complementing the understanding obtained from empirical evaluation studies (see Abbring, Van den Berg and Van Ours, 2005; Van den Berg and Van der Klaauw, 2006). In an economic or so-called structural model individual behaviour is made explicit. Participation in a programme is modelled along with the outcomes, and therefore participation depends on behavioural rules. This implies that by incorporating the policy into a structural model, the impact of the treatment can be studied on multiple outcome variables simultaneously and can be extrapolated to somewhat different economic environments and institutional settings. A structural model allows us to compare the impact of treatment to the effects of related treatments, differing, for example, with respect to the target population or institutional settings. Using a structural model, it is possible to formulate conditions for a policy to be successful and to predict policy impacts. In such a setting the results from the empirical evaluation studies are mainly used to guide the direction of the economic theory and to test the validity of the structure imposed by economic theory (see Todd and Wolpin, 2003). The empirical evaluation estimators improve the knowledge about economic mechanisms, while the economic theory improves the understanding of the results obtained by the empirical evaluation studies.

The evaluation of policy interventions often suffers from self-selection into the programme (see Heckman, LaLonde and Smith, 1999). That is, individuals only choose to participate in a programme if they expect to benefit from it. Comparison of individuals participating in a programme with individuals not participating is more likely to reflect the differences between these groups than the causal effect of the programme itself. Only in the case of a social experiment, can such a comparison of participants and non-participants provide a proper estimate for the causal effect of the treatment (see Gorter and Kalb, 1996; Van den Berg and Van der Klaauw, 2006). Except for this traditional self-selection, in the context of unemployment policies there is a second type of self-selection. Unemployment policies often do not start immediately an individual becomes unemployed, but sometime during the spell of unemployment. For example, to participate in the British Restart programme individuals should be unemployed for at least 6 months (Dolton and O'Neill, 1996). This means that only the selective group of unemployed workers who have not found work prior to the start of the programme actually participate in it. When focusing on policy interventions targeted at increasing individual re-employment rates, the dynamic nature of policy interventions can be exploited to correct for selective participation. Under some restrictions, such as no anticipation of the exact moment of the intervention, correcting for unobserved characteristics in a non-experimental setting is possible. This has the advantage that an existing or recently introduced programme can be evaluated without denying a randomly selected group of workers access to the programme; only some randomization should be introduced at the moment when individuals enrol in a programme (and they should not be aware of the exact moment).

In many situations empirical evaluation estimators can provide an estimate of the effect of a policy intervention. However, both social experiment and non-experimental estimators only provide an estimate of the impact of the treatment as compared to not providing the treatment within a given economic environment. The results can therefore not be used straightforwardly to give an indication of the impact of related treatments or to abstract from the economic situation and the institutional settings at the moment of collecting the data. For instance, an active labour market policy that is very successful in a recession is not necessarily effective during economic expansion. The effect of providing similar training programmes at different locations can be dealt with, however. Hotz, Imbens and Mortimer (2005) show that after correcting for individual characteristics (including pre-treatment outcomes), the impacts of the training programmes are similar across the different locations. This implies that policy-makers can learn a lot from looking at training programmes elsewhere, as long as they keep in mind the exact content of the programme and the target population.

Using results from empirical evaluation studies to modify treatments or to change the target population is more troublesome. Furthermore, empirical treatment evaluation estimators often investigate the causal effect of the treatment on each outcome variable independently of the other outcome variables. In most economic situations there are multiple outcomes that are of interest and these are often interrelated. Participating in a training or schooling programme affects the duration of the worker's unemployment, post-unemployment wage and subsequent employment duration.

In this chapter we try to learn more about the dynamics of unemployment and the evaluation of policy interventions aimed at preventing human capital loss by stimulating re-employment. We integrate empirical evaluation estimators and economic theory. In particular, we use simple job search models to improve our understanding of unemployment dynamics and to guide interpretation on the results from empirical evaluation studies. In section 11.2 we provide a brief outline of job search theory. Section 11.3 discusses the relation between business cycle variation and unemployment dynamics. In section 11.4 we discuss the evaluation of policy interventions aimed at restricting human capital loss by reducing the duration of unemployment, and in section 11.5 we provide some results from empirical policy evaluation. Finally, section 11.6 provides some policy recommendations.

11.2 Job search framework

In this section we discuss a simple theoretical model for the behaviour of unemployed workers. This model guides interpretation for the empirical results discussed in the sections below. A relatively easy economic framework for modelling re-employment of unemployed workers is the job search model (see Mortensen, 1986). Search for work is a time-consuming and expensive activity. An unemployed worker devotes effort to job search, which might reflect the hours spent or the number of application letters written. Due to the existence of labour market frictions it takes time before a worker searching for a job matches a vacancy. The intensity at which job offers come to the unemployed worker increases with the amount of search effort. The relationship between search effort and the arrival of job offers represents search efficiency in the labour market, i.e. when efficiency is high a job application is likely to result in a job offer.

For simplicity we assume that the only relevant characteristic of a job is the wage. A job offer is thus a wage offer, which is a draw from the wage offer distribution. An unemployed worker follows a simple decision strategy by selecting suitable jobs. Only if the wage associated with a job offer exceeds the reservation wage does the unemployed worker accept the job. The probability that the unemployed worker accepts a job offer equals the probability that the associated wage exceeds the reservation wage.

The job-finding of an unemployed worker thus depends on the probability of receiving a job offer and the probability that this job offer is acceptable to the unemployed worker. The transition rate from unemployment to employment (or the re-employment rate) depends on the behaviour of the individual, i.e. the search effort (generating wage offers) and the reservation wage. Increasing the search effort increases the probability of receiving a job offer. If the unemployed worker increases the reservation wage, he becomes more selective about job offers, which reduces the re-employment rate but increases the expected wage in the first accepted job.

The exact solution to the decision process of the unemployed worker depends on all elements of the model, which we do not discuss in detail. The optimal search effort and the reservation wage depend, for example, on the level of unemployment benefits, the specification of the cost function of search effort and the possibility for on-the-job search. Furthermore, the information available to the unemployed worker at any moment during the unemployment spell is important. If, for example, an unemployed worker knows that within a short time his unemployed benefits will be cut, he will increase his search effort and will be less selective about wage offers.

11.3 Unemployment dynamics over the business cycle

So far we have been vague about what the relevant measure of time is. Most obvious is to think of time as the unemployment duration (with the origin at the moment of becoming unemployed). However, transition rates from unemployment to employment display strong fluctuations over the business cycle; see Abbring, Van den Berg and Van Ours (2002). The average duration of unemployment is usually found to be countercyclical. One can think of two competing hypotheses why aggregated exit rates from unemployment are lower during recessions. This may be either because in a recession the probability of exit from unemployment decreases for all workers, or because in a recession the composition of the (heterogeneous) inflow into unemployment shifts towards individuals who have low exit probabilities anyway, i.e. the low-skilled or poorly educated workers. In the first case the business cycle has a true effect on the structural elements of the job search model (the job offer arrival rate and the wage offer distribution). In the second case the structural parameters of the job search model do not vary over calendar time. For public policy it is important to distinguish between these hypotheses. If during recessions the composition of the inflow into unemployment shifts towards the more disadvantaged, such as poorly educated workers, policy should be aimed at stimulating the re-employment of these workers. However, if all unemployed workers are hampered by recession, public policy should not be targeted at specific groups of workers.

Van den Berg and Van der Klaauw (2001) study the effect of the business cycle on unemployment dynamics in a reduced-form setting. Typically, survey (micro) data do not cover a sufficiently long time period to investigate how the exit probabilities and the inflow composition vary over the business cycle. Macro data have the disadvantage of not being very informative on individual characteristics. Therefore, macro data do not allow the identification of the determinants of the individual duration distribution and the composition of the inflow.

Van den Berg and Van der Klaauw (2001) combine micro data and macro data for France. Their empirical results suggest that the counter-cyclicality of the aggregated mean unemployment duration originates from the fact that the individual exit probabilities vary over the cycle for all types of individuals. The effect of changes in the composition of the inflow on the cyclical behaviour of the mean duration is small. This implies that the persistence in unemployment after a negative shock is not primarily due to an increased inflow of disadvantaged workers with low individual-specific exit probabilities. On the contrary, even workers with relatively good qualifications are hampered by a recession if they search for a job. This suggests that policies aimed at bringing the unemployed back to work during a recession should not focus exclusively on the most disadvantaged workers, even though the fraction of low-skilled workers among the inflow into unemployment increases slightly.

The empirical analyses in Abbring, Van den Berg and van Ours (2002) and Van den Berg and Van der Klaauw (2001) are reduced-form analyses. Reduced-form analyses of unemployment durations typically focus directly on the transition rate into employment. A reduced-form analysis tells how transition rates into employment vary over the business cycle, but it cannot tell anything about the underlying mechanism. According to the job search theory discussed in the previous section, variation in transition rates must be caused by variation in either the job offer arrival rate or the wage offer distribution. It is important to distinguish between the causes of fluctuations in re-employment rates as the policy implications differ. A reduction in the job offer arrival rate indicates that finding a job becomes more difficult, for example as a result of a decrease in vacancies. A shift in the probability of accepting a job offer implies that finding work is not more difficult, but that the wage structure on the labour market has changed and therefore more or less jobs are acceptable to individuals. In this latter case, the main cause for longer unemployment spells during recessions is the selectivity of unemployed workers in accepting job offers.

To distinguish between the underlying parameters (and the individual search effort and reservation wage), a structural analysis is required. Van der Klaauw, Van Vuuren and Berkhout (2004) investigate changes in these underlying parameters using a Dutch sample of new entrants on the labour market. The sample consists of college graduates, which is not the most vulnerable group on the labour market, but typically youth unemployment rates are most volatile over the business cycle. The empirical results show that the wage offer distribution is most sensitive to fluctuations in the business cycle, which confirms the common knowledge that wage flexibility is highest for young workers. In particular, a 1% increase in the unemployment rate reduces mean wage offers by around 3%. The job offer arrival rate is less sensitive to business cycle fluctuations, which implies that even in recessions individuals do not suffer too much from a lack of available jobs. Only for new entrants on the labour market is finding a job that offers a high wage more difficult during recessions. Active labour market policies that reduce the selectivity of unemployed workers, such as re-employment bonuses or punitive benefit reductions for not accepting job offers, could therefore be very effective.

So far we have considered calendar time as the most relevant measure of time. However, as mentioned earlier, individual transition rates from unemployment to employment can also vary over the duration of unemployment. Reasons often mentioned for changes in re-employment rates are stigmatization, discouragement and loss of skills. In our simple job search model, stigmatization implies that unemployed workers who are unemployed for a longer period receive fewer job offers (at the same level of job search effort). An unemployed worker who gets discouraged makes less effort to search for work, and loss of skills while being unemployed implies that individuals lose potential productivity and thus receive lower wage offers. These are reasons for decreasing the job search effort during the period of unemployment and eventually quitting the search for work. In this case the unemployed worker leaves the labour force and becomes non-participant. Frijters and Van der Klaauw (2006) have focused on a structural empirical analysis of the transitions from unemployment to employment and to non-participation. Their estimation results for Germany show that during an unemployment spell the rate at which job offers arrive is relatively constant but that the wage offer distribution shifts downwards. This causes reservation wages to decrease over the unemployment duration. This could be the result of loss of skills while being unemployed. In particular, poorly educated workers suffer from duration dependence in the wage offer distribution. For them the probability of finding a well-paid job becomes so low that they become discouraged and decide to become non-participant. Again, the policy implication is that short-term unemployed workers and in particular poorly educated workers should be encouraged to be less selective about job offers.

11.4 Estimating the impact of policy interventions

Recently, in the economic literature many papers have focused on the effects of policy interventions on the duration of unemployment (for recent surveys see Fay, 1996; Fredriksson and Holmlund, 2003). Often the evaluation of policy intervention is complicated by selective assignment of these policy interventions to unemployed workers. Therefore, it is generally believed that using a randomized experiment is the superior method of measuring causal effects. However, in many situations implementing a randomized experiment is not feasible or it takes a long time before data become available. In this section we discuss some methods for evaluating policy interventions in dynamic settings using non-experimental data. We follow Abbring and Van der Klaauw (2002) who give some theoretical considerations concerning dynamic policy evaluation. Since we focus on a dynamic setting, we distinguish the announcement effect of a future intervention from the actual intervention. An actual intervention takes place at the moment a policy parameter changes, for example due to participation in a job search assistance programme. The announcement effect occurs when the individual is informed about the moment at which a policy parameter will change, for example when the individual is told when he has to start participating in a job search assistance programme.

We use the job search model as a guideline for the evaluation of policy interventions. First, we translate the policy intervention into changes in the parameters of the job search model at the moment of the policy intervention. Job search assistance programmes, for example, can be translated into changes in search efficiency (see Van den Berg and Van der Klaauw, 2006). Training and schooling programmes may not only affect job search efficiency, but may also shift the wage offer distribution, depending on the content of the programme. As mentioned above, we should not expect much from schooling and training programmes for unemployed workers. Therefore, in the remainder we take the wage offer distribution as fixed. The behaviour of the unemployed worker depends on the available information. Only if we know when information about the policy intervention was provided to the unemployed worker can we thoroughly evaluate the effectiveness of the policy intervention. Abbring and Van den Berg (2003) stress the importance of specifying the information available to the unemployed workers at any moment in time.

We distinguish two situations. First, the unemployed worker knows the exact moment at which a policy intervention will take place. In this case, the unemployed worker anticipates the policy intervention, i.e. before the actual moment of the policy intervention the intervention is discounted in the search effort and the reservation wage. The best example is the expiration of unemployment insurance benefits. Unemployed workers already know at the beginning of unemployment when their eligibility for unemployment insurance benefits expires. From the start of the period of collecting unemployment insurance benefits the unemployed worker takes into account the moment when the benefits will expire (see Van den Berg, 1990). The intervention thus reflects the moment at which information is revealed to the unemployed worker and becomes relevant in his decision-making rather than the moment at which unemployment insurance benefits actually expire.

The alternative situation is that there is no anticipation, i.e. unemployed workers know that there is a possibility of a policy intervention, but they do not know in advance the exact moment it will take place. An example of an unanticipated policy intervention is a punitive benefit reduction for unemployed workers. Unemployed workers know that they can get a sanction if they do not devote enough effort to job search, but they do not know the exact timing of a sanction in advance (see Abbring, Van den Berg and Van Ours, 2005; Lalive, Van Ours and Zweimüller, 2005; Van den Berg, Van der Klaauw and Van Ours, 2004).

Before we continue it is important to discuss which effect we actually measure. The effect is a partial one, i.e. equilibrium effects are ignored. The effect tells us how the exit rate to work of one individual changes due to the policy intervention, given that other individuals are not affected by it. The model cannot deal with large-scale policy interventions that cause spillover effects between the behaviour and labour market outcomes of individuals. The wage offer distribution and the search efficiency are not explained within the model.

Let us first consider the situation with anticipation, i.e. the unemployed worker knows the exact timing of the intervention. Even before the intervention actually takes place, the unemployed worker anticipates the intervention and adapts his behaviour. An individual, for instance, already knows at the start of unemployment when he has to participate in a programme. If the unemployed worker benefits from participation, he makes less effort to search and has a higher reservation wage prior to participating in the programme (compared to not participating in the programme) to increase the probability of being unemployed at the moment the programme starts. However, if the unemployed worker dislikes the programme or considers it an unwanted interruption of his search activities, he increases his search effort before the programme and decreases his reservation wage. Black, Smith, Berger and Noel (2003) provide an example where the threat of having to participate in a programme is more effective than the actual participation itself.

In the case of anticipation, one can learn a lot about the policy intervention just by comparing exit rates to work just before the intervention with exit rates just after it. Such a comparison is justified from our simple job search model. Consider a job search assistance programme that changes job search efficiency. If the programme is successful, it increases search efficiency. For a group of unemployed workers who are selected to participate in the programme, we can compare the re-employment rates just before and just after the programme starts. At the moment of the intervention, no additional information becomes available to the unemployed worker. Therefore, just before and just after the moment of the intervention, the unemployed worker derives the same utility from working. The reservation wage just before the intervention equals the reservation wage just after it. The effect of the intervention on re-employment rates is therefore only affected by the change in the job offer arrival rates and not by a change in reservation wage and acceptance rates of job offers. The effect of the programme can therefore be summarized by the ratio of the transition rates into employment just before and just after the programme.

In general, search intensities before and after the intervention are not similar if search efficiencies differ. If search after the intervention is more efficient, then the unemployed worker will devote more effort to job search after the intervention than before. The marginal benefits of search are larger after the intervention. Even though the policy intervention changes search effort, the ratio of transition rates is informative on the effect of the policy intervention. If the ratio exceeds 1, the policy intervention improves the search efficiency of the unemployed worker. But if the ratio is less than 1, the policy intervention decreases the search efficiency. Even if there are unobserved characteristics that affect both the re-employment rate and the moment of the intervention, the ratio can be used to test if the policy intervention has a positive or a negative impact. Under some conditions the group of unemployed workers that should participate in the policy intervention and search for work just before the programme starts do not differ from unemployed workers that actually participated in the policy intervention and searched just after the programme started. Therefore, comparing re-employment rates just before and just after the policy intervention provides a good estimate for the ratio of re-employment rates, and this is informative on the effectiveness of the policy intervention.

The analysis can only be conducted if the researcher knows for each individual the exact moment of the policy intervention. Usually data-sets are not sufficiently informative and interventions are often only registered once they have actually been imposed. Under these conditions, the re-employment rate just before the intervention cannot be estimated. Furthermore, to distinguish duration dependence in the job search process from the effect of the policy intervention, it is important that there is sufficient variation between individuals at the moment when the policy intervention is imposed.

Some policy interventions are not anticipated, i.e. the unemployed worker knows about the risk of getting a policy intervention, but he does not know the exact timing of the policy intervention. The unem-ployed worker can therefore only take account of the risk of the policy intervention. An example of an unanticipated policy intervention is the imposition of sanctions (see Abbring, Van den Berg and Van Ours, 2005; Lalive, Van Ours and Zweimüller, 2005; Van den Berg, Van der Klaauw and Van Ours, 2004). Unemployed workers, who do not devote enough effort to job search, might get a sanction in the form of a temporary benefit reduction. Because unemployment insurance agencies and welfare agencies are not capable of perfectly monitoring job search behaviour, there is some randomness involved in imposing sanctions. The search model predicts that, before the sanction, search effort and the reservation wage, and thus the re-employment rate, do not depend on the actual moment of the sanction. The unemployed worker will be surprised by the sanction and will change his search effort and reservation wage.

A simple comparison of re-employment hazards before and after the moment of an unanticipated policy intervention is not possible. The moment of the policy intervention is generally unknown if an unem-ployed worker finds work before the policy intervention. Therefore, there does not exist a simple procedure to determine the re-employment rate just before the policy intervention. Abbring and Van den Berg (2003) provide an alternative method for estimating the causal effect of unanticipated policy interventions. This procedure is less easy than the methods described above for anticipated policy interventions. The estimation method corrects for unobserved differences between unemployed workers with and without the policy intervention. The estimation method exploits variation at the moment of imposing the policy interventions. The estimated effect is the effect of actually imposing the policy intervention and because it is unanticipated there is no announcement effect.

11.5 Empirical results from policy evaluation

In this section we discuss the results from recent empirical studies on the effectiveness of policy interventions aimed at reducing the unemployment duration, and thus preventing human capital deterioration. We focus on policies that target increasing job search effort directly or the efficiency of job search effort. Recall that our model framework imposes strong restrictions on the updating of the information set of unemployed workers. In particular, unemployed workers may be aware of the existence of a policy, but they are not allowed to know the exact timing at which an intervention occurs. Therefore, this framework is not very suitable for investigating the impact of schooling or training programmes, which are often announced to the unemployed worker some time before the training or schooling actually takes place.[1] The policies we discuss are job search assistance, monitoring of search behaviour and punitive benefit reductions.

Abbring, Van den Berg and Van Ours (2005) and Van den Berg, van der Klaauw and Van Ours (2004) investigate the effect of imposing sanctions in the form of punitive benefits reductions on the transition rate from unemployment to work on individuals in the Netherlands receiving unemployment insurance benefits and welfare recipients respectively. Lalive, Van Ours and Zweimüller (2005) investigate the same policy for unemployment insurance recipients in Switzerland. Sanctions are imposed on individuals who do not comply with the minimum job search requirements and administrative rules. An unemployed worker who devotes less than the minimum required effort is at risk of getting a sanction imposed. Sanctions should stimulate job search effort directly.

For some unemployed workers it is optimal to devote less effort to job search than is required. These individuals know that they are at risk of getting a sanction imposed, but prefer this risk over increasing their search effort. A sanction is often accompanied by closer monitoring of search behaviour. This implies that after a sanction has been imposed, an unemployed worker runs a higher risk of getting a second sanction if he does not change his job search effort. Because individuals dislike this higher risk, job search theory predicts that individuals will increase their job search effort after a sanction. Furthermore, the (temporary) reduced benefits increase the acceptance probability of job offers by lowering the reservation wage.

The main problem in the empirical analysis concerns the endogenous selection involved in the imposition of sanctions. Because sanctions are imposed in response to (job search) behaviour, unemployed workers who actually get a sanction imposed most likely differ from unemployed workers who do not get a sanction imposed. The unemployed worker does not anticipate a sanction, and therefore the estimation strategy discussed in the previous section is used to estimate the effect of sanctions. In particular, the process by which unemployed workers get a sanction and the process by which they leave unemployment are modelled jointly to correct for endogenous selection.

The empirical results show that imposing a sanction has a substantial positive effect on individual re-employment rates. The exit rate to work is about twice as large after a sanction has been imposed than before. The results establish that unemployed workers are sensitive to financial punishments, which confirms the simple job search model.[2] Furthermore, the effect of a sanction varies with individual characteristics, which is in agreement with the theoretical prediction that the magnitude of the sanction effect depends on structural determinants of the job search model, such as the discount rate and job offer arrival rate.

The evaluated effect is the effect of imposing a sanction within a system that incorporates sanctions. The evaluation methods discussed in the previous section do not evaluate the effect of having a system with sanctions as opposed to a system without sanctions. Theoretical analysis (see Boone and Van Ours, 2000) shows that unemployed workers are expected to have a higher transition rate to work in a system with sanctions even though they have not (yet) been given a sanction. This implies that the estimated sanction effect is basically a lower bound of the overall effect of a system with sanctions vis-à-vis a system without sanctions. To quantify the 'ex-ante' effect of having a system with sanctions we need additional data from a period with a system without sanctions. Alternatively, we would need sufficient information to estimate a job search model.

Sanctions are often accompanied by stricter monitoring of job search behaviour. In the presence of sanctions, monitoring is expected to increase the transition rate from unemployment to work. Monitoring of job search effort is often not easy for the unemployment insurance agencies. Job search effort is not a univariate measure and unemployed workers can use various job search channels like job advertisements, public employment agencies, open application letters, etc. This complicates the process of job search since individuals not only have to decide how much effort they will devote to job search, but also how to divide it along the different job search channels. Van den Berg and Van der Klaauw (2006) extend the job search model to multiple search channels to show that stricter monitoring can shift search effort from informal job search channels to formal job search channels. Only if the unemployed worker is forced to devote more effort to job search is stricter monitoring an efficient policy intervention for increasing exit rates to work.

Monitoring often starts at the beginning of unemployment. Therefore, the policy cannot be evaluated using the empirical methods described in the previous section. To evaluate the effect of stricter monitoring, often randomized experiments are used (see Ashenfelter, Ashmore and Deschênes, 2005; Gorter and Kalb, 1996; Van den Berg and Van der Klaauw, 2006). These experiments show that monitoring does not have a large effect on the re-employment rates of individuals just after becoming unemployed. At the beginning of unemployment individuals have many opportunities to substitute effort between different search channels. Therefore stricter monitoring (of one search channel) does not increase the total amount of search effort and thus does not affect re-employment rates. From economic theory we can learn that stricter monitoring can be a useful policy at a later stage of unemployment. Long-term unemployed workers often do not use informal search anymore, and therefore stricter monitoring increases their total amount of search effort.

Monitoring and sanctions try to increase the search effort of the unemployed worker; counselling tries to increase the job search efficiency. For example, counselling includes job interview training, improving CVs and application letters and pointing out suitable vacancies. In the simple job search model counselling increases the search efficiency. This is explicitly recognized in Gorter and Kalb (1996) and Van den Berg and Van der Klaauw (2006). It turns out that low-intensity counselling does not have an effect on exit rates to work. Meyer (1995) points out that the success of counselling mainly depends on the intensity of the programme and the population of unemployed workers who receive the counselling. More disadvantaged unemployed workers seem to profit more from counselling than unemployed workers with relatively good labour market prospects. Dolton and O'Neill (1996) stress that, like stricter monitoring, counselling can only be successful if non-compliance is punished financially.

11.6 Conclusion and discussion

While being unemployed the human capital of workers depreciates. Recent studies have shown that schooling and training programmes have not been very successful at directly increasing the human capital of the unemployed worker. At most, schooling and training programmes have a modest impact on re-employment rates and post-unemployment earnings. Therefore, public expenditure on these programmes has very low rates of return. Other active labour market policies might be more successful. Stimulating re-employment directly will reduce the duration of unemployment, and thus reduce loss of human capital and it may restore the worker's participation in on-the-job training. However, there is serious heterogeneity in the effectiveness of the programmes. Empirical studies have shown that almost all unemployed workers respond to financial incentives such as re-employment bonuses and punitive benefit reductions. The monitoring of job search behaviour is effective if it is targeted at disadvantaged and long-term unemployed workers, but can be harmful to the re-employment rates of short-term unemployed workers with relatively good labour market prospects. This requires a supporting profiling system for unemployed workers. The effectiveness of job search assistance programmes depends on the intensity of the programme. In particular, policy-makers should not expect too much from cheap and low-intensity programmes.

Notes

1. Exceptions are Albrecht, Van den Berg and Vroman (2005) and Richardson and Van den Berg (2001), who both study the effect of adult

education for poorly educated workers in Sweden on re-employment. The timing at which a worker is assigned to the training is determined by the case worker, which means that the exact timing of training is unknown to unemployed workers. The empirical results indicate small positive effects from the training on the re-employment of unemployed workers, but no effects on earnings. This suggests that human capital accumulation due to the training is absent.

2. Unemployed workers are not only sensitive to financial punishment, but the bonus experiments discussed in Meyer (1995) show that providing bonuses significantly reduces the duration of unemployment.

References

Abbring, J. H. and G. J. van den Berg (2003). The nonparametric identification of treatment effects in duration models. *Econometrica*, 71: 1491–1517.

Abbring, J. H. and B. van der Klaauw (2002). Analyse van activerend arbeidsmarktbeleid in dynamische modellen. *Daadwerkelijk effectief, Prestatiemeting van Reïntegratie en Activering*, TNO Arbeid, Hoofddorp.

Abbring, J. H., G. J. van den Berg and J. C. van Ours (2002). The anatomy of unemployment dynamics. *European Economic Review*, 46: 1785–1824.
    (2005). The effect of unemployment insurance sanctions and the transition rate from unemployment to employment. *Economic Journal*, 115: 602–30.

Albrecht, J., G. J. van den Berg and S. Vroman (2005). The knowledge lift: the Swedish adult education program that aimed to eliminate low worker skill levels. Discussion Paper, IZA, Bonn.

Ashenfelter, O., D. Ashmore and O. Deschênes (2005). Do unemployment insurance recipients actively seek work? Randomized trials in four U.S. states. *Journal of Econometrics*, 1–2: 53–75.

Black, D. A., J. A. Smith, M. C. Berger and B. J. Noel (2003). Is the threat of reemployment services more effective than the services themselves? Evidence from random assignment in the UI system. *American Economic Review*, 93: 1313–27.

Boone, J. and J. C. van Ours (2000). Modeling financial incentives to get unemployed back to work. Discussion Paper, IZA, Bonn.

Dolton, P. and D. O'Neill (1996). Unemployment duration and the Restart effect: some experimental evidence. *Economic Journal*, 106: 387–400.

Fay, R. G. (1996). Enhancing the effectiveness of active labour market policies: evidence from programme evaluations in OECD countries. Working Paper, OECD, Paris.

Fredriksson, P. and B. Holmlund (2003). Improving incentives in unemployment insurance: a review of recent research. Working Paper, University of Uppsala.

Frijters, P. and B. van der Klaauw (2006). Job search with nonparticipation. *Economic Journal*, 116: 45–83.

Gorter, C. and G. R. J. Kalb (1996). Estimating the effect of counseling and monitoring the unemployed using a job search model. *Journal of Human Resources*, 31: 590–610.

Heckman, J. J., R. J. LaLonde and J. A. Smith (1999). The economics and econometrics of active labor market programs, in O. Ashenfelter and D. Card (eds.), *Handbook of Labor Economics*, vol. IIIA. Amsterdam: North-Holland.

Hotz, V. J., G. W. Imbens and J. H. Mortimer (2005). Predicting the efficacy of future training programs using past experience at other locations. *Journal of Econometrics*, 1–2: 241–70.

Keese, M. and J. P. Martin (2002). Improving labour market performance: lessons from OECD countries' experience. Presentation at the Warsaw Conference on Economic Policy Directions in the OECD, 21–22 March.

Lalive, R., J. C. van Ours and J. Zweimüller (2005). The effect of benefit sanctions on the duration of unemployment. *Journal of the European Economic Association*, 3: 1–32.

Machin, S. and A. Manning (1999). The causes and consequences of long-term unemployment in Europe, in O. C. Ashenfelter and D. Card (eds.), *Handbook of Labor Economics*, vol. IIIC. Amsterdam: North-Holland.

Meyer, B. D. (1995). Lessons from the U.S. unemployment insurance experiments. *Journal of Economic Literature*, 33: 91–131.

Mortensen, D. T. (1986). Job search and labor market analysis, in O. Ashenfelter and R. Layard (eds.), *Handbook of Labor Economics*, vol. II. Amsterdam: North-Holland.

OECD (2003). *Employment Outlook*. Paris: OECD.

Richardson, K. and G. J. van den Berg (2001). The effect of vocational training on the individual transition rate from unemployment to work. *Swedish Economic Policy Review*, 8: 175–213.

Todd, P. E. and K. I. Wolpin (2003). Using a social experiment to validate a dynamic behavioral model of child schooling and fertility: assessing the impact of a school subsidy program in Mexico. Working Paper, University of Pennsylvania, Philadelphia.

Van den Berg, G. J. (1990). Nonstationarity of job search theory. *Review of Economic Studies*, 57: 255–77.

Van den Berg, G. J. and B. van der Klaauw (2001). Combining micro and macro unemployment duration data. *Journal of Econometrics*, 102: 271–309.

(2006). Counseling and monitoring of unemployed workers: theory and evidence from a controlled social experiment. *International Economic Review*, 47: 895–936.

Van den Berg, G. J., B. van der Klaauw and J. C. van Ours (2004). Punitive sanctions and the transition rate from welfare to work. *Journal of Labor Economics*, 22: 211–14.

Van der Klaauw, B., A. van Vuuren and P. Berkhout (2004). Labor market prospects, search intensity and the transition from college to work. Working Paper, SCHOLAR, Amsterdam.

12 | Can we stimulate teachers to enhance quality?

IB WATERREUS

12.1 Introduction

Teachers are the backbone of schools, and the inputs in the production of human capital. It is therefore no surprise that parents, school boards and policy-makers have a strong interest in the availability and the quality of teachers. In this chapter we consider compensation as a policy instrument to influence the volume and the quality of teacher supply.

Often, compensation of teachers at a given rank is mainly determined by tenure. Furthermore, the risk of being laid off declines with tenure. One may wonder whether such incentives effectively contribute to the supply, quality and motivation of teachers. Many other incentive schemes are conceivable, which are put into practice not only in the private sector but also in the public education sector in some countries.

What kinds of pay criteria are possible and what kinds of effects do they generate? The following pay criteria are discussed: fixed pay, performance-related pay, relative compensation, team compensation, and work–life incentives. The empirical literature regarding the use of these different payment schemes for teachers is also discussed.

A review of the literature makes clear that teachers are sensitive to incentives. At the same time it shows that education is a complex organization, where strong, explicit incentives could do more harm than weak, implicit incentives. This may also explain the lack of powerful incentives in most existing arrangements and the failure of most merit pay experiments. On the other hand there seems to be room for improvement.

This chapter aims to draw conclusions about the possibilities and effects of different financial incentives for teachers in secondary education. It starts with a review of the literature, followed by some of my own empirical work regarding the impact of teacher incentives. The chapter concludes with some recommendations for policy and further research.

189

12.2 Review of the literature

In education payment usually occurs according to input, based on the number of teaching hours. The measurement of teacher quality is hard and costly, as the outcomes of education are difficult to measure and lesson supervision is costly. Furthermore, teachers are a homogeneous group as they have all followed a similar type of education. Finally, because of the specific investment in a teaching qualification they are not likely to have many alternative high-paid job opportunities.

In some countries large differences may exist between teachers in different subjects. These differences are not related to performance but to outside opportunities. As teachers in certain subjects (like maths and science) have better outside opportunities than teachers in other subjects (like history and physical education), they have to be better paid in order to attract teachers of the requisite quality. If wages are not differentiated in this way (some countries have uniform wages for teaching), teacher quality may differ by subject. Experiences in other sectors have shown that performance-related pay can be very effective when output can be easily measured, but pay related to the performance of individual teachers appears to be highly problematic. In this respect, objective performance measurement requires clear and measurable goals. As teachers face multiple (and often competing) tasks there is the risk that they focus their efforts on performance measurement indicators at the expense of other educational goals.

Murnane (1996) refers to the absence of merit pay (and the failure of most merit pay plans) in education as evidence that performance-related pay for teachers does not work. The costs may simply exceed the benefits. On the other hand, Ballou (2001) points to the fact that in the United States merit pay is much more common in non-religious private schools than in public schools. This could mean that specific circumstances in public education, notably the opposition of teaching unions, also play a role in the failure or prevention of merit pay plans.

Eberts et al. (2002) provide a case study of a natural experiment of merit pay in a US county where one high school piloted a merit pay system that rewarded student retention and student evaluation of teachers, while another comparable high school maintained a traditional compensation system. The merit pay system did indeed reduce dropout, but at the expense of pass rates. Furthermore daily attendance and grade point averages remained virtually unchanged. Although this case study has to be interpreted with care, the results do confirm Dixit's (2002) claim that incentives in education may produce unintended and misdirected results. As he also suggests, the use of implicit incentives such as relative compensation may be more appropriate.

Recently, Lavy (2003) evaluated an experiment with a rank-order tournament for teachers of English and mathematics in Israel, which rewarded teachers with pay bonuses for (above-average) improvements in their pupils' exam performance. Using three alternative identification strategies Lavy consistently finds a significant positive effect for these performance incentives on students' achievements in English and mathematics. The programme is very cost-effective compared to other experiments with monetary and non-pecuniary interventions, and Lavy does not find evidence of any negative spillover effects on untreated subjects.

As this experiment was abandoned after a year, the question remains whether these effects are stable over time or just a temporary 'Hawthorne' effect of the experiment. For instance, teachers can be expected to respond strategically by selecting pupils for certain classes. In addition, although no spillover effects are found for other subjects, teaching to the test may still take place within a subject. Alternatively, relative compensation could be based on subjective evaluations. School principals may very well be able to identify good teachers and assess all the relevant dimensions of teaching. However, in practice the system may have to be formalized to be acceptable to the teachers (and their unions). This would then invoke the standard problem of defining and measuring the relevant dimensions, and the risk of focusing on just a limited subset.

Compensation based on relative performance can take the form of straight pay rises (or bonuses), or promotion to higher ranks. As schools tend to be very flat organizations, such ranked systems have to be deliberately created. Indeed, a number of countries have attempted to create career ladders for teachers by introducing junior and senior teaching posts, etc. However, like the merit pay initiatives mentioned above, most of these systems have failed.

For example, in the early 1990s, Australia introduced the post of advanced skills teacher (AST), with the explicit intention of keeping excellent teachers in the classroom by offering them better rewards. In practice, promotion often took place without a strict performance appraisal. For instance in the state of Victoria 93% of all AST candidates were promoted to AST 1, because no quota had been fixed. As the AST allowances were provided by the state without any limit, the school-based selection panels had no incentive for a rigorous selection process. As a result AST received the nickname 'automatically selected teachers'.

Other states such as New South Wales (NSW) imposed a quota for the number of ASTs. In NSW this quota was set at 30% in 1992 and increased to 45% in 1995. However, as a result of the more rigorous selection process in these states, a lot of teachers felt the benefits (wage spread) of becoming an AST did not outweigh the costs of obtaining AST status. The teaching union also perceived the quotas as unfair. Furthermore, although the AST programme was meant to reward good teachers who stayed in the classroom, in practice teachers with advanced skills in New South Wales ended up with more administrative tasks. Eventually, this has led to the abolition of the scheme in most Australian states (Ingvarsson and Chadbourne, 1997).

So in practice all kinds of safeguards and procedures are introduced to ensure that teacher evaluations are accepted and to eliminate inconsistency. This involves costs that could outweigh the benefits. Furthermore, benefits may be reduced if mutual cooperation is jeopardized by teachers who have to compete for a wage increase.

A bonus for high-performance schools or teams of teachers could be a more promising option. A major advantage of team-based pay is that it stimulates cooperation between teachers, but this system has similar drawbacks to individual performance-related pay, in the sense that schools may also focus at certain performance indicators at the expense of other goals.

In education, team compensation could be applied on the 'cooperative production' of a small group of teachers: for instance, in primary schools where the number of teachers is small (around ten) or in small sections by subject in secondary education where cooperation is important.

Teachers' pay could be (partly) determined by team compensation on the basis of the number of pupils or school results. Of course the same problems of output-related pay apply, apart from measuring the individual contributions of teachers.

Nevertheless, another study by Lavy (2002) suggests that forms of team-based pay may enhance the quality of education. In 1995 Israel started an experiment in a large number of secondary schools, awarding monetary incentives to teachers in the top third of high-performing schools. Evaluation of this experiment showed significant gains in all five achievement measures of high school graduates, including average test scores and the dropout rate.

Unfortunately, it is unknown whether these effects would persist in the long term. Hawthorne effects cannot be excluded, in particular because the impact of the bonuses was surprisingly large given their small size ($200–$715 per teacher). Experience of a similar school accountability programme in Dallas gives rise to caution as well: although Ladd (1999) reports positive effects like higher pass rates and lower dropout rates, almost all of the positive effects were found before the programme was in full effect.

Further, strong incentives to achieve certain test results may be successful at the expense of other educational goals. It is therefore crucially important to measure all relevant school results and the contribution of the schools towards them. For instance, in Texas, a wide gap emerged in the development of two different test scores. Schools rapidly achieved an improvement in the state test, which forms the basis for inspection reports and school awards, but there was no parallel upturn in other national tests (Klein et al., 2000). Jacob (2002) finds similar effects for public schools in Chicago. In addition, he finds that teachers also respond to incentives by taking other strategic actions, such as placing more pupils in special education and substituting away from low-stakes subjects.

A recent evaluation of a randomized experiment in Kenya finds test score gains in the short run without any persistence of the gains in the post-programme year (Glewwe et al., 2003). In this programme among a random group of low-performing primary schools, both schools with the best performance and those showing most improvement were eligible for awards, with teachers at about half of the best-performing schools receiving prizes ranging from 21% to 43% of a monthly teacher's salary. Pupils who did not take part in the tests were assigned low scores, in order to discourage dropouts, but apart from higher exam participation no effects on dropout rates were found. Finally, apart from an increase in the number of test preparation sessions, teachers did not significantly change their teaching behaviour. The above examples clearly indicate that schools are likely to engage in 'test-oriented teaching', which may harm other – unmeasured – educational goals.

12.3 Work–life incentives

It is generally assumed that teachers' productivity increases sharply during the first years of teaching, after which it remains fairly constant. At least it is very unlikely that the yearly wage increases throughout the teaching career reflect equal increases in productivity. Therefore Lazear's (1995) theory of deferred compensation seems a plausible explanation for the use of seniority pay in education in most countries. Given the lack of opportunities for promotion, the prospect of future wage increases could keep teachers motivated.

To be effective as an incentive, seniority pay should be accompanied by a regular appraisal of performance and the possibility of dismissal in case of a poor assessment. Otherwise seniority pay may induce adverse selection in the sense that only the most talented teachers are likely to leave the profession, as they are able to earn more elsewhere. However, in most countries regular appraisal is not very common and teachers cannot easily be laid off. For that reason, rent seeking by teaching unions is often referred to as an alternative explanation for the structure of teachers' compensation. Lazear (2001) argues that elimination of tenure is unrealistic, in particular in Europe where the probability of lay-off is very low outside education as well. It might be more effective to increase the probationary period for teachers in order to select the best ones.

To sum up, table 12.1 provides an overview of the potential incentives and risks, as well as the optimal conditions for the different pay criteria described above. Although further research is needed, incentives for teachers can definitely be improved given the weak incentives in the widely used system of seniority pay for teachers. However, as the costs of measuring absolute performance are very high, it makes more sense to look at relative performance. Apart from introducing elements of relative compensation, schools can also vary teachers' pay between subjects and lengthen the probationary period for teachers to improve the opportunities for schools to recruit and retain better teachers.

12.4 Teachers' pay and teacher quality: an international comparison[1]

An investigation of international experiences with teachers' pay, quality and supply in seven western countries suggests that the level of pay

Table 12.1 Characteristics of different pay criteria

Pay criteria	Incentives	Risks	Conditions
Fixed pay (payment by input)	Weak	Negative sorting	Performance measurement costly, homogeneous workers, possibility of selection and dismissal
Performance-related pay (payment by output)	Strong	Strategic behaviour	Absolute performance measurement at low cost
Relative compensation (rank tournament)	Strong	Strategic behaviour	Relative performance measurement at low cost, optimal wage spread
Team compensation	Dependent on team size and composition	Free-riding	Team performance measurement at low cost, cooperation important, small group size, peer pressure
Work–life incentives	Weak	Negative sorting	Performance measurement costly, homogeneous workers, possibility of selection and dismissal, mandatory retirement

(relative to the earnings of other highly educated employees) seems to be an important determinant for the quality and supply of teachers, although other factors are also likely to play a role, such as the workload and the level of unemployment.

In order to determine the attractiveness of the teaching profession it seems relevant to look at the level of teachers' pay relative to other highly educated employees. For this reason, earnings profiles of male and female (secondary school) teachers are compared to earnings of highly educated men and women employed in other sectors. In general this shows that teaching is a more attractive career option for women than for men. This is confirmed by the fact that a majority of teachers are female in most countries.

In all countries the variation of teachers' pay is low compared to other professions. This variation in earnings could be interpreted as a measure of risk, which people might want to avoid. As a result, the low earnings risk attached to teaching may provide an important asset in times of economic hardship. However, it also makes it more difficult to recruit high-ability teachers, in particular when unemployment is low and other sectors offer jobs with better career opportunities. This is due to the fact that teachers' earnings in most countries only rise slowly with seniority, and the compensation structure provides few performance incentives.

It is quite difficult to compare the workload of teachers to the workload in competing professions, as a teacher's workload is often calculated in teaching hours instead of working hours, and the additional non-teaching activities at school or at home differ between countries. In addition, the workload is also determined by class size, which also differs between (types of) schools and countries.

Nevertheless, teachers in most countries have long school holidays (although always in the high season), and outside teaching hours they have some flexibility in performing their additional tasks. This eases the combination of work and family, which may also add to the popularity of the teaching profession among women.

Apart from the similarities great differences also exist between countries in the relative level of pay and the workload of teachers. Although (in 1999) in most countries the level of teachers' pay was fairly competitive with the average employee in other sectors, teachers in Germany, the United States and Australia seemed to be relatively well paid, whereas Swedish teachers were relatively poorly paid. On the other hand, the workload of Swedish teachers in terms of hours and pupils was very low, as it is in France and to some extent in Germany and Australia. The workload for teachers is higher in England and the United States, and in particular in the Netherlands. As a result, only France, Germany and Australia appear to do well on both indicators.

With regard to teacher incentives, France is the only country concerned here that has a tradition of performance-related pay for teachers. The performance of each French teacher is assessed by both the head of the school (weight 40%) and the inspectorate (weight 60%). It is a system of relative compensation where teachers with the highest performance marks see their pace of promotion increased.

Recently, Sweden, England and the Netherlands have introduced some kind of relative compensation for teachers, providing the school with the opportunity to reward some of its teachers with additional pay rises. Apart from the (local) experiments in the United States and Australia mentioned above, pay is not directly related to performance in the other countries. Even though seniority pay rises may also be conditional upon performance, teachers are rarely refused such a standard pay rise.

The relative employment conditions of teachers can be confronted with indicators of the supply and quality of teachers in each country. One would expect the relative wage and the workload to strongly affect both the supply and quality of teachers. Performance incentives seem particularly relevant for the quality of teachers, by influencing the selection of certain types of teachers.

Effects on teacher supply

To some extent all countries considered have problems recruiting teachers for specific subjects or regions. In France and Germany shortages are rare, whereas England and the Netherlands have recently experienced more or less general shortages. In all countries the difficulties have been unevenly distributed across regions and subjects. It is clear that relative teacher wages do matter, even if they can only explain part of the shortage problems: shortages increase when unemployment declines and shortages are worse in subjects with better alternative career options, like maths and science. Further, the regional differences in shortages are often related to the regional costs of living or the share of disadvantaged pupils. In fact, several countries try to compensate teachers for these circumstances by paying additional allowances.

Dutch teacher shortages are lower in general upper secondary education, where pupils are 'easier' and schools used to have more opportunities to award higher salaries. In contrast, schools with a lot of disadvantaged pupils in the big cities are having the greatest problems in recruiting and retaining teachers. Obvious explanations are a heavy workload due to difficult pupils and high costs of living (in particular housing). As a result of a recent rise in unemployment, general teacher shortages in the Netherlands have disappeared. Nevertheless, shortages are expected to return in the near future as many teachers are approaching the age of retirement. Similar demographic developments pose a threat to teacher supply in other countries as well.

In spite of apparently competitive working conditions, Australia, the United States and Sweden have increasing recruitment difficulties, especially in remote and difficult city areas and in subjects like maths and science. A possible explanation might be that the economic boom at the end of the 1990s increased pay in other sectors relative to teachers' pay. This might be combined with a decline in the value attached to the job security offered in education, due to a lower level of unemployment. This seems to be confirmed by the fact that unemployment levels decreased by a third in these countries between 1994 and 2000.

In countries where unemployment is still relatively high such as Germany and France, the supply of teachers is still abundant. In France only 10–20% of the participants in the competitive examinations for the different teaching qualifications were admitted in 1999. Nevertheless, there are great differences between subjects, for instance in philosophy only 2.5% are admitted, whereas in the classical languages and some technical subjects over 50% are admitted. For a few subjects, there may not be enough qualified candidates for the number of available places. Shortages only occur in some subjects and regions. For example, mobility is very high in remote areas and at schools with many disadvantaged pupils.

Apart from the number of teachers entering the profession, supply is also determined by the number of teachers leaving the profession. In France and Germany, attrition among teachers at the beginning of their careers appears to be very low. Less than 5% of new German teachers and an insignificant share of French teachers leave teaching during the first years of their career. By contrast, of those entering teaching in

England 40% are said to leave their job within the first three years. In the United States attrition is also very high, as around 30% of teachers leave the school system within five years.

In sum, the level of teachers' pay is an important determinant of the supply of teachers. Teacher shortages are lower in countries and subjects where teachers have good working conditions, compared to alternative career options. In addition, the job security offered by education makes teaching more attractive when unemployment levels are high.

Effects on teacher quality

Teacher quality can be defined as a teacher's ability to contribute to pupils' achievements. In most economic production functions of education, pupils' achievements are generally considered to be the output of interest, with teacher quality as one of the important inputs. However, even under the assumption of pupils' achievements as the main educational objectives it has proved difficult to find good indicators for teacher quality.

At first glance, the share of qualified teachers may seem a reasonable indicator of teacher quality. However, in order to contribute to teacher quality, teacher certification should fulfil a number of conditions. First, those who pass certification should be better teachers than those without certification. This may have been achieved by improving the skills of prospective teachers through training, but this is not necessary. The certification process may also serve as a selection mechanism. In that case, the certification process functions as a filter to distinguish good and bad teachers. Of course, if this filter does not function properly, bad teachers may also become certified.

At the same time, a certification requirement has an impact on the quality of prospective teachers. For instance, if it requires a costly investment it could also deter good potential teachers. In this way talented teachers without the right certification could be lost to education. As a consequence, strict qualification requirements do not automatically guarantee better teachers. This may apply to the United States in particular, where there are huge quality differences between universities. In the United States a master's degree may not serve as a signal of quality, as it can be easily obtained at some universities. This explains why the selectiveness of a college may serve as a better proxy of quality. In most of continental Europe, by contrast, (academic) subject degrees may function more as a signal of quality, as quality differences between universities are much smaller.

We should distinguish between the quality of the applicants for teacher training and the quality of those who ultimately become (and stay) teachers. The quality of the applicants is likely to be influenced by the level of teachers' pay, whereas the final quality of the teaching population depends on the further selection process as well. Of course, in order to be able to select the best teachers, there should be sufficient supply in the first place. As a result, concern about teacher supply is accompanied by concern about teacher quality.

It is important to note that there are essentially two different models of teacher selection. They can either be centrally employed by the state and allocated to schools, or directly employed by local schools. In the central model (for example in France, Germany and Australia) selection takes place during teacher training. In combination with special allowances, this model seems successful in providing geographically or socially disadvantaged schools with sufficient supply, but at relatively high costs. As wages are equal across subjects, teachers in most subjects are offered a wage above the market clearing level in order to attract enough teachers for all subjects.

A decentralized model (as, for example, in England, the Netherlands and Sweden) more flexibly adapts to local needs, as schools have the opportunity to select teachers themselves. As a result, the selection during teacher training is less crucial and entry barriers to the teaching profession can be lower. However, balancing teacher demand and supply for all schools requires that teachers' wages reflect local labour market conditions. As the working conditions of teachers strongly depend on political budget decisions, they do not quickly respond to changing labour market conditions. This explains why most of these countries have difficulties finding teachers at times when unemployment is low.

We assume that average teacher quality is relatively high in France and Germany, because of the high number of candidates and the selectivity of teacher training.[2] Although we cannot entirely exclude the possibility that the quality of candidates is below average, as we have no direct measures of teacher quality, this seems highly unlikely and the selection procedure should filter out the best candidates. Of course this relies on the assumption that selection is based on criteria that are related to teacher quality.

Further, it is important to note that in France the opportunity costs for talented students to become teachers are limited. Students receive a salary in the second year of teacher training as well as a job guarantee and students with the highest grades receive favourable treatment when they are allocated to a school.

The system of performance-related pay for French teachers during their career may help in retaining high-quality teachers. At the same time the French system of teacher evaluation is criticized, as the evaluations by the inspectorate are not carried out on a regular basis. Teachers may have to wait for over ten years to be inspected, and the outcomes of the subjective evaluations are sometimes felt to be rather arbitrary. As mentioned in the review of the literature, this shows a clear dilemma between introducing subjective evaluations or not. For these evaluations to be accepted and to avoid arbitrariness, a lot of safeguards and procedures are often put in place. However, this involves high costs (inspection, management), which may outweigh the benefits.

In the other countries there is at least concern about the quality of teacher-training students. Australia is not attracting the same number of high-quality teachers as in the past. The minimum required level of examination results to enter teacher training has declined over the years. Further, over half of teacher-training students appear to be in the bottom quartile of school leavers starting at university. Therefore, centralized employment by itself does not provide a guarantee of teacher quality.

A study by Webbink (1999) confirms the concerns about teacher quality in the Netherlands. He estimates a multinomial logit model for the choice of teacher studies, and finds that enrolment is dominated by females, graduates from senior secondary general education (as opposed to pre-university education) and students with 'no mathematics' packages. Unfortunately no similar analyses are available for other countries.

Although little is known about the effectiveness of the teacher selection process in most countries, there is some evidence for Texas. A comparison of Scholastic Aptitude Test (SAT) scores shows that prospective teachers in Texas have lower than average test scores. However, as not all prospective teachers pass the Examination for the Certification of Educators in Texas (ExCET), certified teachers tend to have above-average SAT scores. On the other hand, the average SAT scores of certified teachers are higher for those who do not enter teaching than for those who actually teach.

For Sweden there is no direct evidence of the level of teacher quality. For most teacher-training courses the number of applications is still slightly larger than the number of places available, but still not high enough as Swedish students apply for different studies at the same time and teacher training is less popular than most other studies. As a result, the share of unqualified teachers has greatly increased over the last ten years, from around 5% to almost 20%.

Nickell and Quintini (2002) find some evidence for the influence of relative pay on the quality of male teachers in the United Kingdom. UK teachers aged between 31 and 50 showed a fall of between 7 and 12 percentage points between 1975 and 1995 in their average percentile position in the overall earnings distribution of the same age and sex grouping. At the same time average test score percentile rankings for male teachers declined by 11 to 13 percentage points. However, no such pattern emerged for female teachers, perhaps due to the increased participation rate of women. This increase in the supply of female teachers might also explain the decline in relative teacher pay, and the subsequent decline in the quality of male teachers.

To improve teacher quality England has recently introduced skills tests in literacy and numeracy in the final year of initial teacher training, and an induction programme for the first year of teaching. The number of applicants for initial teacher training falls short of the targets for secondary education. As a result, the number of unqualified teachers is rising. Although only 1% of all secondary teachers is unqualified, the share of unqualified teachers reaches 6% in some areas of London.

Finally, the first results of the English performance-related pay scheme seem to confirm that it is hard to measure teacher quality. No fewer than 95% of those who applied have passed the test, and have been promoted. Not only would a general wage increase probably have been cheaper, but it would also have prevented the remaining 5% from becoming strongly demotivated. Their failure is now highlighted because they are such a tiny minority. Even if it was the objective to discourage this group from teaching, other procedures were likely to have been more effective and less costly. For the others, the new pay scheme is unlikely to provide an incentive effect.

Teachers' salaries and working conditions relative to other job opportunities are also important for teacher quality. In order to be able to select the best teachers, the supply of teachers has to be sufficient in the first place, but the selection process also deserves serious attention, not only at job entrance but also during the career.

12.5 Full-time premium: a cost-efficient trick to make part-timers work extra hours

Dutch secondary schools are increasingly having problems recruiting teachers. In contrast to the beginning of the 1990s, when there were hardly any vacancies, in recent years the demand for teachers has increased rapidly. This is due to a growing number of pupils, a reduction of standard working time, and the ageing of the teacher population, leading to an increased outflow of teachers into (early) retirement.[3]

Attracting new teachers by improving the attractiveness of the teaching profession may be one way to solve the labour shortages. However, this will take considerable time and is especially difficult under conditions of labour market shortages of highly educated people in general. Increasing the number of hours worked by the teachers who are already in the profession provides an alternative, as a lot of teachers are working part-time. The average teaching job as a percentage share of a full-time position in 1997 was 91% for men and 69% for women.

There can be important differences between part-time and full-time jobs, such as fewer chances of promotion or lower wage rates. However, teachers in Dutch secondary education face few adverse consequences from their choice of working hours: wage rates increase with tenure irrespective of the number of working hours. Teachers also have little scope for promotion, and therefore their risk of forgoing promotion by working part-time is small. In fact, wages of full-time teachers are lagging behind other sectors, whereas the wages of part-time teachers are higher than in other sectors.

Policy-makers and other participants in the public debate are calling for a general rise in teachers' salaries to attract more supply. However, a large general wage increase is costly and not likely to produce much effect. When the income effect dominates the substitution effect, teachers may even decide to work fewer instead of more hours. Alternatively, working more hours can be made more attractive by increasing the hourly wage rate with the number of hours worked. Such a premium increases the incentive for teachers to work more hours, as this leads to a more than proportional wage increase. At the same time the premium creates a disincentive to work fewer hours, as this results in a more than proportional wage decrease. An extreme version of such a measure is a premium on working full-time. The effect that such measures will have depends on the labour supply elasticity of teachers with regard to their wages.

Typically, the labour supply elasticity of males aged between 25 and 55 is found to be very small. Most men tend to work full-time regardless of their wage level, while traditionally the labour supply of women is found to be more responsive to wage changes, with the substitution effect dominating the income effect. Recent work, however, suggests that the labour supply elasticities of women are decreasing, converging with those of men. Most recent empirical studies (for various countries) find uncompensated wage elasticities between 0 and 0.2 for men and between 0 and 1 for married women. Most income elasticities lie between –0.3 and 0 for men and between –0.4 and 0 for women (Blundell and MaCurdy, 1999).

To assess the consequences of attractive policies, we have used a survey of Dutch secondary school teachers to estimate supply elasticities. We estimated the effect of teachers' net marginal wages on their number of hours worked, using an IV approach, to correct for endogeneity of wage and virtual income.[4] The resulting uncompensated wage elasticity is significantly positive and has a value of 0.2 for males and 0.4 for females at their average number of working hours. At the same time a significant negative income elasticity of –0.06 is found for men and –0.20 for all women.

With these elasticities we can calculate the effect of wage increases on working hours by teachers already in the profession. A general wage increase is not a very cost-effective way to reduce teacher shortages, as teachers already working full-time cannot increase their number of working hours. In this way half the potential effect is lost, as more than half of teachers are working full-time. As a consequence a general wage increase of 5% has a very small effect on the number of hours that teachers work (only 0.6% increase), whereas the total additional wage costs are 110 million euros. Even a wage increase of 20% would increase hours with only 2.3% whereas costs are over 450 million euros. It should be noted, however, that these simulations only refer to direct effects on the number of working hours of current teachers. In addition over the long run new teachers may be attracted by these wage increases, in particular when they are large. Nevertheless, this simulation makes clear that solving the teacher shortage in this way would

Table 12.2 Comparison of the estimated costs (in millions of euros) of an increase in the number of hours worked of a general wage increase and a full-time premium

Increase in hours worked	1%	2%	3%	4%	5%	6%	7%	8%
Costs of general wage increase (in millions of euros)	190	390	590	770	950	1,140	1,360	1,590
Costs of full-time premium (in millions of euros)	30	70	100	120	150	170	200	230

require wage increases of more than 50%, and would lead to a cost of more than a billion euros.

An alternative measure is to give a bonus to teachers working full-time. The large distinction with the previous measure (a general wage increase) is that in the case of a full-time premium the negative income effect does not occur. The reason for this is simple: the premium can only be gained by working extra hours, and is lost as soon as teachers decide to work less than full-time. As a result, in the case of a full-time bonus only the positive substitution effect holds, which results in a larger elasticity. Table 12.2 gives a comparison of the two policies, calculated as the wage cost needed to obtain a given increase in hours worked.[5]

From the table it is clear that a full-time premium produces a much larger effect than a general wage increase at lower costs. For the total additional wage cost of 200 million euros the full-time premium produces an effect that is almost seven times larger (7% against just over 1%). Still, it should be noted that the potential effect of full-time premiums is reduced by the fact that all teachers that were already working full-time (about half of the teacher population) receive a full-time premium without an increase in their number of working hours. Therefore, even a full-time bonus does not seem a very cost-effective measure: to induce one teacher to work more hours, about two teachers are given a full-time bonus. We have estimated that the gross premium needs to be over 1,000 euros a year to create an effect large enough to solve the expected teacher shortage. At least 6% increase in hours worked is needed, which requires a premium equal to 3% of the current average gross full-time teacher salary.

In addition to the policy measures discussed, one can think of other instruments to increase the labour supply of teachers. The main short-coming of the above measures is that they can only increase the supply of teachers currently working part-time, while the majority of teachers work full-time: two-thirds of males and a quarter of female teachers. In such a situation it seems worthwhile to consider an increase in the maximum number of hours worked per week. Even at the current wage rate we can expect that some of them are willing to work more than their present number of working hours.

Around 20% of secondary teachers recently indicated they were pre-pared to give up their recent reduction of working time and work extra hours. Suppose that 20% of full-time teachers are willing to work 40 instead of 38 hours: this will result in an increase of 0.9% of hours worked, and would cost about 20 million euros. Although increasing the working week could never totally solve the expected teacher shortages (a working week of more than 40 hours seems unlikely), it is a very cost-effective contribution to reducing the teacher shortage. It costs 20 million euros per percentage increase in supply, whereas the full-time premium costs 30 million euros per percentage supply increase. Moreover, it will increase the potential effects of other measures: if a full-time bonus is introduced simultaneously with an increased working week the effects will be much larger than presented in table 12.2.

Apart from monetary incentives one can think of other instruments to improve the attractiveness of the teaching profession, such as the provision of child care facilities. Such measures may be especially useful for female teachers, of which currently only a quarter work full-time. Unfortunately, however, our dataset includes poor informa-tion on presence and age of children in the teacher's household, and we therefore dare not speculate on the potential effect of these measures.

We conclude that the usual call for general wage increases in the case of insufficient supply is often short-sighted. Specific wage increases to reward only additional hours supplied can be a much more cost-effective measure. We have shown this for the case of the Netherlands, but no doubt the results generalize to other countries.

12.6 Conclusion and discussion

Countries with relatively high levels of teachers' pay, such as Germany, are able to attract more applicants to teacher training than the number of places available. The same holds for France where competitive teacher salaries are combined with small classes and a low number of working hours. Further, these countries have the opportunity to select the best teachers through competitive examinations. In most other countries there is concern about the supply and quality of teachers.

The fact that countries with apparently competitive wages also have problems with teacher quality and supply suggests that other factors may also play an important role. For instance, when unemployment levels are low (high), employees may attach less (more) value to the job security offered by education and care more (less) for the career opportunities outside education.

Another finding is that teacher quality and teacher shortages tend to be unevenly distributed over subjects and regions. Shortage subjects and schools with disadvantaged pupils are more likely to end up with lower-quality teachers or with no teacher at all. In a number of countries special allowances are used to prevent such shortages, but permanent allowances for specific subjects are non-existent.

We conclude that teachers' salaries and working conditions relative to other job opportunities are important to attract sufficient supply and sufficient quality. Ignoring this basic economic wisdom has clearly produced problems in some European countries.

Regarding pay criteria for teachers, the omnipresence of seniority pay and the difficulties experienced with merit pay can be understood from the characteristics of the profession. Although a system of merit pay could seem attractive, it is very hard to measure all the relevant dimensions of education with sufficient reliability. The costs of the evaluation procedures involved in these systems often seem so high that they could outweigh the benefits. This could be partly due to demands for costly safeguards and procedures by teaching unions. The certification requirements and the high level of employment protection in most countries also provide support for the hypothesis of rent-seeking by teaching unions. In order to determine the optimal compensation structure for teachers, further research is needed which takes the political economy of the teacher labour market into account.

Shortages in the supply of teachers are often accompanied by a call for a general wage increase. An alternative to attracting more teachers into the teaching labour force is to increase the supply of the teachers currently working part-time. Working more hours can be made attractive for individual teachers by giving a premium to those working full-time.

This kind of premium provides part-time teachers with a greater incentive to work full-time, as the negative income effect does not occur. Simulation results show that such a premium produces an effect that is almost seven times larger than a general wage increase. In Dutch secondary education, a general wage increase of almost 1.6 billion euros would be needed to increase the number of hours worked by 8%, whereas a full-time premium would produce the same effect for 230 million euros.

Some studies have shown benefits for performance-based pay, although not without qualification. Strong incentives to improve test scores may result in teaching to the test, at the expense of other educational goals. Therefore, the introduction of teacher incentives should be accompanied with scientific evaluation, using (quasi-)experimental designs.

Empirical evidence on the impact of teacher incentives is growing but is still scarce. There is need for further empirical investigations into the impact of incentive pay for teachers. In particular, little is known about the relation between teachers' pay and teacher quality. Ideally we would like to measure the value-added of teachers in the learning process of students. However, as it is already hard to measure the contribution of schools, it is even harder to measure the impact of an individual teacher.

In practice the share of certified teachers is often used as an indicator of the quality of the teaching workforce, whereas this provides little information about the quality of students that choose teacher training and the effectiveness of their teaching. In this respect the teacher training and licensing practices in most countries deserve a critical assessment. Teacher training is often the only entrance to the teaching profession; a teacher-training certificate is necessary as a licence to teach. Consequently, teacher training has a positive and a negative function with regard to selection: it sets the minimum requirements for new teachers, but at the same time the costly investment (often on top of academic study) may be perceived as a barrier by prospective (high-quality) teachers.

Finally, although some experimental studies suggest that incentive pay for teachers may result in better teacher performance in the short run, we know little about the impact in the long run. First, we cannot completely exclude the existence of a Hawthorne effect (teachers may be motivated by the attention provided by the experiment regardless of the incentives) that may disappear over time. Second, apart from an incentive effect, performance-related pay may have a selection effect in the long run if more talented individuals are attracted to teaching.

Although earlier studies failed to find a clear relation between teachers' pay and teacher quality, more recent studies come up with evidence that the level of teachers' pay does matter. At least higher wages seem important for recruiting and retaining (talented) teachers. However, this does not automatically mean that it is socially optimal to set wages at a level that would attract the most talented individuals, as they would have to be withdrawn from other sectors. Recruitment should be aimed at those talented individuals with a comparative advantage in teaching. It would be valuable to find a way of attracting exactly those individuals as teachers.

Notes

1. This section focuses on the following western countries: France, Germany (North Rhine-Westphalia), the Netherlands, the United States (Texas), Australia (New South Wales), England and Sweden.
2. In France students must have followed at least three years of university training to be admitted to a two-year teacher-training course. At the end of the first year of teacher training a competitive examination has to be passed to go on to the second year. During this second year teachers receive a full salary while they are teaching part-time and following courses at the same time.

   In Germany prospective teachers have to follow three and a half (for lower secondary schools) to four and a half (for upper secondary schools) years of teacher training, followed by two years of preparatory service. To be admitted to the preparatory service, students have to pass the First State Examination, and at the end of the preparatory service the Second State Examination has to be passed.
3. In 1998 38% of all teachers in secondary education were over 50 years old.
4. Technical details can be found in Waterreus and Dobbelsteen (2001).
5. The necessary amount for an increase in working hours is the number of full-time premiums for those already working full-time plus the number of full-time premiums for those who choose to work full-time as a result of this premium. For a small increase in working hours a small premium will be sufficient, as only teachers who are already working almost full-time have to be reached. In order to get teachers working fewer hours the full-time premium has to be larger.

References

Ballou, D. (2001). Pay for performance in public and private schools. *Economics of Education Review*, 20 (1): 51–61.

Blundell, R. and T. MaCurdy (1999). Labor supply: a review of alternative approaches, in O. Ashenfelter and D. Card (eds.), *Handbook of Labor Economics*, vol. III. Amsterdam: North-Holland, pp. 1559–695.

Dixit, A. (2002). Incentives and organizations in the public sector: an interpretative review. *Journal of Human Resources*, 37 (4): 696–727.

Eberts, R., K. Hollenbeck and J. Stone (2002). Teacher performance incentives and student outcomes. *Journal of Human Resources*, 37 (4): 913–27.

Glewwe, P., N. Ilias and M. Kremer (2003). Teacher incentives. NBER Working Paper 9671.

Ingvarsson, L. and R. Chadbourne (1997). Reforming teachers' pay systems: the advanced skills teacher in Australia. *Journal of Personnel Evaluation in Education*, 11 (1): 7–30.

Jacob, B. A. (2002). Accountability, incentives and behavior: the impact of high-stakes testing in the Chicago public schools. NBER Working Paper 8968, Boston.

Klein, S. P., L. S. Hamilton, D. F. McCaffrey and B. M. Stecher (2000). *What Do Test Scores in Texas Tell Us?* Santa Monica: RAND.

Ladd, H. F. (1999). The Dallas school accountability and incentive program: an evaluation of its impact on student outcomes. *Economics of Education Review*, 18 (1): 1–16.

Lavy, V. (2002). Evaluating the effect of teachers' group performance incentives on pupils' achievement. *Journal of Political Economy*, 110 (6): 1286–317.

(2003). Paying for performance: the effect of teachers' financial incentives on students' scholastic outcomes. CEPR Discussion Paper 3862, London.

Lazear, E. P. (1995). *The Economics of Personnel*. Cambridge, MA: MIT Press.

(2001). Paying teachers for performance: incentives and selection. Mimeo.

Murnane, R. J. (1996). Staffing the nation's schools with skilled teachers, in E. A. Hanushek and D. W. Jorgenson (eds.), *Improving America's Schools, the Role of Incentives*. Washington: National Academy Press, pp. 241–58.

Nickell, S. and G. Quintini (2002). The consequences of the decline in public sector pay in Britain: a little bit of evidence. *Economic Journal*, 112 (477): F107–18.

Waterreus, J. M. (2003). Lessons in Teacher Pay: Studies on Incentives and the Labor Market for Teachers. PhD thesis, University of Amsterdam.

Waterreus, J. M. and S. H. A. M. Dobbelsteen (2001). Wages and teachers' hours of work. *De Economist*, 149 (3): 277–98.

Webbink, D (1999). *Student Decisions and Consequences.* Amsterdam: SEO.

13 | Optimal tax and education policies and investments in human capital

BAS JACOBS[1]

13.1 Introduction

When one starts to think about schooling and training as investments in human capital, one realizes that public policies are particularly important for the incentives to acquire human capital. First of all, progressive taxes on labour income, taxes on capital income and taxes on consumption are major sources of government revenue. Furthermore, a large part of taxation is used for social insurance and redistributional purposes. In 2006 the total tax and non-tax revenue in OECD countries amounted about 38% of GDP (Netherlands: 49%) (see OECD 2005). Clearly, taxation affects the economic incentives to acquire skills in various ways. Education is highly subsidized by most governments. Public contributions to the direct costs (school buildings, teachers' wages, etc.) are substantial. In OECD countries governments contribute about 87% to the direct costs of education (Netherlands: 93%). Average public spending on education in OECD countries is about 4.6% of GDP (Netherlands: 4.3%) (see OECD, 2003). Furthermore, outlays on education are among the most important public spending categories of most governments. Clearly, the government must have important motivations to subsidize education to this large extent.

13.2 Brief review of the literature

After some important early studies on taxation and human capital formation (Boskin, 1975; Heckman, 1976; Kotlikoff and Summers, 1979; Eaton and Rosen, 1980; Driffil and Rosen, 1983), theoretical interest remained somewhat slack for a decade or so until endogenous growth theories came to the fore. Endogenous growth theories attributed an important role to human capital in the process of economic growth (Lucas, 1988) or technological change (Romer, 1990). At the beginning of the 1990s the literature really boomed. (See, for example,

Milesi-Ferretti and Roubini (1998) for an overview of this literature and Jacobs (2002a) for more references.) Findings from the literature are somewhat extreme. On one side of the spectrum we have the analyses by Boskin (1975) and Heckman (1976). They argue that labour taxation is generally not important for human capital formation. On the other side of the spectrum, Trostel (1993) concludes: 'Thus the conclusion that taxation significantly discourages investment in human capital seems inescapable.' This may seem very odd, but there are five mechanisms which are relevant to understanding all the results in the literature: (1) tax progression, (2) endogenous leisure demand decisions, (3) non-deductible costs of education, (4) distortions in inputs invested in human capital, and (5) implicit subsidies deriving from capital income taxes.

First, more tax progression harms investments in human capital because the benefits of learning, i.e. increases in future wage incomes, are subject to higher taxes than the costs, i.e. forgone earnings, of learning, and vice versa. If the tax system is flat, future earnings are subject to the same rate of tax as forgone earnings, so that the labour tax does not distort the educational investment decision. In the real world one would expect this effect to be present because tax rates on forgone earnings while enrolled in college are typically lower than on future earnings.

Second, taxes may have an indirect effect on human capital formation through labour supply decisions. Taxation of labour incomes induces individuals to work less if the substitution effect in labour supply is dominant.[2] Consequently, at lower levels of labour supply, the utilization rate of acquired human capital falls, and the returns on human capital investments are reduced accordingly. Therefore, investments in human capital fall when taxes are increased.

Third, non-tax deductibility of resources invested in education also harms investments in human capital. Examples are: tuition costs, costs of books and computers, effort costs, etc. The intuition is that the returns of education are taxed whereas the costs are not deductible at the same rate. Hence, education is taxed on a net basis. If, however, resources invested in education are tax-deductible, all costs and benefits are taxed at the same rate so that the tax becomes non-distortionary. In the same way, the government may subsidize these resource costs.

Fourth, the tax system distorts the optimal composition of investments in human capital if the tax treatment of different inputs is different. For example, resources invested in education are not deductible, whereas the costs of time invested in education are deductible, since forgone earnings are taxed. Consequently, higher income taxes will make the costs of time invested in education smaller relative to the non-deductible inputs invested in education. Therefore, the optimal composition of inputs invested in education is distorted and individuals will invest too much time in education, and too little effort or direct resources, which are non-deductible. Thus, if the government subsidizes the time spent in education a lot, students will work less hard to finish in time.

Fifth, higher capital taxes increase investments in human capital since financial savings become less attractive relative to human savings. Three equivalent intuitions for this result can be given. First, the rate at which future earnings are discounted decreases so that the present value of the returns to investments in human capital increases. Consequently, investments in human capital increase. Second, a lower return on financial savings implies that the return on human savings should fall, since arbitrage between financial savings and human savings should hold in an optimizing framework. This can only be accomplished by investing more in human capital, since there are diminishing returns to investments in human capital. Third, effective borrowing costs to finance investments in human capital decrease when these costs are reduced by the capital tax and investments in human capital increase. In any case, a capital tax acts as an implicit subsidy on investments in human capital.

The existence of these five channels implies that taxes will have no effect on human capital accumulation except under special circumstances that are likely to be violated in practice: (i) labour taxes are flat; (ii) labour supply is not affected by labour taxation; (iii) direct costs of education are either absent or fully deductible; (iv) tax treatment of all inputs invested in human capital is equal, and (v) capital income taxes are absent. Consequently, it is hard to argue that taxes on labour and capital income have no effect on investment decisions in human capital, at least from a theoretical perspective. Finally, education subsidies are not very much discussed in the taxation literature, although these are the natural complements to taxes. Education subsidies encourage human capital formation and may therefore be used as an instrument to offset negative incentives on learning through the tax system.

Empirically, the impact of taxes depends on the elasticities of investments in human capital with respect to the taxes. Unfortunately, empirical work regarding the effects of taxes on human capital formation is extremely scarce. Structural models developed by Heckman et al. (1998) suggest that human capital investments can in principle react quite substantially to policy changes.[3] Also, Leuven and Oosterbeek (2005) find empirical evidence for the elasticity of training investments with respect to income taxes that are of the same magnitude as conventional labour supply elasticities. We also know that graduates respond to changes in tuition rates, forgone earnings and future earnings in their decision to enrol in education (see, for example, Leslie and Brinkman, 1987; Cameron and Heckman, 2001; Hilmer, 1998, and others). Since the taxes (subsidies) directly affect, for example, forgone earnings, future earnings and education costs, taxation is therefore of empirical importance.

The literature on the economics of education mainly discusses three arguments to subsidize education and skill formation: external effects, capital and insurance market failures, and merit or public good arguments. We discuss each of them below.

First, and often mentioned, large subsidies on education are justified on the basis of perceived externalities of education. Parents and students do not take into account that their investments in human capital may be of social value above the private return on education, so that they underinvest in human capital. If the government gives subsidies on education, it can internalize the externality.[4] The problem with the externalities argument is that it is empirically impossible to detect positive externalities from education, certainly at current levels of education: see, for example, Krueger and Lindahl (2002) and Ciccone and Peri (2006).

Second, subsidies on education may also restore incentives to invest in human capital if there is underinvestment in human capital due to failing capital and insurance markets. Human capital is generally regarded as illiquid and bad collateral: see also Friedman (1962). Individuals cannot sell a claim on their future earnings to banks. Therefore, they cannot use human capital as collateral. Consequently, in case individuals default on their loans, banks are not allowed to 'own' the human capital embodied in the individual, and banks cannot force the individual to do work for them so as to repay debts as a consequence. Legal restrictions, that is, non-slavery considerations, effectively block trade in (future) claims on human capital. For similar reasons, as credit markets fail, insurance of the income risks associated with investments in human capital is also impossible. Insurance of human capital risks would require a so-called 'state contingent claim' on future earnings: in good states (when lucky) the individual promises to pay a certain amount of income as an insurance premium to the insurance company, whereas in bad states (when unlucky) the individual receives compensation from the insurance company. Again, it is very difficult for the insurance company to force the individuals in the good states of nature to pay their premiums, when they have decided not to do so. Consequently, underinvestment is likely to occur due to capital and insurance market failures.

Furthermore, even if capital markets and insurance markets are present, they would probably not function very well due to asymmetric information between banks and borrowers and between insurance companies and the insured. If banks cannot assess the economic risks of their loan applicants, the high-risk borrowers may drive the low-risk borrowers out of the market, since the latter finance the costs of default through a premium on the interest rate. Consequently, adverse selection occurs and banks may even ration credit so as to keep the pool of loan applicants healthy (see Stiglitz and Weiss, 1981). Also income insurance is subject to problems with asymmetric information. The individuals with low risks of a low income may voluntarily underinsure themselves to avoid income redistribution to high-risk individuals. Again, adverse selection effects are important here. Also moral hazard may give rise to failures in capital and insurance markets. If banks and insurance companies cannot observe whether individuals exert enough effort to avoid default or an accident, costs of financing loans or the price of insurance increases, and underinvestment may result as well (see Arnott and Stiglitz, 1990).

Recently, some economists have begun to argue that capital market imperfections are not that important (see Carneiro and Heckman, 2003). The seemingly non-importance of capital market imperfections is highly controversial, however, and the empirical jury is still out. For example, Plug and Vijverberg (2005) find, after careful estimation, evidence for the importance of liquidity constraints in education choices.

Whether insurance markets fail to insure risks in human capital is a complicated empirical question. The average returns on human capital are in the range of the returns on equity. This could indeed reflect the large risk of investments in human capital. However, it is quite hard to believe that the returns on education are that high because of systematic macroeconomic shocks (like the returns on equity). Graduates typically suffer less from macroeconomic shocks, resulting in, for example, lower unemployment, sickness and disability rates, than non-graduates. As such, education serves as an insurance device against macroeconomic uncertainty and the risk premium for macroeconomic risk would be negative (see also Gould et al., 2000). Consequently, to justify the large returns on human capital, risks in human capital are probably individual risks, rather than macroeconomic risks which cannot be insured. Large returns could then indeed be evidence for the failing of the insurance market. However, the fact that individuals cannot insure themselves may also be the result of moral hazard problems in the insurance market. Hence, non-insurability of income risks may also reflect a rational market response. This is a version of the 'human capital premium puzzle' (see also Judd, 2000). Again, the jury is still out. Empirical research is extremely scarce and more research is certainly needed here, as is pointed out in chapter 8.

The third and final argument is that education is also often viewed as a merit or public good with intrinsic and non-monetary values such as promoting citizenship, contributing to culture, etc. To the extent that society values education, above the private valuations of education, there is an argument for subsidizing education. Also political mechanisms may explain why education is subsidized. In this research, we abstract from these issues.

13.3 Income redistribution and human capital

Income redistribution seems to have vanished totally from the literature on taxation and human capital formation, since none of the aforementioned studies considers redistributional concerns. Most analyses have been cast in the framework of the representative agent without distributional concerns.[5] The lack of attention to income distribution contrasts heavily with the more traditional analyses on taxation and labour supply that originated from the Nobel Prize-winning article by Mirrlees (1971). This can be considered a serious drawback. In our opinion, the ultimate reason for having distortionary taxes is to correct inequalities in income distribution, otherwise governments would use individualized lump-sum taxes (or, equivalently, Tinbergen's talent tax). Therefore, one could say that the scientific debate has turned its attention away from the ultimate reasons for having distortionary taxes.

A related issue is the distributional impact of education subsidies. Although education subsidies are generally justified to guarantee access to education for the students from poor backgrounds, one may doubt whether they are really that equitable, especially education subsidies to higher education. The incidence of education is highly unequal, since most of the students enrolled in higher education belong to the wealthiest socioeconomic classes. And, on average, students turn out to belong to the wealthiest income groups after graduation due to the high financial returns on human capital investments.

13.4 Our contribution to the international literature

13.4.1 The core question

In our research we take a typical public finance perspective. The central, normative question is how the government should design tax and education policies. 'First-best' (perfect markets, no information problems, no distributional issues, etc.) is generally not attainable. Therefore, second-best considerations become important and trade-offs between policy objectives appear, such as the trade-off between equity and efficiency. Crucial to our exposition is that income redistribution is the important justification for using distortionary tax instruments since we rule out individualized lump-sum taxes (or Tinbergen's talent tax). The ultimate reason is that the government cannot observe ability or earnings capacity, only earned income (see also Mirrlees, 1971; Stiglitz, 1982). Furthermore, we pay attention to the role of potentially important non-market distortions arising from imperfect capital and insurance markets.

Up to now, standard public finance has largely ignored human capital decisions and related issues such as the failing of financial markets. By adding human capital formation to the models of optimal income taxation and redistribution we attempt to fill this gap. In doing so, this research integrates the literature on education policy and public finance. Further, we show that second-best reasoning may actually explain some salient features of current policies that cannot be understood by relying on first-best arguments. For example, why do governments subsidize education whereas externalities cannot be found and capital market imperfections can be solved by means of loans? Why do many people believe that education subsidies (to higher education) are equitable whereas they appear to be completely perverse from a redistributional perspective? Why do governments levy positive capital income taxes whereas insights from public finance dictate that capital should not be taxed at all?

13.4.2 Optimal labour income taxation

How progressive should the income tax be? The answer to this question is one of the main questions in the optimal tax literature. The standard optimal taxation model with endogenous labour supply shows that there is a fundamental trade-off between achieving equality in after-tax incomes and efficiency in labour supply decisions. In the standard linear taxation model the government optimizes the combination of a flat marginal tax rate and a lump-sum transfer (or negative income tax). The income tax schedule is more progressive when the marginal tax rate is larger so as to allow for a larger lump-sum transfer. The optimal marginal tax rate increases with the desire to redistribute incomes which is, in turn, determined by social preferences. The optimal income tax decreases with the elasticity of labour supply because taxation erodes the tax base, and more so when labour supply is more elastic.

Once the optimal linear taxation model is extended with endogenous human capital formation, the elasticity of the tax base with respect to the marginal tax rate on labour income substantially increases (Bovenberg and Jacobs, 2001, 2005; Jacobs, 2002c, 2005). The reason is that not only is labour supply affected by taxation, but also human capital decisions. Labour supply and investments in human capital are complementary. The more labour is supplied, the higher will be the utilization rate of acquired human capital, and, therefore, the larger will be the return to investments in human capital. Therefore, welfare costs of marginal taxes increase when human capital formation is endogenous. The optimal linear tax rate is reduced, which is in accordance with standard Ramsey intuitions: lower taxes when the tax base becomes more elastic. Numerical evidence in Jacobs (2005) shows that reductions in optimal taxes are indeed substantial when endogenous human capital formation is taken into account.

The linear taxation model is a convenient vehicle to understand the main trade-off between equity and efficiency. But in real life tax schedules are generally differentiated and not flat. Bovenberg and Jacobs (2005) generalize the optimal linear tax results to a pure non-linear income tax in the spirit of Mirrlees (1971). They also allow for imperfect substitution between tax-deductible inputs (like forgone earnings) and non-tax-deductible inputs (effort costs and direct costs) in the production of human capital. Taxes will then not only reduce the level of investment in human capital, but will also distort the optimal composition of investments in human capital. In particular, a higher income tax gives incentives to substitute the non-tax-deductible investments for tax-deductible investments in human capital. Thus a more progressive income tax may reduce the individual's efforts in learning, and increase the number of years spent in education. Consequently, the welfare costs of the income tax increase if substitution between various inputs in skill formation is easier. Bovenberg and Jacobs (2003) show that, in a dynamic setting, the tax progression effects will give rise to another tax distortion. Individuals creep up to higher tax brackets when they become more educated. Therefore, the marginal benefits of education are taxed at higher rates than the costs in the form of (taxed) forgone earnings. As a result, welfare costs of labour taxation increase and optimal marginal taxes should be lowered accordingly.

13.4.3 *Optimal labour income taxation and market failures*

When borrowing is impossible, (poor) individuals are prevented from investing optimally in human capital. Jacobs (2002c) shows – using the linear income tax model – that the optimal tax on labour is progressive from a pure efficiency point of view, i.e. in the absence of distributional concerns. A progressive tax schedule redistributes incomes from the old (or the rich parents) to the young (or their poor parents) so that the liquidity constraints for the young are relaxed. At the optimum the government strikes a balance between, on the one hand, reducing the adverse consequences of capital market failures, and, on the other hand, reducing investments in human capital as a consequence of higher marginal tax rates. Numerical simulations show that optimal taxes substantially increase due to capital market failures even if credit constraints are binding for only 25% of the population. Therefore, the presence of capital market imperfections substantially lowers the welfare costs of progressive income taxes.

If individuals cannot insure the risks in their future incomes, there will be underinvestment in human capital if individuals are risk averse. Also a progressive income tax is optimal from a pure efficiency point of view (Jacobs and Van Wijnbergen, 2005). The reason is that a redistributive graduate tax mimics income insurance by redistributing incomes from lucky to unlucky graduates. Future income risks are insured and underinvestment in human capital is mitigated. Thus we confirm earlier theoretical findings by Eaton and Rosen (1980) to a setting where we explicitly modelled the underlying sources of the insurance market imperfection resulting in underinvestment and adverse selection. Again, welfare losses of progressive income taxes are mitigated when non-insurable income risks are present.

13.4.4 Optimal labour and capital income taxation

There is a general consensus in the public finance literature that capital incomes should not be taxed under quite general conditions.[6] Nevertheless, capital income taxes are part of virtually any existing tax system. Theoretical predictions on the optimality of zero capital income taxes are therefore not met in practice. By allowing for the interaction between human and financial capital formation, Bovenberg and Jacobs (2001) and Jacobs and Bovenberg (2005) show that the optimal capital income tax is indeed positive, rather than zero. The reason for this result is that the capital income tax reduces the tax distortions on human capital formation arising from the labour income tax. By taxing capital incomes the government reduces the incentives to save too much in financial form and individuals substitute towards savings in human form. The capital tax should be used especially if distortions in the lifetime financial saving decisions are small. However, if these distortions are large, then the capital tax loses its benefits in boosting learning, since the welfare costs of employing the instrument increase. A trade-off emerges between distorting the labour market and the acquisition of human capital, on the one hand, and distorting the capital market, on the other hand. The more important labour market distortions become, the more the government relies on capital taxes to stimulate investment in human capital, rather than burdening employment prospects. Similarly, the more distortionary the labour tax with respect to investments in human capital, the higher the optimal capital income tax. We show numerically that a synthetic income tax where capital and labour incomes are taxed at equal marginal rates appears to be roughly optimal. This result contrasts with the conventional wisdom in public finance but can explain why capital income taxes are so commonly observed.

13.4.5 Optimal labour and capital income taxation and optimal education policies

First-best arguments cannot explain the commonly observed practice of progressive income taxes and education subsidies. Redistributive governments would abstain from giving regressive education subsidies which increase the need to redistribute income through the tax system. Moreover, education subsidies need to be financed by raising distorting income taxes. In the absence of externalities or other reasons to subsidize education, this would be inefficient as well. Consequently, societies would be better off in terms of equity and economic efficiency by simultaneously lowering education subsidies and income taxes. Why, then, do virtually all governments both give regressive subsidies to education and levy progressive income taxes?

If first-best arguments, such as capital market failures and externalities, cannot justify large education subsidies, we show that substantially positive education subsidies are typically an ingredient of the optimal tax system. The reason is that education subsidies are able to offset distortions on human capital decisions caused by the tax system. If all learning efforts can be perfectly observed, and therefore subsidized, subsidies can ensure that learning decisions are efficient and not distorted by income taxes. The efficiency losses of more progressive income taxation are lowered if education subsidies are allowed for. Therefore, the optimal labour tax is more progressive with education subsidies. Education subsidies therefore allow the government to better approach the ideal individualized lump sum or talent taxes (Plug et al., 1999). Even though education subsidies are regressive, the combination of progressive taxes and education subsidies yields more equality since non-observed ability rents are effectively taxed at higher rates. Hence, education subsidies and redistribution of incomes are Siamese twins. The more the government wishes to redistribute incomes, the larger education subsidies are even if they are regressive. Numerical calculations reveal that tax distortions may go a long way towards explaining the current level of education subsidies.[7] The second-best interactions between redistributive income taxes and education policies can therefore provide a solid reason why governments should subsidize education even if first-best arguments are not relevant.

The argument holds for linear as well as for non-linear tax schedules. Marginal taxes are generally highest at the bottom of the skill distribution due to the presence of the poverty trap. Poor individuals face high marginal tax burdens because poverty programmes are phased out as individuals start to earn higher incomes. As a result, individuals lose their eligibility to tax credits, rent assistance, health care costs, exemptions from local taxes, and so on. We show that education subsidies should therefore be highest for the individuals who face the highest marginal tax rates on their incomes. We do not need to resort to paternalism, externalities or merit motives to justify high education subsidies for primary and secondary education. We only need redistributional motives (Bovenberg and Jacobs, 2003, 2005). Individuals are less likely to get stuck in the poverty trap when governments combine poverty reduction with education policies that keep individuals out of poverty.

If education subsidies are available to offset tax distortions on human capital formation, governments do not rely on alternative tax instruments to boost learning, such as taxes on unskilled labour, or on taxes on capital to reduce tax distortions on investments in human capital. In contrast to education subsidies, the latter instruments cause distortions in labour and capital markets. So the government can do better by employing education subsidies that avoid these distortions (Bovenberg and Jacobs, 2001, 2003; Jacobs and Bovenberg, 2005).

If not all educational efforts can be observed, however, education subsidies can be given only on observed inputs in human capital formation (notably years spent in education). Thus, education subsidies will tend to distort optimal investments in human capital away from non-subsidized to subsidized inputs in human capital formation. For example, students may put less effort (non-observed investment) and more time (subsidized investments) in human capital formation if the government subsidizes time invested in education a lot. Thus, education subsidies lose their power as an instrument to offset tax distortions on human capital formation if substitution between various inputs in human capital formation is easier (Bovenberg and Jacobs, 2005). If not all educational efforts can be observed, the case for taxes on capital incomes is not lost (Jacobs and Bovenberg, 2005). The capital tax will then be an instrument to boost investments in human capital as well, and the synthetic income tax remains approximately optimal.

13.4.6 Optimal financing of education

Many people hold firm beliefs that the government should subsidize (higher) education to guarantee universal access, especially for students from lower socioeconomic backgrounds. However, it is debated whether subsidies are really the most efficient instruments if accessibility problems originate from failures in financial markets. A priori it seems to be more efficient to tackle failures in financial markets directly by making sufficient resources available to students through income-contingent loans or a graduate tax instead of giving large tax-financed subsidies which end up in the pockets of the affluent. For these reasons, Australia introduced income-contingent loans in the 1990s (the Higher Education Contribution Scheme) and students now pay over one-third of the real costs of education themselves. Prime Minister Tony Blair introduced income-contingent loans in the UK, although he almost stumbled over his plans. Also, the Dutch government has now introduced income-contingent loans. The insights from our research have contributed to this policy change to a significant extent.

From a theoretical perspective we show that an equity-participation model implemented by the government does indeed tackle both the capital and insurance market imperfections arising from adverse selection and the impossibility of trading income-contingent contracts (Jacobs and Van Wijnbergen, 2005). Further, income risks can be pooled by the government, so that it can recoup the losses it makes on the unlucky graduates through higher 'dividend payments' from the lucky graduates. Hence the government does not need subsidies to overcome liquidity constraints and combat risk aversion.

Education subsidies are not an efficient instrument to restore inefficiencies caused by capital and insurance market failures. First, education subsidies allocate resources to individuals who are not credit-constrained. Moreover, most students are not credit-constrained in a lifecycle sense, since the returns to education are high, and students are generally better off than the average taxpayer. Further, education subsidies are not effective at all in reducing income risks; consequently most of the subsidies will be directed towards students with relatively safe earnings prospects. Since education subsidies have to be financed from general tax revenues, these deadweight losses are costly because government revenues can only be obtained through distortionary taxes.

An equity participation scheme features no subsidies, and thereby avoids the efficiency costs of distortionary taxes to finance subsidies. Under an equity participation scheme, the government buys shares in students' human capital by funding the costs of their education and obtaining a claim on the future returns of education. In other words, graduates repay a part of their incomes as dividend to the government. Moreover, an equity participation scheme can be defended on equity grounds as well. The majority of students come from the wealthiest classes and will belong to the most wealthiest classes after graduation. Equity participation avoids perverse redistribution of incomes from the average taxpayer to students.

Equity participation can be implemented through a graduate tax. Under a graduate tax, the dividend payout is incorporated into the income tax system. Under a pure equity-financing regime, there is no individual link between the size of equity stake and the dividend payouts to the government. An income-contingent loan scheme is a combination of equity and debt financing of higher education. It may be desirable to introduce some element of debt financing in order to give students sufficient incentives to study hard and work hard after graduation. Moral hazard problems under 100% equity financing are reduced by restoring the individual link between repayments and funds received to study.

Jacobs (2002b) illustrates the theory for the Netherlands. He studied the switch from a system with mainly subsidies to education to a system where graduates pay part of the costs of education through a graduate tax (GT) or an income-contingent loan system (ICL). Substantial reductions in government outlays can be achieved. The costs of protecting students from lower socioeconomic groups can be substantially lowered without erecting barriers to students from these groups. The reason is twofold. First, no subsidies are directed towards graduates who have sufficiently high incomes over the lifecycle to finance the costs themselves. Second, no external subsidies to cover the default risks from those with insufficient incomes are needed if the risks of default on loans are pooled amongst graduates. If, however, the costs of default are not shared amongst graduates, but financed from general tax revenue, the savings on government outlays are less, since ex ante subsidies to every student are replaced by ex post subsidies to the graduates who default.

13.5 Directions for future research

Although this research project has given some important and policy-relevant insights, loose ends still remain. In the following we discuss some issues which seem to be interesting for future research.

Dynamic aspects and the intergenerational distribution of welfare

We have only studied the intragenerational distribution of welfare. However, as Heckman et al. (1998) and Heckman (2000) have pointed out, learning and human capital formation are by their very nature activities taking place over the entire lifecycle. In order to get a better understanding of the effects on tax and education policies it is only a natural extension of this research to look at the intergenerational distribution of welfare as well, in a multi-period model with human capital formation. An important further extension is to add formation of human capital within the family (cf. chapter 6). Most analyses have generally neglected intergenerational transfers of human capital. Heckman (2000) forcefully argues that these intergenerational effects are important ingredients for incentives to acquire skill over the life-cycle ('skill-begets-skill' and 'learning-begets-learning'); see also chapter 9. Another important extension in this respect is a more elaborate analysis of the role of credit constraints. Parents may also respond to credit constraints through savings and bequests. As a result, (means-tested) subsidies on education and capital income taxes may distort parental incentives to save for their children's education.

General equilibrium effects

We have assumed perfect substitutability of individuals' factor supplies. Wage differentials then only reflect differences in units of human capital and not intrinsic differences between the types of skills. Clearly, this is not the case in the real world. A skilled worker is not equal to twice an unskilled worker. Empirically, general equilibrium effects on wages are important (see, for example, Hartog et al., 1993; Leuven et al., 2004; Jacobs, 2004). Recently, Dur and Teulings (2001) have argued that education subsidies can be used to provoke general equilibrium effects on wages. By subsidizing human capital formation, the supply of skilled workers increases and wage inequality between skilled and unskilled workers diminishes, because skilled workers become less scarce. As such, the government may want to subsidize education to reduce inequality. Nevertheless, the jury is still out on whether this mechanism is indeed robust. Saez (2003) has – in contrast – argued that the government should refrain from exploiting general equilibrium effects to achieve a more equal distribution of incomes by resorting to the Diamond and Mirrlees (1971) production efficiency theorem which suggests that subsidies/taxes on intermediate goods, like different types of labour, should optimally be avoided. Therefore, for future research it is interesting to explore the optimal taxation of labour incomes and optimal education policies in the presence of general equilibrium effects on wages.

Moral hazard and the optimal financing of education

In our analysis of optimal financing of education in the presence of capital and insurance market imperfections we have abstracted from problems with moral hazard in the financing of education. We expect that the presence of moral hazard may give rise to a weaker case for equity financing of education, and combinations of debt and equity will probably be optimal. This may point to a stronger case for income-contingent loans since this financing system contains both debt and equity elements. Therefore, more research is needed where moral hazard is introduced in models of optimal educational financing.

Time consistency of optimal policies

Individuals may anticipate that the government may change its behaviour after announcing a set of policies. The setting of second-best policies is not credible if the government cannot pre-commit to the announced policies, such as the setting of the tax (see, for example, Andersson and Konrad, 2003). In the case of setting the optimal tax, a hold-up problem emerges: people know that the government engages in excessive taxation after the investments in human capital have been made. Based on this expectation of government intervention, people reduce investments in human capital. The government should take this behavioural response into account when setting optimal taxes. Due to the time-inconsistency of its policies the optimal tax structure has become 'third-best'. The government can (partly) escape this problem by means of education subsidies. This may be an additional explanation for the use of education subsidies. More research may shed light on the presumed optimality of education subsidies under time-inconsistent government policies.

Human capital equity premium puzzle

Although we think that risk-aversion is very important for graduates, it could be that risk-aversion arguments may not be sufficient in explaining a real rate of return to human capital in the order of 8–9%. Empirical work is largely lacking on the causes of the high return on human capital and the effects of risk on investments in human capital (see also chapter 8). From the equity premium literature we know that conventional rates of risk-aversion are not able to produce a risk premium of 4–5%. Moreover, education is arguably less liquid than equity and options in human capital may be important, since one cannot sell a piece of human capital. That is, investments in human capital are to a large extent irreversible. Maybe the illiquidity of human capital can explain why students borrow so little. Clearly, future research should shed more light on this topic. Moreover, these issues have large practical and policy implications. For example, is there underinvestment in education and should education be subsidized more in light of the high return on human capital investments? Or are students borrowing so little for solid, rational reasons?

Notes

1. I thank Casper van Ewijk, Lans Bovenberg and Hessel Oosterbeek for their comments. Further, I thank Joop Hartog for his extremely constructive advice and suggestions, both literary and economic. Finally, I am very grateful to Henriëtte Maassen van den Brink for her support and continuous efforts to keep me in the SCHOLAR research group. This chapter is based on the introductory and concluding chapters of Jacobs (2002a).
2. This seems to be the case empirically: see Blundell and MaCurdy (1999).

3. Policy effects might, however, be countered by changes in the economic environment, such as changes in the wages due to changes in the supply of skills. These are so-called general equilibrium effects.
4. This presumes that the subsidy can be financed in lump-sum fashion, otherwise a trade-off would appear between internalizing the externalities and distorting economic incentives with taxes to finance the subsidy.
5. There are some older papers in the spirit of Mirrlees (1971) on optimal taxation and education (see, for example, Ulph, 1977; Hare and Ulph, 1979), but they all have in common that the tax system does not affect educational choices.
6. See, for example, the excellent overview by Bernheim (2002).
7. This finding implies that education decisions should be efficient if possible, even if the government wants to redistribute incomes. Tobin (1970) has argued that education policy could be useful to 'limit the domain of income inequality'. However, this research has shown that this argument is incorrect, for both efficiency and equity reasons. To 'limit the domain of inequality' is equivalent to tax education on a net basis, especially at the top end of the income distribution. We admit, though, that Tobin only considered elementary and secondary education. We show that education should be subsidized, not taxed, in the presence of a redistributive tax scheme to offset the distortions on learning, and, if possible, maintain total efficiency in human capital investments.

References

Andersson, Fredrik and Kai A. Konrad (2003). Human capital investment and globalization in extortionary states. *Journal of Public Economics*, 87 (7–8): 1539–55.

Arnott, Richard and Joseph E. Stiglitz (1990). The welfare economics of moral hazard. NBER Working Paper 3316, Boston.

Bernheim, B. Douglas (2002). Taxation and saving, in Alan J. Auerbach and Martin Feldstein (eds.), *Handbook of Public Economics*, vol. III. Amsterdam: North-Holland, chapter 18.

Blundell, Richard and Thomas MaCurdy (1999). Labour supply, in Orley Ashenfelter and David Card (eds.), *Handbook of Labour Economics*. vol. IIIA. Amsterdam: North-Holland, pp. 1586–1607.

Boskin, Michael (1975). Notes on the tax treatment of human capital. NBER Working Paper 116, Boston.

Bovenberg, A. Lans and Bas Jacobs (2001). Redistribution and education subsidies are Siamese twins. CEPR Discussion Paper Series 3309, London.

(2003). On the optimal distribution of education and income. Mimeo: University of Amsterdam/Tilburg.

(2005). Redistribution and education subsidies are Siamese twins. *Journal of Public Economics*, 89: 2005–35.

Cameron, Stephen and James J. Heckman (2001). The dynamics of educational attainment for Black, Hispanic, and White males. *Journal of Political Economy*, 109: 455–99.

Carneiro, Pedro M. and James J. Heckman (2003). Human capital policy, in James J. Heckman and Alan B. Krueger (eds.), *Inequality in America: What Role for Human Capital Policies?* Cambridge, MA: MIT Press.

Ciccone, Antonio and Giovanni Peri (2006). Identifying human capital externalities: theory with an application to US cities. *Review of Economic Studies*, 73: 381–412.

Diamond, Peter A. and James A. Mirrlees (1971). Optimal taxation and public production I: production efficiency. *American Economic Review*, 61: 8–27.

Driffil, E. John and Harvey S. Rosen (1983). Taxation and excess burden: a life cycle perspective. *International Economic Review*, 3: 671–83.

Dur, Robert and Coen N. Teulings (2001). Education and efficient redistribution. Tinbergen Institute Discussion Paper 090/3, Amsterdam.

Eaton, Jonathan and Harvey S. Rosen (1980). Taxation, human capital and uncertainty. *American Economic Review*, 70 (4): 705–15.

Friedman, Milton (1962). *Capitalism and Freedom*. Chicago: University of Chicago Press.

Gould, Eric D., Omer Moav and Bruce A. Weinberg (2000). Precautionary demand for education, inequality, and technological progress. *Journal of Economic Growth*, 6 (4): 285–316.

Hare, Paul G. and David T. Ulph (1979). On education and distribution. *Journal of Political Economy*, 87: S193–S212.

Hartog, Joop, Hessel Oosterbeek and Coen N. Teulings (1993). Age, wage, and education in the Netherlands, in P. Johnson and K. Zimmerman (eds.), *Labour Markets in an Aging Europe*. Cambridge: Cambridge University Press.

Heckman, James J. (1976). A life-cycle model of earnings, learning and consumption. *Journal of Political Economy*, 84: S11–S44.

(2000). Policies to foster human capital. *Research in Economics*, 54: 3–56.

Heckman, James J., Lance Lochner and Christopher Taber (1998). Explaining rising wage inequality: explorations with a dynamic general equilibrium model of labour earnings with heterogeneous agents. *Review of Economic Dynamics*, 1: 1–58.

Hilmer, Michael J. (1998). Post-secondary fees and the decision to attend a university or a community college. *Journal of Public Economics*, 67: 329–48.

Jacobs, Bas (2002a). Public Finance and Human Capital. PhD thesis, University of Amsterdam.

(2002b). An investigation of education finance reform: income contingent loans and graduate taxes in the Netherlands. CPB Discussion Paper 9, CPB Netherlands Bureau for Economic Policy Analysis, The Hague.

(2002c). Optimal taxation of human capital and credit constraints. Tinbergen Institute Discussion Paper 2002.044/2, Amsterdam.

(2004). The lost race between schooling and technology. *De Economist*, 152 (1): 47–78.

(2005). Optimal income taxation with endogenous human capital. *Journal of Public Economic Theory*, 7 (2): 295–316.

Jacobs, Bas and A. Lans Bovenberg (2005). Human capital and optimal positive taxation of capital income. CEPR Discussion Paper Series 5047, London.

Jacobs, Bas and Sweder J. G. van Wijnbergen (2005). Capital market failure, adverse selection and optimal financing of higher education. Tinbergen Institute Discussion Paper 05–036/3, Amsterdam.

Judd, Kenneth L. (2000). Is education as good as gold? Mimeo, Hoover Institute.

Leslie, Larry L. and Paul T. Brinkman (1987). Student price response in higher education: the student demand studies. *Journal of Higher Education*, 58 (2): 181–204.

Kotlikoff, Laurence J. and Lawrence H. Summers (1979). Tax incidence in a life cycle model with variable labour supply. *Quarterly Journal of Economics*, 93: 705–18.

Krueger, Alan B. and Mikael Lindahl (2002). Education and growth: why and for whom? *Journal of Economic Literature*, 39, (4): 1101–36.

Leuven, Edwin and Hessel Oosterbeek (2005). The effect of tax-deductibility on human capital investment: direct evidence from a panel of individual tax returns. Mimeo, University of Amsterdam.

Leuven, Edwin, Hessel Oosterbeek and Hans van Ophem (2004). Explaining international differences in male wage inequality by differences in demand and supply of skill. *Economic Journal*, 144: 478–98.

Lucas, Robert E. Jr. (1988). On the mechanics of economic development. *Journal of Monetary Economics*, 22: 3–42.

Milesi-Ferretti, Gian Maria and Nouriel Roubini (1998). On the taxation of human and physical capital in models of endogenous growth. *Journal of Public Economics*, 70: 237–54.

Mirrlees, James A. (1971). An exploration in the theory of optimum income taxation. *Review of Economic Studies*, 38: 175–208.

OECD (2003). *Education at a Glance*. Paris: OECD.

(2005). *OECD Economic Outlook*, 77. Paris: OECD.

Plug, Erik J. S. and Wim Vijverberg (2005). Does family income matter for schooling outcomes? Using adoption as a natural experiment. *Economic Journal*, 115 (506): 880–907.

Plug, Erik J. S., Joop Hartog and Bernard M. S. van Praag (1999). If we knew ability, how would we tax individuals? *Journal of Public Economics*, 72: 183–211.

Romer, Paul M. (1990). Endogenous technical change. *Journal of Political Economy*, 98: S71–S102.

Saez, Emmanuel (2003). Direct or indirect instruments for redistribution: short-run versus long-run. *Journal of Public Economics*, 88: 503–18.

Stiglitz, Joseph E. and Andrew Weiss (1981). Credit rationing in markets with imperfect information. *American Economic Review*, 71 (3): 393–410.

Tobin, James (1970). On limiting the domain of inequality. *Journal of Law and Economics*, 13 (2): 263–77.

Trostel, Philip A. (1993). The effect of taxation on human capital. *Journal of Political Economy*, 101: 327–50.

Ulph, David T. (1977). On the optimal distribution of income and educational expenditure. *Journal of Public Economics*, 8: 341–56.

Epilogue: some reflections on educational policies

R OUGHLY speaking, some 20% of all government spending in western countries is on education. Western countries are increasingly aware that a well-educated labour force is essential for maintaining standards of living and to compete in global markets. Within the EU, the Lisbon Declaration, with its emphasis on education and training, has become a mantra for politicians and policy-makers. Can they learn something from this book?

As we have documented extensively, education has substantial returns, both privately and socially. The cross-section average returns to a year of education are, internationally, between 5 and 15%. Even in a job that does not fully utilize an individual's education, with returns lower than in the perfect match, they are still substantial. Moreover, mismatches are often temporary and seldom last for an entire working life. The return to education for entrepreneurs, rarely estimated before, is in the high end of the interval, at an average of approximately 14%. Investments in education are important for maintaining one's health. Indicative calculations suggest that these effects are substantial, bringing an additional benefit of 15–60% of the wage return to education. Even offspring benefit, as more educated parents have more successful children.

We have shown good reasons to doubt that the routinely estimated returns to schooling are truly causal effects for an average individual. They are usually measured in a cross-section of different cohorts of individuals, instead of during an individual's working life. Other factors, such as motivation and ability, play a role. And there is self-selection by individuals who decide on schooling or not on the basis of expected benefits. Research has not yet produced robust easy-to-summarize conclusions on direction and magnitude of the bias that results from these factors. We are quite confident that the true return to education is still substantial. Empirical research that allows for individual variation in returns shows that returns are seldom negative, and the same holds for simulations based on realistic parameter values.

However, one cannot bluntly conclude from high estimated returns to post-compulsory education that the government should invest, or invest more, in education. The classical motivations for government interventions are market failure and concern for the distribution of welfare among citizens. Market failure would be manifest in external effects, i.e. benefits from education that do not accrue to the investor and that would lead to underinvestment. We have shown that the case for external effects is weak, and cannot be a basis for government intervention. Market failure in training is also far less likely than has often been assumed. High measured returns to on-the-job training appear sometimes due to selection effects, where the differences in productivity between participants and non-participants are mistakenly viewed as the effects of the training. Controlling for selectivity reduces the returns to training to normal levels and thus undermines the argument that high returns signal underinvestment in training that should be cured by government stimuli. Moreover, there is experimental evidence that the hold-up problem (underinvestment in training because benefits from a joint investment will be robbed by the other party) is less serious than orthodox theory suggests: it is effectively countered by reciprocity and norms of fairness.

Capital markets may fail, and individuals may be unable to finance their education. If so, the government may step in and act as a banker. But note that this would motivate a system of loans rather than grants. The argument for capital market intervention is interwoven with distributional concerns, as richer families will have no problem financing their offspring's education. Indeed, distributional concerns may be the prime argument on which to base government subsidies for education. There is evidence that wages compensate for the risk associated with an education, but this compensation may be too low for children in poor households, which suggests that the government may share the risk, by a loan system where redemption is conditional on labour market success.

A general policy lesson from this book is thus that market failure and external effects are generally insufficient reasons for government subsidies to education. The taste for equity may be a much more convincing argument for interventions. Indeed, the conclusion is that interventions for young children from disadvantaged families to attend school at a younger age have clearly beneficial effects.

While this conclusion calls for a critical attitude towards the broad and sweeping calls for government interventions, there is also good reason for critical assessment of specific interventions. With government intervention as a fact of life, one may require that these interventions by themselves are cost-effective. This seems to be an obvious and trivial statement, but in practice this is not so. Scrutiny of actual policies can suggest important improvements.

This book contains two examples. Teachers' salaries and working conditions are important in attracting a sufficient supply of high-quality teachers, and in the specific situation of the Netherlands a premium to stimulate working full-time rather than part-time is a much cheaper method for reducing shortages in the supply of teachers than a general increase in all teachers' wages. The second example concerns actions to prevent the loss of skills because of unemployment. Active labour market policies such as re-employment bonuses or punitive benefit reductions for not accepting job offers could be very effective.

The studies in this book have emphasized that the key issue in policy assessment is the identification of the counterfactual: what would have happened in the absence of the actual policy, or under an alternative policy. This may be formulated as a second general conclusion: in policy evaluation studies one should always critically assess the presumed counterfactual. Different approaches may lead to dramatically different conclusions. If one is seriously interested in the effects of policies, one should search for possibilities to create a good counterfactual. Often this can be accomplished by an experimental design where subjects cannot freely decide on their participation in a programme. This is a plea to policy-makers to allow for a careful evidence-based strategy in implementing new policies. Immediate full implementation for the entire target population will make assessment very difficult. Initial stages allowing proper distinction between treatment and control groups can generate essential information on the effectiveness of the massive spending that is often involved. Sometimes, the distinction is given accidentally, as with an age limit for subsidies in cases where one may trust that the populations around the limit are essentially identical. But much can be gained if testing the effect is a strategic element in the design of a policy.

A note on econometrics

Methodological concerns, on the proper estimation of parameters of interest, are prominent in many chapters of this book. Full details on these issues are given in textbooks, such as the widely used *Econometric Analysis of Cross-section and Panel Data*, by Jeffrey Wooldridge (Cambridge, MA: MIT Press, 2002), or in 'Empirical strategies in labor economics', by Joshua Angrist and Alan Krueger, chapter 23 of *The Handbook of Labor Economics*, ed. Orley Ashenfelter and David Card (Amsterdam: North-Holland, 1999). Here, we just set out and define some core concepts.

If we estimate the parameters of an econometric model, we want a method to yield consistent parameter estimates, that is, estimates that converge to the true population value if the sample size goes to infinity. The common method of estimating the parameters in a regression model is the method of ordinary least squares (OLS). With qualitative data or ordinal variables ordered probit regression is an adequate technique. OLS or ordered probit regression only generate consistent parameter estimates if certain conditions are met. A key condition is exogeneity of the regressors: regressors and error term are independent. The assumption of exogeneity will generally not hold in three situations: omitted variables, measurement error and simultaneity. An omitted variable will be subsumed in the error term and cause problems if it is correlated with a regressor. For example, in an earnings equation containing the individual's education as a regressor, individual ability may not be observed, while it will most certainly be correlated with attained education. There may be measurement error in the dependent variable (such as an individual's wage rate) or in the regressor (such as years of working experience). Measurement errors can lead to inconsistent parameter estimates if they are correlated with a regressor, such as when the measurement error in wages is related to education, or when the measurement accuracy in years of experience is related to the true length of experience. Simultaneity occurs when at least one

236

explanatory variable is determined simultaneously with the dependent variable. An obvious case is an earnings function that includes education, employment status (employee or self-employed) or participation in a government training programme as explanatory variable: education, employment status and participation will be determined in part by the wage effect they generate. These are examples of *selectivity or self-selection*: individuals are selected into particular values of the explanatory variables with an eye on the effect on earnings, by their own motivation or by programme administrators. Generally, the errors in the equation that determines the explanatory variable (the selection equation) and the errors in the equation of interest (the earnings equation) will be correlated. This violates the assumption of exogeneity: error term and explanatory variables are correlated and inconsistent parameter estimates result.

Instrumental variable estimation (IV) is a method to deal with the problem of endogeneity (absence of exogeneity). Suppose we want to estimate an equation that has several exogenous explanatory variables and one endogenous variable. We then look for an instrument for the endogenous variable. An instrumental variable or instrument has to satisfy two conditions. The instrument must be uncorrelated with the error term in the equation that we want to estimate. And the instrument must be correlated with the endogenous variable after the effect of the other (exogenous) variables has been taken into account. Essentially, the method works because we observe a change in the dependent variable that is triggered by an exogenous change in the instrument, while the instrument can have its impact through only one channel: its effect on our explanatory variable of interest. The challenge of applying the method is finding a good instrument, i.e. a variable that satisfies both conditions. Sometimes one may find an instrument from a *natural experiment*: a situation where an otherwise endogenous variable, unintentionally, varies exogenously. One example is quarter of birth as an instrument for education in an earnings equation. Quarter of birth has no direct influence on earnings, but it will be correlated with education if there is compulsory education up to a particular age: quarter of birth determines when a child starts school and compulsory school regulation determines when it ends for children who no longer want education. Results of IV estimation are very sensitive to the quality of the instruments. Another way to deal with endogeneity is to set up an experiment where individuals are randomly assigned values of the explanatory variables.

Index

Aakvik, A. 12
Abbring, J. H. 176, 178, 181, 182
Abraham, K. G. 45
Acemoglu, D. 32, 33, 68
adoption studies, successful parents as
    secret to success 90, 92–3
adverse selection 216
age
    effect of tax deduction of training
        costs on training participation
        of older workers 160–1
    overeducation and 102
    relation between health and
        education and 68, 73–4
alcohol 67
Alessie, R. 31
allocative efficiency 69
Altonji, J. G. 45
Amsterdam, University of 1
Angrist, J. 10, 11, 32, 33, 158, 164
Antonovics, Kate 90
Ashenfelter, O. 11, 15, 16
asymmetrical information 216
Australia, education
    financing 224
    private rate of return 10
    stimulation of teachers to enhance
        quality 191–2, 196, 197,
        198, 200

Bajdechi, S. 18, 137, 138, 139
Baker, R. 76
Ballou, D. 190
Barro, R. J. 24, 26, 29
Barron, J. 42
Bartel, A. 46
Becker, Gary 1, 23, 39, 40, 69
Behrman, Jere 90
Belzil, C. 136
Benhabib, J. 27

Berger, M. C. 180
Berkhout, P. 176
Björklund, Anders 90
Black, D. A. 180
Black, Sandra 91
Blau, F. 15
Blundell, R. 46
Boskin, Michael 213
Bound, J. 76
Bovenberg, A. Lans 220, 221
Brown, J. N. 38
Büchel, F. 102
business cycle, unemployment in
    175–7

Canada, private rate of return on
    education 14
capital markets 216, 234
capital taxation 214, 221–4
Card, D. 60
causality, relation between health and
    education 67–70, 71, 73, 75
Chevalier, Arnaud 91
children
    divorce and 156
    education levels of parents and health
        of children 70, 71, 72, 74, 75
    successful parents as secret to success
        81–2, 92–4
    estimation of family background
        effects 82–7
    family income and 88–9
    gender of parent and 85, 87,
        89–92, 93–4
    importance of inherited abilities
        87–8
    meaning of results of study 87–8
Chile, private rate of return on
    education 14
Ciccone, A. 33

class *see* socioeconomic status
class sizes in schools 155–6, 158
Cohen, D. 29
competitive theory, returns on training
and 39–40
compulsory education
private rate of return on 11, 12
social rate of return on 32, 33
successful parents as secret to success
and 91
contracts, labour market 113–14
counselling 184–5
counterfactuals 235
private rate of return on education
10–11
cumulative risk 68
Cunha, F. 146
Czech Republic, private rate of return
on education 14

damages 127
data quality issues 2
de la Fuente, A. 29, 33
deferred compensation 194
Denmark, risk compensation in wages
143, 144, 146
depreciation of human capital,
prevention policies 170–3,
185, 235
empirical results from policy
evaluation 182–5
estimation of impact
177–82
developing countries, returns on
education
private rate 8
social rate 21
Devereux, Paul 91
Diamond, Peter A. 227
Diaz Serrano, L. 137
divorce 156
Dixit, A. 191
Dolton, P. 185
Doménech, R. 29
Dominitz, J. 135, 146
Duncan, J. 101, 108

earnings/wages
education and 7, 17–19, 156
basic schooling model 7–9

contributions to international
literature 13–17
earnings variance by education
137–8
recent developments 10–13
risk compensation in wages 140–4
family income and successful parents
as secret to success 88–9, 93
income redistribution 217–18
income taxation 213, 214, 219–24
job search framework and 174
overeducation and 102
returns on training 38–9, 48
estimation issues 42–5
international literature 46–7
measurement of training 40–2
summary of literature 45–6
theory on 39–40
risk compensation in wages 140–4
stimulation of teachers to enhance
quality 189, 206–9, 235
full-time premium 203–6, 207–8
international comparisons 194–203
review of literature 190–3
work–life incentives 194
underinvestment in training study
117, 118–19
Eaton, J. 135, 221
Eberts, R. 190
econometrics 236–7
education 212, 233–5
class sizes 155–6, 158
financing of 224–6, 227
health and 65–6, 77–8
contributions to international
literature 71–5
instrumental variable approach
75–6
monetary measure of health effect
of education 76–7
review of literature 66–70
optimal policies
financing of education 224–6, 227
future research directions 226–8
review of literature 215–17
taxation and 222–4
overeducation 101–3, 110–11
dynamics of skill mismatches
109–10
survey and meta-analysis 103–9

education (cont.)
  policies to prevent depreciation of
      human capital 171
  empirical results from policy
      evaluation 182–5
  estimation of impact 177–82
  private rate of return on 7, 17–19
    basic schooling model 7–9
    contributions to international
        literature 13–17
    dispersion in rates of return 138–40
    entrepreneurs and 53–62
    recent developments 10–13
  risks of investment in 134–5,
      147–8, 217
    dispersion in rates of return
        138–40
    earnings variance by education
        137–8
    educational choice under risk 135–7
    research agenda 144–7
    risk compensation in wages 140–4
  social rate of return on 21–2, 33–4
    findings from early growth
        literature 26–7
    human capital and macroeconomic
        theory 22–6
    measurement errors and
        specification issues 27–9
    new literature using cross-country
        data 29–31
    new literature using individual and
        within-country data 31–3
  stimulation of teachers to enhance
      quality 189, 206–9, 235
    full-time premium 203–6, 207–8
    international comparisons 194–203
    review of literature 190–3
    work–life incentives 194
  subsidies 215, 219, 223, 224–5, 227
  successful parents as secret to success
      81–2, 92–4
    estimation of family background
        effects 82–7
    family income and 88–9
    gender of parent and 85, 87,
        89–92, 93–4
    importance of inherited abilities
        87–8
    meaning of results of study 87–8

  using (quasi-)experiments to evaluate
      interventions 155–7, 166–8
    effect of extra funding for ICT for
        schools with disadvantaged
        students 163–5
    effect of extra funding for
        personnel for schools with
        minority students 161–3
    effect of extra time in school on
        early test scores 165–6
    effect of financial incentives on
        students' achievements 159–60
    effect of tax deduction of training
        costs 160–1
    review of related studies 157–8
efficiency 69
Ellingsen, T. 128
empirical work 2
endogenous growth model 24–6, 212
entrepreneurs 52–3, 59–62
  contributions to analysis 56–9
  meta-analysis of earlier evidence on
      53–6
equity participation schemes 225
equity premium puzzle 228
ethnic minorities
  effect of extra funding for ICT for
      schools with disadvantaged
      students 163–5
  effect of extra funding for personnel
      for schools with minority
      students 161–3
  effect of extra time in school on early
      test scores 165–6
  private rate of returns on
      education 8
expectation damages 127
experimental studies
  promotion rules and skill acquisition
      120–2
  underinvestment in training 125–8
  using (quasi-)experiments to evaluate
      education interventions
      155–7, 166–8
    effect of extra funding for ICT for
        schools with disadvantaged
        students 163–5
    effect of extra funding for
        personnel for schools with
        minority students 161–3

effect of extra time in school on
early test scores 165–6
effect of financial incentives on
students' achievements
159–60
effect of tax deduction of training
costs 160–1
review of related studies 157–8
externalities
returns on training and 40
social rate of return on education and
21–2, 32–3, 34

Farber, H. S. 45
Fehr, E. 128
Feinstein, L. 68
Ferrer-i-Carbonell, A. 148
financial incentives
effect on students' achievements
159–60
stimulation of teachers to enhance
quality 189, 206–9, 235
full-time premium 203–6, 207–8
international comparisons
194–203
review of literature 190–3
work–life incentives 194
financing of education 224–6, 227
France, stimulation of teachers to
enhance quality 197, 198,
200, 201, 207
Frazis, H. 42, 46
Frijters, P. 170, 177
Fuchs, V. 70
full-time premium 203–6, 207–8

gender
education and
overeducation 107, 110
private rate of return on 8, 13
relationship between health and
education 71–2, 73, 74
social rate of return on 26–7
labour supply elasticity 204
successful parents as secret to success
and 85, 87, 89–92, 93–4
general equilibrium effects 226–7
Germany, education in
entrepreneurs 54, 55
private rate of return 15, 54, 55

risk compensation in wages 142
stimulation of teachers to enhance
quality 196, 197, 198, 200, 206
Goldberger, Arthur 90
Gorter, C. 185
Griliches, Zvi 92
Groeneveld, S. 102
Groot, W. 68, 70, 71, 77, 101, 102,
103, 104, 108, 109, 111, 136
Grossman, M. 65, 67, 69

Hammond, C. 68
Hansen, J. 136
Hanushek, E. 157, 158
Harmon, C. 15, 147
Hartog, J. 17, 18, 101, 102, 103, 111,
137, 138, 139, 146, 148
Hause, J. C. 140
health, education and 65–6, 77–8
contributions to international
literature 71–5
instrumental variable approach 75–6
monetary measure of health effect of
education 76–7
review of literature 66–70
Heckman, James 9, 76, 167, 213, 215
Herrnstein, Richard 87–8
Hewlett Packard 116
Hoffman, S. 101, 108
Hogan, V. 136, 147
Hotz, V. J. 173
human capital theory 4
development of 1
macroeconomic theory and 22–6
endogenous growth model 24–6
neoclassical growth model 22,
23–4
technology adoption 26
see also individual topics
Hungary, private rate of return on
education 14

IBM 116
Imbens, G. W. 173
immigration, relationship between
health and education and 72
incentives *see* financial incentives
income *see* earnings/wages
information 69
asymmetries 216

information technologies, effect of
    extra funding for ICT for
    schools with disadvantaged
    students 163–5
insurance 216
intelligence (IQ) 85, 87–8, 93
intergenerational distribution of
    welfare 226
investment
  risks of human capital investment
    134–5, 147–8, 217
    dispersion in rates of return
      138–40
    earnings variance by education
      137–8
    educational choice under risk 135–7
    research agenda 144–7
    risk compensation in wages 140–4
  underinvestment in training 113–15,
    128–30
    overview of other experimental
      studies 125–8
    promotion rules and skill
      acquisition 115–25
Israel, education in
  effect of extra funding for ICT for
    schools with disadvantaged
    students 164–5
  experimental studies 158
  stimulation of teachers to enhance
    quality 191–2
Italy, private rate of return on
    education 14

Jacob, B. A. 193
Jacobs, Bas 135, 146, 219, 220, 221
Jaeger, D. 76
Japan, promotion policies 116
job search framework 173–4, 178, 180,
    182–3, 184, 185
Johannesson, M. 128
Johnson, S. 68
Jonker, N. 16, 148

Kaestner, R. 65, 67, 69
Kahn, L. 15
Kalb, G. R. J. 185
Keese, M. 170
Kenya, stimulation of teachers to
    enhance quality 193

King, A. G. 142
Kodde, D. 135
Krueger, A. 10, 11, 27, 158
Kyriacou, G. 29

labour market 146–7
  contracts 113–14
  overeducation in 101–3, 110–11
    dynamics of skill mismatches
      109–10
    survey and meta-analysis 103–9
  see also unemployment
Ladd, H. F. 193
Lalive, R. 182
Lavy, V. 158, 164, 191, 192
Lazear, E. 55, 61, 194
Lee, J. W. 29
Leigh, J. 70
Leuven, E. 14, 15, 46, 47, 48, 129, 130
Levhari, D. 135
lifestyle, education and 67
Lincoln Electric 116
Lindahl, Mikael 27, 90
liquidated damages 127
Lisbon Strategy 62, 233
List, J. A. 128
loans for education 224, 225
Lochner, L. 9
Loewenstein, M. 42, 46
Low, S. 142
Lucas, Robert 23, 24, 25, 26

Maassen van den Brink, H. 68, 70, 71,
    77, 101, 102, 103, 104, 108,
    109, 111
McGoldrick, K. 141, 142, 143
Machin, S. 170
macroeconomic theory, human capital
    and 22–6
  endogenous growth model 24–6
  neoclassical growth model 22, 23–4
  technology adoption 26
Maier, M. 147
Mankiw, N. G. 23, 24, 27
Manning, A. 170
Manski, C. 135, 146
market failures 234
  taxation and 220–1
Martin, J. P. 170
Medoff, J. 45

Meghir, C. 12
merit pay 190
Mertens, A. 102
methodological issues 2–3, 236–7
Meyer, B. D. 185
Mincer, Jacob 1, 7, 8, 18
minorities *see* ethnic minorities
Mirrlees, James A. 217, 220, 227
monetary measure of health effect of
   education 76–7
Moore, M. 77
moral hazard 216, 227
Moretti, E. 32, 33
Mortimer, J. H. 173
Mulligan, C. 69
Murnane, R. J. 190
Murray, Charles 87–8

Nelson, R. 26
neoclassical growth model 22, 23–4
Netherlands 155
   education 166–7, 212
      dispersion on rates of return 139
      effect of extra funding for ICT for
         schools with disadvantaged
         students 163–4
      effect of extra funding for
         personnel for schools with
         minority students 161–3
      effect of extra time in school on
         early test scores 165–6
      effect of financial incentives on
         students' achievements
         159–60
      entrepreneurs and 58–9, 60
      financing 225
      overeducation 101, 103, 109
      private rate of return on 13–14, 18
      relationship between health and
         71, 75
      risk compensation in wages 142,
         144
      social rate of return on 21
      stimulation of teachers to enhance
         quality 197, 198, 200, 203,
         235
   taxation 212
   training
      effect of tax deduction of training
         costs 160–1

returns on 46
underinvestment in 120, 129–30
unemployment
   dynamics over business cycle
      175–7
   policies to prevent depreciation of
      human capital 170
Nickell, S. 202
Noel, B. J. 180
Norway, private rate of return on
   education 12

Olsen, L. 142
O'Neill, D. 185
Oosterbeek, H. 14, 15, 16, 17, 46, 47,
   116, 136
ordinary least squares method 2
Oreopoulos, Philip 91
Organization for Economic
   Cooperation and
   Development (OECD) 170
Ormiston, M. B. 142
outside option principle 126
overeducation 101–3, 110–11
   dynamics of skill mismatches 109–10
   survey and meta-analysis 103–9
over-identification test, returns on
   education, private rate 12

Page, Marianne 91
Palme, M. 12
Parent, D. 46
parents
   education levels and health of
      children 70, 71, 72, 74, 75
   intergenerational distribution of
      welfare 226
   successful parents as secret to success
      81–2, 92–4
      estimation of family background
         effects 82–7
      family income and 88–9
      gender of parent and 85, 87,
         89–92, 93–4
      importance of inherited abilities
         87–8
      meaning of results of study 87–8
Parker, S. 58
performance-related pay 190, 191–2,
   193, 197, 201, 202

Peri, G. 33
Pfeiffer, F. 147
Phelps, E. 26
physical capital 23
Plug, Erik 89, 90
Pohlmeier, W. 147
Poland, returns on education, private
    rate 14
Portela, M. 31
Portugal, risk compensation in
    wages 142
primary education, rate of return on 8
Pritchett, L. 27
private rate of return on education 7,
    17–19
  basic schooling model 7–9
  contributions to international
    literature 13–17
  dispersion in rates of return 138–40
  entrepreneurs and 53–62
    contributions to analysis 56–9
    meta-analysis of earlier evidence
      on 53–6
  recent developments 10–13
productive efficiency 69
promotion rules and skill acquisition
    115–25
  different promotion rules 118–20
  economic environment 116–18
  experimental results 120–2
  scope for reciprocity 124–5
  stay-or-stay promotion policies 119,
    124, 125
  up-or-out promotion policies 115,
    119, 122–3, 125
  up-or-stay promotion policies 116,
    119, 123–4, 125
Psacharopoulos, G. 8
publication bias 16

quality of data 2
quality of life, relationship between
    health and education 71–2, 77
quality of teachers, stimulation to
    enhance 189, 206–9, 235
  full-time premium 203–6, 207–8
  international comparisons 194–203
  review of literature 190–3
  work–life incentives 194
Quintini, G. 202

redistributional issues 217–18
reliance damages 127
rent seeking 194
reporting heterogeneity 73
research 1, 2, 3
returns on education 233–4
  overeducation 101–3, 110–11
    dynamics of skill mismatches
      109–10
    survey and meta-analysis 103–9
  private rate 7, 17–19
    basic schooling model 7–9
    contributions to international
      literature 13–17
    dispersion in rates of return 138–40
    entrepreneurs and 53–62
    recent developments 10–13
  social rate 21–2, 33–4
    findings from early growth
      literature 26–7
    human capital and macroeconomic
      theory 22–6
    measurement errors and
      specification issues 27–9
    new literature using cross-country
      data 29–31
    new literature using individual and
      within-country data 31–3
returns on training 38–9, 48
  estimation issues 42–5
    evaluation framework 42–3
    exploiting exogenous variation in
      training 44–5
    standard regression approach 43–4
  international literature 46–7
  measurement of training 40–2
  summary of literature 45–6
  theory on 39–40
risks
  cumulative risk 68
  human capital investment 134–5,
    147–8, 217
    dispersion in rates of return 138–40
    earnings variance by education
      137–8
    educational choice under risk 135–7
    research agenda 144–7
    risk compensation in wages 140–4
Robinson, J. 68
Robst, J. 141, 142

Romer, D. 23, 24, 26, 27
Rosen, H. S. 135, 221
Rosenzweig, Mark 90
Rouse, C. E. 165
Rubb, S. 102, 108

Sacerdote, Bruce 90
Saez, Emmanuel 227
Sala-i-Martin, X. 24, 26
salaries *see* earnings/wages
Salvanas, K. 12
Salvanes, Kjell 91
Sander, W. 70
scale of reference bias 73
SCHOLAR Institute 1, 82, 157
schooling *see* education
Schultz, Theodore 1, 23, 65
self-employment *see* entrepreneurs
seniority pay 194
Shakotko, R. 45
Shefrin, H. M. 142
Sicherman, N. 101, 102
Silva, O. 55–6, 61
Singer,B. 76
Sloof, R. 126, 127
Slovenia, private rate of return on
      education 14
Smith, Adam 134, 140, 148
Smith, J. A. 180
smoking, education and 70
social rate of return on education 21–2,
      33–4
   findings from early growth literature
      26–7
   human capital and macroeconomic
      theory 22–6
      endogenous growth model 24–6
      neoclassical growth model 22,
         23–4
      technology adoption 26
   measurement errors and specification
      issues 27–9
   new literature on
      using cross-country data 26–7
      using individual and within-
         country data 26–7
socioeconomic status 75, 155
   effect of extra funding for ICT for
      schools with disadvantaged
      students 163–5

effect of extra time in school on early
      test scores 165–6
successful parents as secret to success
      81–2, 92–4
   estimation of family background
      effects 82–7
   family income and 88–9
   gender of parent and 85, 87,
      89–92, 93–4
   importance of inherited abilities
      87–8
   meaning of results of study 87–8
Solow, R. M. 22
Soto, M. 29
Spain, risk compensation in wages 142
Spiegel, M. M. 27
state-dependent-reporting bias 73
stay-or-stay promotion policies 119,
      124, 125
Stevens, Anne Hu 91
subsidies, education 215, 219, 223,
      224–5, 227
Sweden
   education
      private rate of return 10, 12, 14
      social rate of return 21
      stimulation of teachers to enhance
         quality 196, 197, 198, 200, 202
   successful parents as secret to success
      81, 91
Switzerland
   policies to prevent depreciation of
      human capital 182
   private rate of return on education 14

taxation
   capital taxation 214, 221–4
   effect of tax deduction of training
      costs 160–1
   optimal taxation policies 212, 218–19
      education policies and 222–4
      future research directions 226–8
      income redistribution 217–18
      income taxation 213, 214, 219–24
      market failures and 220–1
      review of literature 212–15
teachers, stimulation to enhance
      quality 189, 206–9, 235
   full-time premium 203–6, 207–8
   international comparisons 194–203

teachers, stimulation (cont.)
   review of literature 190–3
   work–life incentives 194
team compensation 192–3
technology
   effect of extra funding for ICT for
      schools with disadvantaged
      students 163–5
   human capital and technology
      adoption 26
   neoclassical growth theory and 23
tenure 189, 194
Teulings, C. 31
time consistency 227–8
time horizons, education and 68, 71
time preferences, education and
      69–70
Todd, P. 9
Topel, R. 45
trade unions 194
training
   effect of tax deduction of training
      costs 160–1
   overeducation and 102
   policies to prevent depreciation of
      human capital 171
      empirical results from policy
         evaluation 182–5
      estimation of impact 177–82
   returns on 38–9, 48
      estimation issues 42–5
         evaluation framework 42–3
         exploiting exogenous variation
            in training 44–5
         standard regression approach
            43–4
      international literature 46–7
      measurement of training 40–2
      summary of literature 45–6
      theory on 39–40
   underinvestment in 113–15, 128–30
      overview of other experimental
         studies 125–8
      promotion rules and skill
         acquisition 115–25
Trostel, Philip 9, 213
twin studies
   private rate of return on education 10
   successful parents as secret to
      success 90

underinvestment in training 113–15,
      128–30
   overview of other experimental
      studies 125–8
   promotion rules and skill acquisition
      115–25
      different promotion rules 118–20
      economic environment 116–18
      experimental results 120–2
      scope for reciprocity 124–5
      stay-or-stay promotion policies
         119, 124, 125
      up-or-out promotion policies 115,
         119, 122–3, 125
      up-or-stay promotion policies 116,
         119, 123–4, 125
unemployment
   dynamics over business cycle 175–7
   job search framework 173–4, 178,
      180, 182–3, 184, 185
   policies to prevent depreciation of
      human capital 170–3, 185, 235
      empirical results from policy
         evaluation 182–5
      estimation of impact 177–82
United Kingdom
   education
      financing 224
      stimulation of teachers to enhance
         quality 197, 199, 200, 202
   policies to prevent depreciation of
      human capital 172
   private rate of return on
      education 10
   successful parents as secret to
      success 91
United Nations 69
   Human Development Report 65
United States of America
   education
      dispersion on rates of return 139
      entrepreneurs and 54, 55, 57, 58,
         59, 60, 61
      experimental studies 158
      health and 65
      overeducation 104
      private rate of return 8, 10, 14,
         15, 18
      risk compensation in wages
         142, 143

social rate of return 32, 33
stimulation of teachers to enhance
quality 190–1, 193, 196,
198, 199
promotion policies 116
returns on training 45
successful parents as secret to success
81, 90, 91
university education, rate of return on 8
up-or-out promotion policies 115, 119,
122–3, 125
up-or-stay promotion policies 116, 119,
123–4, 125

Vaage, K. 12
van den Berg, G. J. 175, 176, 178, 181,
182, 185
van der Klaauw, B. 170, 175, 176, 177,
178, 182, 185
van der Sluis, J. 54, 56, 58
van Ophem, H. 14, 17, 18, 137, 138, 139

van Ours, J. C. 176, 182
van Praag, C. M. 54, 56, 58
van Rens, T. 31
van Vuuren, A. 176
van Witteloostuijn, A. 56, 58
Vijverberg, Wim 54, 89, 146
Viscusi, W. K. 77

wages *see* earnings/wages
Wagner, J. 61, 5555
Walker, I. 9, 136, 147
Webbink, D. 16, 138, 146, 201
Weil, D. N. 23, 24, 27
Weiss, Y. 135, 140
welfare benefits, unemployment 179
White, H. 142
Williams, J. 136
Woolley, P. 9
work–life incentives 194

Zweimüller, J. 182